THE FIXED INCOME ANSWER BOOK

for SENIORS®

Publisher's Note

He raises the poor from the dust and lifts the needy from the ash heap; he seats them with princes and has them inherit a throne of honor. For the foundations of the earth are the Lord's; on them he has set the world.

1 Samuel 2:8 (NIV)

FC&A Publishing®
103 Clover Green
Peachtree City, GA 30269

Produced by the staff of FC&A
ISBN 978-1935574736

Table of contents

Calendar of savings: Put over $25,000 back in your pocket this year

January: Spectacular savings on furniture — and more . . .1

February: Track down free samples to save
thousands on prescriptions 3

March: Fresh discounts for your homeowners
insurance policy 5

April: Need a tax break? Don't miss these
money-saving tips for caregivers 7

May: Small improvements reap big returns
in home sales 9

June: Penny-wise strategies for the savvy shopper 11

July: Jump into a pool of summer water savings 13

August: Reap the savings on fresh produce
at harvest time 15

September: Seal your house to save on winter
heating bills 17

October: Take advantage of cost-saving plans to
put thousands back in your pocket 19

November: Save hundreds on holiday gifts with
these tried-and-true tactics 21

December: Pay rock bottom for your next car 23

Smart money moves to build a richer retirement

Chart your path to financial freedom 26

Social Security simplified: Unravel the secrets
to a steady income 32

Pension payout: How to maximize your benefits 43

Rock-solid savings: Make the most of your
401(k) and IRA 46

Investment success: Wise ways to help your
money grow 53

Taxes: Refunds and rip-offs you don't want to miss 59

Earn extra cash to boost your retirement budget 69

Boost your credit and banking power

Reap the benefits of a better credit score 78

Credit cards: Safe and smart ways to take control
of your plastic 86

Beat the bank fee blues 94

Estate planning to secure your family's future

Life insurance: The right protection at
    the right price 102

Wills and trusts: Expert advice to safeguard
    your money 108

Bid farewell to the high cost of funerals 118

Top-notch defense against financial fraud

ID theft: Lock down your data to protect
    your privacy 122

Clever tricks to scam-proof your wallet 133

Battle the high cost of health care

Medicare and more: Quality coverage without
    spending a fortune 144

Rx essentials: Stop paying too much for meds 154

Vitamins, minerals, and herbs: Spend your
    supplement dollars wisely 162

Doctor visits: Get more, pay less 167

Take a bite out of dental costs 172

Loud and clear savings for your eyes and ears 176

Simple cures for soaring hospital bills 180

Long-term care: Affordable solutions for
    your retirement years 184

Real estate secrets help you buy, sell, or rent like a pro

Your mortgage road map: Navigate home
    loans with ease 190

Ready, set, sell: Cash in on your home's value 194

Stretch your home-buying dollars 199

Keys to a smart move for less 205

Home sweet home: Open the door to better
    insurance rates 211

Property taxes: How to save on the homefront 216

Unlock the value of rental properties 219

Stretch your utility savings with smart home hacks

Bright ideas to power down your electric bill 224

Put the freeze on high heating and cooling costs 234

Plug the leaks in your water budget 242

Handy hints to make your home last a lifetime

Clean sweep: How to make your home
sparkle for pennies 248

Around the house: Budget-friendly guide to easy
fix-its and fix-ups 255

Frugal food tips slash your grocery bill

Shopping secrets: How you can outsmart
the supermarket 264

Grow your own food for less 281

Kitchen hacks that save you money 288

Dine out in style without breaking the bank 298

Your road map to owning a car for less

Insurance essentials: Steer your way to
cheaper rates 304

'Auto'-matic savings: Put the brakes on costly
care and repair 310

Buy, sell, or lease: Rev up the savings on
your next car deal 317

Money-saving tricks to master technology

Hang up on high cellphone bills 326

Cutting-edge gadgets at rock-bottom prices 333

First-class fun on an economy budget

Cable, satellite, and streaming: Ways to watch
that save you more 340

Cheap and easy entertainment at your fingertips 350

Savvy travel: Great escapes at the right price 356

Index 365

January

Spectacular savings on furniture — and more

Timing is everything. Whether it's buying a house, putting in your retirement papers, or investing in the stock market, success often hinges on when you take action. Retail shopping is no different. In fact, you can save money on everything you buy — if you know the right time of year to strike a deal.

Just ask Louise, who saved $416 by postponing the purchase of a sofa. She originally wanted to buy it in time for Christmas, when her in-laws visited.

"What we had was so ratty," she complained. "I wanted to impress them with something new."

So Louise visited several furniture stores and finally found what she was looking for — a two piece, dark brown sectional for $1,388. Wanting a second opinion, she snapped a photo and sent it to a friend.

"Love it. But can you wait another month?" the friend responded. "You'll wind up saving so much money."

That's when Louise learned that furniture retailers discount their year-end stock by 25% or more in January. Why? They need to clear warehouse and showroom space to make room for new products.

Louise thought it over and concluded that it made sense to wait. So she covered her old sofa with red and green blankets and waited until mid-January to return to the store. Sure

Calendar of savings

enough, she found the same sectional marked down to $972 — a 30% discount on the original price.

Louise bought it on the spot. She plans to use the money she saved to buy a new coffee table and throw rug. And her in-laws? "They had so much fun playing with the grandkids that they never even sat on the sofa," Louise says.

Figuring out the best month to get a discount shouldn't require a lot of time and energy. Fortunately, you don't have to depend on a friend to help.

This handy calendar section has all the best deals for each month, telling you what you should buy, when, for maximum savings. You'll never again have to wonder if it's the right time to shop.

Smart deals of the month

Christmas and New Year's Eve are over and it's time to recharge. Why not take a break and sleep in late? There's even a Jan. 3 holiday set aside — Festival of Sleep Day — for catching up on your ZZZ's.

Retailers are all too happy to help make your day a success, offering big discounts on bedding throughout the month.

Don't be caught dozing, though, when it comes to these other January sales.

- carpeting
- gym memberships
- men's suits
- hotel stays
- toys
- rugs
- motorcycles
- towels

February

Track down free samples to save thousands on prescriptions

Valentine's Day is on the horizon. Boxes of heart-shaped chocolates line the shelves and every florist in town is offering deals for a dozen red roses. And while you'd like to shower your special someone with gifts, your budget is tight this year. After spending thousands on prescription drugs, you just don't have a cent to spare.

Maybe you should follow Francine's example. She managed to hang on to an extra $6,800 this year. And all she did was ask the simple question, "Do you have any free samples?"

Francine's doctor prescribed several expensive drugs throughout the year to treat her various health problems. She thought Medicare would cover most of the costs, but that wasn't the case. A single dose of one asthma drug fetched an eye-popping $3,000. And her doctor prescribed six injections. Later she needed three shots of another asthma drug, which was $3,700 a dose. The price tags of two prescription creams for eczema were pretty steep, too.

Fortunately, some of the costs were covered by Medicare. But Francine still had to deal with a hefty coinsurance payment. Here's a breakdown of what her yearly out-of-pocket drug expenses would have been without the free samples.

- first asthma drug — $3,600
- second asthma drug — $2,220
- first eczema cream — $700
- second eczema cream — $280

Calendar of savings

All in all, Francine would have had to pay almost $7,000 out of pocket for those prescriptions throughout the year.

The drug companies offered coupons and discount programs that would make these medicines more affordable. In some cases, the programs could erase the out-of-pocket costs entirely. But there was a slight hitch. Because Francine was on Medicare, she was ineligible for these discount programs. She would have to shoulder all the out-of-pocket costs herself.

But Francine simply told her doctor that insurance wouldn't cover these pricey medications. So he got on the phone with the drug manufacturers and convinced them to send out enough free samples to cover most of Francine's treatments.

And this trick works for more than just specialty prescriptions. Francine saved hundreds more on other creams, steroids, and allergy drugs by asking for free samples.

Smart deals of the month

Do you enjoy the convenience of canned peaches and creamed corn? You can thank Napoleon Bonaparte. The French military needed a steady supply of rations, so Napoleon offered 12,000 francs to anyone who came up with a way to preserve large amounts of food. Voila! A French candymaker won the prize after inventing a method of boiling and sealing food in airtight jars.

February is National Canned Food Month, so stock up and save on tinned fruit, pie filling, soups, vegetables, and tuna. You'll also find discounts this month on these items.

- winter clothes
- candy after Valentine's Day
- interior paint
- last-minute ski trips
- home goods
- humidifiers

March

Super savings: $565.25

Fresh discounts for your homeowners insurance policy

March is the month when most of the nation springs forward for daylight saving time. It's also your cue to check the batteries in your smoke detectors. Did you know having smoke detectors can lower your homeowners insurance by 5%?

And it's not the only discount you can find. Mike and Caryn saved $565.25 on their annual insurance premium just by amping up their home security and simplifying their billing process. In all, they discovered 10 different ways they could save on homeowners insurance every month for the rest of their lives.

Install a monitored security system. Mike and Caryn's system pays for itself because they earn a 20% discount for having it. That amounts to $452.20 off of their $2,261 annual premium.

Automatically save with auto pay. As their agent factored in the first discount, she asked if they minded going paperless for an additional 5% savings. Since they had already shifted to paying most of their bills online, that decision was easy. They bagged another $113.05 in yearly savings.

Mike and Caryn's discounts capped at 25%, but they are going to tell their friends and family to ask their agents about these additional savings.

Bundle up. Lois next door will be glad to know she can save 20% by combining her auto and homeowners insurance in one policy.

Stay loyal. Caryn's cousin has been with her insurer for 10 years, so she may be eligible for 10% off.

Calendar of savings

Renew early. Their nephew can get rewarded for his organizational skills. By planning ahead and renewing his policy before it expires, he may get 10% off.

Cash in on retirement. Their neighbors, who are over 55, should claim their retiree discount of 10% later this year when they officially hang up their hats.

Don't smoke. Mike's brother, Jeff, just gave up his smoking habit. He can probably get 15% off of his homeowners policy.

Renovate and upgrade. The Davis family across the road just installed an impact-resistant roof and will qualify for a renovation discount of up to 10%.

Resist the urge to make small claims. Mike's mother hasn't filed a claim in 12 years. She gets rewarded with 20% off.

Pay it all at once. Caryn's brother pulls in a great salary. He can pay his premium annually instead of monthly for a 5% discount.

Smart deals of the month

Busy on March 14? Hope not. You'll miss out on National Pi Day, the annual salute to the mathematical concept of pi — the ratio of the circumference of a circle to its diameter — whose infinite digits are usually rounded to 3.14.

Lots of supermarkets and restaurants honor the occasion with free deals or reduced prices on bakery pies and pizzas. Just don't ask the staff to explain the meaning of pi. They might go on forever.

Be sure to keep an eye out for these other smart buys.

- luggage
- ski and snowboard gear
- tax software
- cleaning products
- air purifiers
- space heaters

Super savings: $2,281

Need a tax break? Don't miss these money-saving tips for caregivers

Tax season has always been stressful for Gladys. Every April she worries about owing a large amount to Uncle Sam, a situation that would leave her scrimping and saving to pay the bills.

This tax year, though, her circumstances have changed. Gladys has begun to look after the daily needs of her aging mother. That means she can take advantage of important tax breaks.

Just how much can she save? This year Gladys gets to keep an extra $2,281 in her pocket. Here's how.

Filing as head of household. Gladys, a single woman earning $39,000 a year, can now file her taxes as head of household because she pays for more than half of her dependent mother's living expenses.

That means Gladys can take a higher standard deduction — $18,350 instead of the $12,200 that she previously took as a single filer. To top it off, her income is now subject to wider tax brackets, meaning more of her money is taxed at lower rates.

The result? Her tax bill just dropped from $3,022 to $2,201. That's a savings of $821 — more than enough to cover Gladys' cellphone bill for a year.

Claiming the dependent care credit. Gladys also paid someone to care for her mother while she was at work. That makes her eligible for a dependent care credit of up to $1,050. The credit covers costs for things like home health nurses and adult daycare.

Gladys' adjusted gross income qualifies her for a $960 credit — nearly the same amount the two women spend on groceries every couple of months.

Taking the credit for other dependents. Gladys was about to sign her tax return when a friend told her she was allowed to take a new tax credit for dependents who don't qualify for the child tax credit.

The $500 bonus — enough to pay the women's electricity bill for six months — is meant to assist people looking after disabled or senior family members.

What does all this mean for Gladys? Her tax bill for the year was just $741. That's 75% lower than what she would have paid if she were still a single filer without the larger deduction and credits.

Smart deals of the month

April may well be known for Tax Day, but it's also National Lawn and Garden Month. Why not celebrate by getting ready for mowing and planting season? After all, spring is already here and summer is right around the corner.

April is one of the best times of year to take advantage of seasonal markdowns on lawn mowers and tractors.

Be sure you're also on the lookout for these discounted items.

- vacuum cleaners
- thrift store items
- athletic shoes
- gardening supplies
- post-Easter candy
- pressure washers
- spring clothes
- big-screen televisions

Small improvements reap big returns in home sales

Thinking of selling your house? Experts say May is the best time to do it. People who list in this beautiful spring month earn an average of $1,600 more on their sale price with fewer days on the market.

Want some simple ideas on how you can boost your asking price even more? Follow the advice of the Rogers who netted an extra $7,951 on their $200,000 home by improving their curb appeal and listing in May. Here are the profit-boosting projects they took on to get their best offer.

Front door. The Rogers painted their front door black, a color that not only has a stately air but can also improve sale price by as much as $6,271. They chose a premium, semi-gloss exterior paint that only needed one coat. This simple, inexpensive upgrade cost them a little time and around $40 but increased the value of their home by thousands.

Exterior paint. The couple also decided to hire someone to paint the exterior of their house gray-beige, otherwise known as "greige." Houses this color on average sell for $3,500 more than those that are tan or medium brown, making their $3,000 investment worthwhile.

Garage door. Replacing the garage door is the big ticket item the Rogers stretched for. A new door costs about $3,600, but it was expected to recoup at least 97.5% of its value and add to the home's overall attractiveness.

Calendar of savings

Landscaping. Depending on size, trees in front lawn landscaping can add to curb appeal. The couple thought their front yard looked a little bare, so they invested $300 in several younger trees from a nearby nursery. For ease of care they picked native plants.

Overall charm. The Rogers wanted their home to look its best so they freshened the exterior by trimming bushes, sweeping the driveway, weeding, and cleaning the gutters and mailbox. They knew curb appeal could boost their sale price 3% to 5%, so they took care to make sure everything looked welcoming.

Once they completed these projects, the Rogers had added $13,291 of potential value to their home. With the help of the $1,600 May price boost, they listed and sold their house for $214,891. Taking into consideration the $6,940 they invested in their improvements, that's an extra $7,951 profit.

Smart deals of the month

Cinco de Mayo, which is Spanish for the fifth of May, is a holiday that honors the Mexican army's victory over French troops in an 1862 battle.

Oddly enough, Cinco de Mayo isn't widely celebrated in Mexico. But the holiday has taken on a life of its own north of the border. That's why lots of restaurants in the U.S. mark the occasion by offering Cinco de Mayo specials, including coupons and discounts on Mexican-style food and drink.

But don't let the good times stop there. You can also save on these expenses in May.

- Mother's Day gifts
- freezers
- party supplies
- windows
- exterior paint
- exercise clothes

Super savings: $71.68

Penny-wise strategies for the savvy shopper

June is one of the shorter months of the year, but it's a prime time for buying gifts for dads and grads. And if you're like most consumers on a budget, shopping can be downright stressful.

Just ask Suzanne, who browsed the malls and the internet in search of Father's Day and graduation gifts.

"I'm on a fixed income with not much extra money to spare," she says. "I really had to be creative to keep my spending within reason."

The extra work paid off. Suzanne, who managed to save $71.68, recommends that you give the following strategies a try.

Go online for discount codes. Like to shop at Macy's or Target? Google the retailer and "promo code" or go to *retailmenot.com* or *befrugal.com* for coupons, cash-back offers, and deals on gift cards.

And remember, lots of retailers will match competitors' lower prices or give you a refund on items you bought that later went on sale.

Another option? Go to online sites like *amazonwarehouse.com* or *blinq.com* for deep discounts on returned items in good condition that can't be sold as new.

Suzanne found a Sony digital camera on one of the sites, spending $67.76 on her niece's graduation gift. Buying online at *amazonwarehouse.com* saved her $22.23 off the suggested retail price.

Calendar of savings

Claim your senior discount. Did you know that lots of department stores offer senior discounts on certain days of the week? Kohl's, for example, takes 15% off your bill on Wednesdays if you're age 60 or older.

Ross Dress For Less, meanwhile, offers a 10% discount on Tuesdays to shoppers 55 and older. Be sure to call ahead to see if your local store participates in a similar program.

Suzanne saved a small fortune when she took advantage of Stein Mart's senior discount — 20% off the price of clearance items on the first Monday of every month.

Scouring through the men's section, she found a $75 Ben Sherman watch marked down for clearance to $31.94. With her senior discount, Suzanne paid just $25.55 for her Father's Day gift. That's $49.45 off the suggested retail price.

Smart deals of the month

You won't want to miss this opportunity to reel in a freebie. The first week of June is National Fishing and Boating Week, when many states allow you to fish on public waters for free — no license required.

Activities and dates vary, so call your state's fish and wildlife department for information.

Angling for more savings in June? Don't forget to look into these bargains.

- exercise equipment
- summer sports gear
- cookware
- dinnerware
- Father's Day gifts
- tools

July

Super savings: $175+

Jump into a pool of summer water savings

You could spend big bucks in July watering your lawn and plants. To keep your water bill from skyrocketing, try conserving water elsewhere in the house. That's what Ben and Laura Taylor have done. They followed the suggestions below to save more than 1,900 gallons of water each month and over $175 for the year.

Cut out bath time. The average bathtub uses 36 gallons of water to fill. Switching from baths to showers saved the Taylors 288 gallons of water each month and cut $25.56 off their annual $540 bill.

Shorter showers save. If you take a 10 minute shower with an average flow shower head you use around 25 gallons of water. The Taylors dedicated themselves to halving their showering time to save 600 gallons of water every month and a yearly savings of $53.26.

Don't let the water run. About a gallon of water per minute streams from your bathroom faucet, so turn it off when you brush your teeth to save up to 8 gallons of water per day. The Taylors did that and together saved 448 gallons of water in a month and $39.77 for the year.

Scrape your plate and skip the pre-rinse. Your kitchen faucet uses about 1.5 to 2 gallons per minute, so if you pre-rinse you could waste up to 6 gallons of water before your dishwasher does its job.

Instead, just scrape off the food first. The Taylors gave up pre-rinsing and saved 280 gallons each month for an annual savings of $24.85.

Calendar of savings

Focus on full cycles. Unless you have a special water-saving dishwasher or an especially old model, you will typically use around 6 gallons per cycle. Make sure you've filled your dishwasher to avoid waste, and if possible, run it less often.

The Taylors committed to filling up their dishwasher before running it, saving them two loads every week and 48 gallons of water every month. Their $4.26 annual savings may be small, but they know every little bit helps.

Load up in the laundry room. If you have a new washing machine, you probably use 25 gallons per load, but the Taylors have an old model that uses about 40 gallons.

To help save water, they try to wash two fewer loads each week and make sure they're all full. This saves them 320 gallons of water every month and $28.41 for the year.

Smart deals of the month

July is National Blueberry Month, a great time to eat this juicy fruit that's high in nutrients and antioxidants but low in calories — just 80 calories per cup.

Look for purple-blue to blue-black colored berries that are firm, plump, and smooth-skinned. Stock up in July when they're at their freshest and least expensive.

You'll find other savings this month on these items.

- video games
- large appliances
- dehumidifiers
- swimsuits
- home decor
- last-minute travel

August

Reap the savings on fresh produce at harvest time

Ah, summer. Luscious tomatoes eaten right off the vine. Crisp lettuce, cucumbers, and green peppers filling your salad bowl. If you have a home garden, you know the joy — and savings — of a bountiful harvest.

But even if you don't, August is the perfect time to save money on fresh produce. Janice will save over $100 on her grocery bill during the coming months just by doing two simple things — stocking up on produce now and freezing it for later.

Buy a bunch fresh while it's everywhere. Janice loves to buy in bulk at the end of the summer because grocers stay well stocked with locally grown produce. It travels the shortest distance with the least handling or processing, which also makes it more affordable.

Plus Janice knows that many grocery prices have stayed low compared to the cost of eating out. The last time she compared prices on her favorite fresh vegetables, she could hardly believe the differences she found at the grocery store from season to season and at the restaurants she sometimes visits.

	Cost per serving		
Produce	Summer	Winter	Restaurant
green beans	$0.48	$0.64	$1.99-$2.89
corn	$0.20	$0.60	$1.99-$2.89
tomatoes	$0.38	$0.75	$2.99

Freeze it fresh. Since she was young, Janice has used simple and affordable flash freeze methods her mother taught her to preserve fruits and vegetables. When she pulls them out of the icebox and serves them up, they taste like they were just picked from the garden.

One serving a week of her favorite fruits and veggies from the freezer saves Janice about $4.35 a meal, or $108.75 over 25 weeks. That's six months of savings on better tasting food. If she eats the same food at a restaurant, she will pay three times that amount, or close to $330.

When Janice is cooking up new ideas for meals, she checks the website for the National Center for Home Food Preservation. Their easy guides tell her which foods freeze best and how they should be prepared.

The drying method for fruits and blanching technique for vegetables locks in flavor perfectly. You can see what they recommend at *nchfp.uga.edu/how/freeze.html*.

Smart deals of the month

Ever hear of National Dollar Day? It's on Aug. 8, the day in 1786 that the Continental Congress established America's monetary system. Think of it as the birthday of the U.S. dollar.

Of course, money went a lot further back then. Why not stretch your dollars to go as far as possible this month? You're sure to save if you buy any of these things in August.

- linens
- patio furniture
- shoes
- summer clothes
- air conditioners
- school supplies

September

Super savings: $354

Seal your house to save on winter heating bills

Your house isn't the only thing that gets a nice lining when you buff up your insulation — your wallet does, too. Put some money back in your pocket, like Michael and Lucy Flowers, using these money saving tips. By sealing off air leaks in September, the Flowers were ready for the cold and saved $354 on their winter heating bill.

Plug teeny openings for a big budget boost. Who would have thought a tiny outlet could cause major air leaks? Just hold your hand over one on an exterior wall and you'll be shocked to feel cold air blowing into your home. This is one place in the house almost nobody thinks to insulate, but it could save you money year after year on heating and cooling.

The Flowers improved insulation in this problem area by adding a foam gasket to each outlet and light switch. All they had to do was pop off the faceplates, line them with the foam insulators, and reattach. You can buy outlet and light switch gaskets online for 11 to 50 cents each.

That deal is hard to pass up once you know this fix could lower your heating and cooling bill by as much as 20%. For Michael and Lucy, that's a whopping $236 off their typical $1,181 winter electric heating bill.

One other easy change is to keep your closet doors shut so you're not wasting your heated air in unnecessary spaces. This is most cost-effective when the closets are on exterior walls.

Calendar of savings

Save hundreds on your energy bill with DIY fall fixes. Michael and Lucy sealed other air leaks with spray foam, caulk, and weatherstripping to save an extra $118. Plug the cracks and crevices in your home and you too might trim 10% off your energy bill.

- Spray foam and caulk. Who knew a spray can and a caulk gun could cut energy use? The Flowers found that these tools are perfect for filling in small holes and gaps around vents and ducts or rim joists.

- Weatherstripping. Expect steep savings for a meager $10 and one-hour investment. Michael and Lucy used nonexpanding foam and V-channel weatherstripping on their windows and decked out their door with a door sweep to stop warm air from leaving their house. And while they had the materials out, they sealed the attic hatch.

Smart deals of the month

Like to grill burgers and socialize before the big game? Then you'll love National Tailgating Day, which always falls on the first Saturday in September.

You might be surprised to learn, though, that the origins of tailgating might date way back to the Civil War. That's when Union Army supporters are said to have brought food and drink in their horse-drawn carriages to cheer Northern soldiers from the sidelines at the Battle of Bull Run.

Headed for the stadium parking lot any time soon? September is the best time of year to get good deals on two modern-day tailgating conveniences — cars and grills. And don't forget about these discounted items.

- mattresses
- office supplies
- small appliances
- bicycles
- airfare
- plants

Take advantage of cost-saving plans to put thousands back in your pocket

The leaves are changing — and so are your health care options. That's because October marks the beginning of Medicare's open enrollment period. You have the opportunity to find a new, money-saving Medicare Advantage plan.

That's just what Shellie did. At 68 years old, she was tired of paying thousands a year in Medicare premiums for services she barely used. So when open enrollment started, she managed to save about $2,000 on health insurance costs by going with a new plan.

Take a look at how much she spent every year on health insurance before making the change.

- Medicare Part B premiums — $135.50 a month (yearly total = $1,626)
- Medicare Part D premiums — $33.19 a month (yearly total = $398.28)
- Total yearly costs — $2,024.28

Because Shellie rarely needed to visit the doctor for anything other than an annual checkup, she opted for a plan with no premiums and a high deductible. On top of that, the plan paid for most of her Part B premium each month. Plus, drug coverage was included, so she could drop her Part D plan.

Medicare Advantage plans are provided by private insurers, which means you have a wide variety of options to choose from. Some plans advertise zero premiums, but still require you to pay your Part B costs yourself. Look for a plan that pays a portion — or all — of your health premiums to get the most savings upfront.

Calendar of savings

Because Shellie's plan has a high deductible, she has to pay more money out of pocket before her benefits kick in. Before you decide to go for a plan like this, think about whether or not you'll have cash on hand in case of sickness or injury.

Many people overlook these potential costs and choose a plan based on monthly premiums alone. Make sure you understand the out-of-pocket limits and how your plan will pay for special services, like hospital and skilled nursing facility stays. Weigh the cost of premiums against these plan features.

When enrolling in any Medicare plan, don't just set it up and forget about it. Plans can change every year, so that means your favorite doctors or preferred prescriptions could be dropped when the next enrollment window comes around. Follow Shellie's lead. She examines her options every October to make sure she'll still save money.

Smart deals of the month

October is Vegetarian Awareness Month, a swell time to learn about the health benefits of eating a plant-based diet. According to the Mayo Clinic, vegetarians tend to eat fewer calories, weigh less, and have a lower risk of heart disease than people who eat meat.

Not sure if you're ready to give up pork chops and steak? You can begin meeting your health goals with small steps like "Meatless Mondays."

Although summer is known for its fresh fruits and vegetables, you'd also be wise to fill up on October's thrifty and nutritious bounty of beets, broccoli, parsnips, sweet potatoes, Swiss chard, turnips, rutabagas, and butternut squash.

Don't miss out on these bargains, either.

- snow blowers
- denim jeans
- smoke detectors
- patio furniture
- camping gear
- snow shovels

Save hundreds on holiday gifts with these tried-and-true tactics

Thanksgiving leftovers aren't even in the fridge before Christmas carols start playing on the radio. And if you're anything like Robert, those holiday tunes mean it's time to make a list of seasonal chores. Buy a tree, hang up the lights, and of course, shop for gifts.

Normally, Robert dreads Christmas shopping. But this year, he managed to save $850 by doing all his gift buying in November, the month experts say is the best time to snag deals on electronics. Here's how.

Get great bargains with Black Friday sales. The day after Thanksgiving is famous for big sales. Robert knew that Black Friday was the perfect chance for him to score a great price on a brand new television for his wife. He found a deal that knocked $100 off a 50-inch 4K ultra HD smart TV.

Black Friday deals change from year to year, but Robert had a good idea of what the sale prices would be. How? Many retailers reveal their deals before the big day. Roger scoured websites like *consumerreports.org* and *BFAds.net* to see if anything he wanted to buy would go on sale.

But if you're not one to fight through crowds at the stores, don't worry. Most retailers offer Black Friday discounts on their websites. And the following Monday — which is often called Cyber Monday — gives you another opportunity to bargain hunt from the comfort of your computer.

Renew your budget with refurbished tech. Robert didn't do all of his shopping during the Black Friday rush. His granddaughter wanted a high-end electronic tablet that wasn't going to be marked down.

Calendar of savings

Instead of paying full price, Robert snagged a refurbished tablet for $250 below retail. That means the pre-owned device was restored, repaired, and tested before being sold at a discounted price.

Make sure you check out each company's policy on refurbished items before you buy, though. Some brands don't do much more than repackage old electronics, while others put their products through rigorous tests.

Look to the past to protect your wallet. Gadgets come out every year with shiny new bells and whistles. And those new features come with a hefty price tag. If you buy older electronics, the products are almost as good. And even better? They're a lot cheaper.

Robert wanted to buy a new phone for himself before the holidays, but a cutting-edge smartphone would cost upwards of $1,000. Instead, he went for last year's edition with similar features. And the best part? It cost $500 less than the latest model.

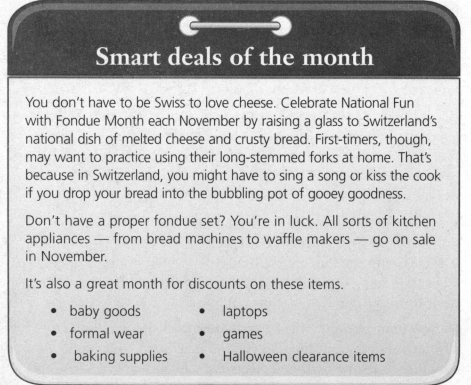

Smart deals of the month

You don't have to be Swiss to love cheese. Celebrate National Fun with Fondue Month each November by raising a glass to Switzerland's national dish of melted cheese and crusty bread. First-timers, though, may want to practice using their long-stemmed forks at home. That's because in Switzerland, you might have to sing a song or kiss the cook if you drop your bread into the bubbling pot of gooey goodness.

Don't have a proper fondue set? You're in luck. All sorts of kitchen appliances — from bread machines to waffle makers — go on sale in November.

It's also a great month for discounts on these items.

- baby goods
- formal wear
- baking supplies
- laptops
- games
- Halloween clearance items

Pay rock bottom for your next car

Quinn discovered that the last really will be first. To get the best deal, that is. While most of his neighbors spent December baking and wrapping presents, he was online researching his options for a sweet new ride. He knew something his friends didn't — that December was the ideal time to buy a car. When they were snoozing after too much feasting, he was at the car dealership saving himself $5,189 on the new electric car he had always wanted.

Buy late and save more — you won't learn this from an auto dealer. Quinn knew his golden opportunity would come late in the year. Car dealers offer some of their best discounts then because they are trying to make their year-end goals and close out the year with strong sales, which will earn them bonuses.

They also need to clear out space for the new cars coming in for the new year. In fact, customers have gotten up to 8.5% off the price of their vehicles just by shopping on New Year's Eve.

Make a list and check it twice to land a fair price. When Quinn stepped onto the lot, he had done his homework on the Kia crossover SUV he had his eye on and was ready to fight for 15% off the $34,594 asking price.

- He knew the Kelley Blue Book fair market and MSRP values, so he could negotiate a good deal based on how much local buyers had paid for the same car.

- He also had figures from Edmunds, another resource that helps you identify a fair price based on local sales data.

Calendar of savings

- Quinn was carrying quotes from other dealers and just needed this dealer to beat them.

- And the most important detail? He knew what his rock bottom price was. And he wasn't interested in talking payments before they settled on the vehicle price.

Get in the right mindset to mine the best deal. Quinn was ready to commit several hours to the process, and he knew he would walk away if he didn't reach the number he believed was fair. After several trips to the manager, the salesperson was really close to Quinn's target price.

When Quinn said he needed to leave and think it over, the dealer made the offer he was looking for. As they closed the deal, he knew his persistence and preparation had really paid off.

Smart deals of the month

Natural pearls used to be so rare that only nobility and the very rich were allowed to wear them. Thankfully, that's no longer the case. Everybody can now celebrate this unique jewel — it's the only gemstone created by a living creature — on National Wear Your Pearls Day each Dec. 15.

If you're looking for a new set of pearls — or any jewelry for that matter — you're likely to see more discounts in December than in the new year.

You'll also save on these finds this month.

- golf clubs
- wedding dresses
- champagne

- pajamas
- gift cards
- post-Christmas holiday decorations

Smart money moves to build a richer retirement

Chart your path to financial freedom 26

Social Security simplified: Unravel
the secrets to a steady income 32

Pension payout: How to maximize
your benefits 43

Rock-solid savings: Make the most
of your 401(k) and IRA 46

Investment success: Wise ways to
help your money grow 53

Taxes: Refunds and rip-offs you
don't want to miss 59

Earn extra cash to boost your
retirement budget 69

Chart your path to financial freedom

Watch out for these budgeting blunders that could sink your savings

"It's important to make the most out of every dollar during retirement," says Bruce McClary, vice president of communications for the National Foundation for Credit Counseling. Consider the big picture as you build your budget to avoid making these common retirement-ruining mistakes.

Retiring based on your age, not your bank account. You've hit that magic age of 65, so it's time to trade your briefcase for a fishing rod, right? Not so fast.

Experts say it's best to determine your retirement age based off of your savings, not some other milestone. If you retire at 65 without enough money to cover your bills, you'll spend years in debt. You might even need to go back to work.

Taking your Social Security too early. Tempted to tap into your Social Security money as soon as you can? That move could cost you thousands over your lifetime.

If you take your benefits at 62 when you become eligible, your monthly check may be up to 30% lower than if you had waited until full retirement age.

Take it from David. He did the math and realized that if he waits until his full benefits kick in at 67, he will receive $440 more each month than if he takes his benefits at 62.

Setting unrealistic expectations for your pension plan or retirement accounts. The days of relying on your pension to pay for retirement are going the way of the dodo bird. If you're lucky enough to still have one, you might not be able to rely on it forever.

New laws have made it easy for companies to buy out your pension. So your monthly check could be swapped for a one-time payment, which makes you responsible for making the funds last through retirement.

Need help building a budget? Reach out to the National Foundation for Credit Counseling (NFCC). "There are free resources online and a nationwide network of counselors available to assist with household budgeting and debt management," says Bruce McClary, vice president of communications for the NFCC. To find more information, go online to *nfcc.org* or call 800-388-2227.

If you're relying on other accounts, like a 401(k), you need to make sure you set realistic standards. Even if you get an 8% return on your investments this year, don't design your budget around it. You'll be in trouble if next year the returns are only 5%.

A post-retirement spending spree will wreck your golden years. You probably have big plans for the first few years of retirement. You've got the time and the energy to take that long-awaited trip to Italy. Or you might want to eat lunch at your favorite cafe every day.

Many seniors splurge during the first few years of retirement, only to see their savings dry up too early. Make a plan and watch your spending so you don't eat through your nest egg.

Forgot to account for inflation? That could come back to haunt you. It might not feel like it's been long since movie tickets were less than $5 per person. But now you're hard pressed to get out of the theater without spending twice that.

And inflation impacts more than just the cost of entertainment. At the average 3% annual inflation rate, your cost of living will double within 25 years. Your retirement budget needs to account for that. Make sure you don't deplete your savings too fast. You should also keep some money in investments that grow faster than the current rate of inflation.

Neglecting your future expenses will cost you down the line. Your budget at 45 was probably pretty different from your budget at 25. So why would you expect your expenses to be the same in 20 years?

As you age, health care costs start to creep up. You might have to take more trips to the doctor or hire a home aide. Leave extra money in the budget to pay for care down the road.

Debts could devastate your budget. Debt is a heavy burden to bear no matter where you are financially. Unfortunately, it's even harder to shed if you retire on a limited income.

> Your retirement income will probably come from multiple sources. Make sure you know when to expect each payment, says Bruce McClary. Some could be monthly, while others are less frequent. If you don't account for the differences, you might build your budget around money that isn't there.

But if you pay off what you owe before you hang up your hat, you'll free up money that could be better spent elsewhere during your retirement. For tips on paying down your balance, see *Dig yourself out of debt and never fall down the hole again* in the chapter *Credit cards: Safe and smart ways to take control of your plastic.*

Dodge disaster — don't put all your eggs in one basket. Risky investments are fine when you're 45. But now that you're not working anymore? You can't balance your budget if you've only invested in stocks and they're not doing well. Work to build a portfolio with a variety of stocks, bonds, and other investments.

Make sure that dream home won't become a costly nightmare.
Too many retirees decide where they'll spend their golden years
before doing any real research. You might love the idea of living
on the beach in the warm summer months, only to find you can't
stand hurricane season.

But by then you'll have sunk hundreds of thousands into buying
and owning a home. And relocating will cost you thousands more.
Do careful research before settling on a destination to avoid making
a costly move.

5 simple steps to a successful retirement

Late starts don't have to slow you down. Take it from Gladys Burrill,
who started running marathons in her 80s. She made history at 92
years old, when she became one of the oldest people to finish a
26.2 mile race.

If saving for retirement sounds just as daunting as running a
marathon, you're not alone. Experts say that nearly half of households headed by someone 55 and over don't have any money saved
for their golden years. Don't fret. Even if you're a late starter, you
can still find a way to retire rich.

Set your goals to kick-start your saving. Before you can set your
retirement plan in motion, you'll have to figure out how much
money you need and where you stand now.

Get an estimate of what your Social Security benefits will be, and
add up your retirement accounts. Next, crunch the numbers to see
what you spend every month. Experts say a good way to see how
much you need to save is to take your annual expenses and multiply
them by 25.

Take advantage of catch-up contributions. After you turn 50,
the IRS lets you stow away even more money in your retirement

accounts. These catch-up contributions let you add an extra $6,000 to your 401(k) and another $1,000 to an IRA.

Those numbers add up. Take it from Mary Beth. After turning 50, she maxed out her IRA contributions. With a 6% return on her investment, she saved up $163,000. Without those catch-up contributions, she'd retire with $23,000 less.

Postpone your retirement plans. A recent study found that working longer is one of the best ways to prep for your retirement. You'll be able to stow away more money, your investments have more time to mature, and you don't have to tap into your savings as early.

In fact, experts say that delaying your retirement by just three to six months has the same impact as saving an additional 1% for 30 years.

Seek out supplemental income. Your home is a smart place to start. Have a spare room? Consider renting it out. Have an attic full of old knickknacks? Host a yard sale. And put the extra cash toward your retirement.

Some experts also recommend tapping into your home's equity to boost your retirement savings. However, this is a serious financial consideration. To learn more about reverse mortgages and refinancing, read *How to turn your home into a cash cow* in the chapter *Your mortgage road map: Navigate home loans with ease.*

Consider an annuity. Many experts suggest plugging the holes in your retirement budget with an annuity. That's when you pay a lump sum to an insurance company in exchange for steady paychecks in the future.

For example, Greg bought a lifetime annuity when he turned 65. He had to pay $75,000 upfront, but in exchange he got $400 a month for the rest of his life. By the time he turns 95, that annuity will have paid out $144,000.

Annuities aren't for everyone, so before you sign the bottom line, be sure you understand the ins and outs.

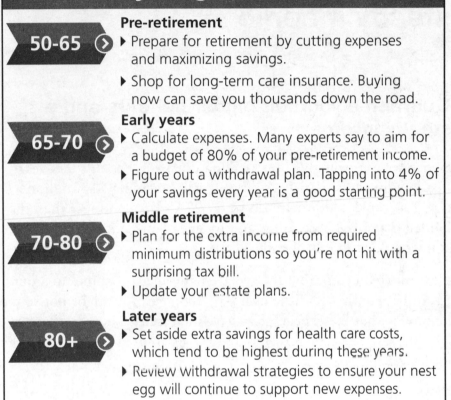

Fine-tune your budget in every stage of retirement

50-65 ⊙

Pre-retirement
- ▸ Prepare for retirement by cutting expenses and maximizing savings.
- ▸ Shop for long-term care insurance. Buying now can save you thousands down the road.

65-70 ⊙

Early years
- ▸ Calculate expenses. Many experts say to aim for a budget of 80% of your pre-retirement income.
- ▸ Figure out a withdrawal plan. Tapping into 4% of your savings every year is a good starting point.

70-80 ⊙

Middle retirement
- ▸ Plan for the extra income from required minimum distributions so you're not hit with a surprising tax bill.
- ▸ Update your estate plans.

80+ ⊙

Later years
- ▸ Set aside extra savings for health care costs, which tend to be highest during these years.
- ▸ Review withdrawal strategies to ensure your nest egg will continue to support new expenses.

Social Security simplified: Unravel the secrets to a steady income

Guarantee yourself bigger benefits and a steady income

Social Security will give out a trillion dollars in benefits this year. Just how much is that? Let's say you start spending $10 million a day. You could continue to do so for 273 years — longer than the United States has been a free and independent nation — and you still wouldn't run out of cash.

How much do you think the average retiree gets? It comes to around $1,460 a month, or a little over $17,500 a year. It might not sound like much, but life expectancies have increased by nearly a decade over the last 50 years. So seniors today get to draw payments for a lot longer than before.

"The value of your Social Security benefits, if you add up what those payments will be over the lifetime of receiving them, is an extremely large amount of money," says Devin Pope, a partner and senior wealth advisor at Albion Financial Group in Salt Lake City, Utah. "We're talking hundreds of thousands of dollars."

That's why, he says, it's so important to form a strategy before claiming benefits. After all, you want to get the maximum amount possible.

With that in mind, Pope advises seniors to consider the following before signing up for Social Security.

- Whether or not you'll be eligible for spousal benefits. For example, married couples can maximize their payments by coordinating the timing of their claims.

- Whether or not you're divorced or widowed. Seniors in those situations often have more options than, say, an older adult who never married.

- How long you expect to live. Older adults in poor health might consider claiming reduced benefits before full retirement age.

- The effect a job can have on your payments. Uncle Sam penalizes seniors who work while claiming benefits before full retirement age.

Determining when to apply for benefits is a personal and complex decision. So where can you go for help? You can tap into the Social Security website, Pope says, but it will provide you with information only. You'll have to go somewhere else for advice on what to do.

"I definitely would recommend working with a fee-only certified financial planner," he says, particularly in the case of married couples who, with a good strategy, could easily see their benefits edge upwards of, say, $700,000.

"Is it worth paying a couple of hundred dollars to have an analysis done so you can make the best decision? It probably is."

Fend off these financial mishaps to plump up future payments

The Social Security Handbook has more than 2,700 rules. No wonder 9 in 10 older Americans can't identify the factors that determine the size of their benefits. If you're among them, you could lose a fortune in payments.

Why not make sure you're getting everything you can from Social Security? After all, you've paid into it for years. Here are five common mistakes and provisions seniors often miss.

Being unaware of spousal perks. The Social Security Administration (SSA) looks kindly upon married seniors, allowing them to choose between the higher of two benefits — their own or up to 50% of their spouse's full retirement amount.

Say you're eligible for $800 a month in benefits based on your work record. But your spouse qualifies for $1,800 each month. You could get $900 a month — an extra $100 — by claiming the spousal payment.

But remember, you aren't eligible for spousal benefits unless your husband or wife is already collecting Social Security. And the government will permanently reduce those benefits if you begin collecting before your full retirement age.

Want to upgrade your monthly Social Security check? If you were born before Jan. 2, 1954, you might be able to take advantage of a little-known provision that lets you claim your spousal benefit at age 66 while your own benefits accumulate delayed retirement credits. This strategy increases your own retirement benefit up to 32%.

Underestimating survivor benefits. Don't claim Social Security benefits before full retirement age without considering the impact it could have on your spouse — particularly if you're the higher earner. That's because widows and widowers are eligible for up to 100% of their deceased spouse's benefits, including any delayed retirement credits that might have accumulated.

Here's a strategy that might work for couples with a big difference in incomes. The lower-earning spouse collects Social Security before full retirement age. The higher-earning spouse, meanwhile, waits until age 70 to claim benefits.

Why? Because Uncle Sam will tack an extra 8% onto that monthly payment for each year the higher earner delays drawing benefits between full retirement age and age 70. If the higher earner dies first, the lower earner will be eligible for 100% of the survivor benefit once they reach full retirement age.

Need help making ends meet? Supplement your income with this secret program

You never imagined anyone would give out free money to help you pay for things like food, clothing, and housing. But Supplemental Security Income (SSI) does just that. To qualify, you must be at least 65 years old, blind, or disabled. The government program, run by the Social Security Administration, limits a single person's maximum monthly payment to $771. Still, that's nearly $5,000 over six months to pay your bills. Eligible couples can get up to $1,157 a month.

Of course, you'll have to meet very strict income limits and have less than $2,000 in assets if you're single — $3,000 if you're married — but your car and home don't count.

Use the Benefit Eligibility Screening Tool at *ssabest.benefits.gov* to find out if you qualify for SSI or other benefits. Lots of people who get SSI are also eligible for food stamps and Medicaid.

Jumping the gun on jumping the broom. Nearing retirement and planning on tying the knot a second time? You may want to hold off a bit. That's because 60 is the age when widows and widowers can begin to collect survivor benefits if they haven't yet remarried. If you wait until age 60 or after to remarry, you're eligible for what could amount to tens of thousands of dollars.

Take the case of Betty. She waited until she turned 60 to remarry so she could collect reduced survivor benefits of $1,200 a month — that's $14,400 in the first year alone.

And surviving spouses like Betty get an added bonus called a restricted application. That means she has the option of collecting survivor benefits while her own benefits continue to grow until full retirement or later. Or she can continue to collect survivor benefits for the rest of her life — whichever makes the most financial sense.

Not checking your earnings record. Everybody slips up. But in the case of the federal government, clerical errors related to your tax return could result in the SSA not recording your income for a given year.

The end result? The SSA doesn't credit you for the Social Security taxes you paid. Losing benefits that are rightfully yours is one of the worst errors you can make, especially if you're on a fixed income.

Check your earnings record by creating your personal Social Security account at *ssa.gov/myaccount*. If you find something amiss, collect documentation — W-2s, pay stubs, or tax returns — and contact the SSA at 800-772-1213.

In most cases, you'll have a little over three years after you earned the income to request a correction.

Hanging up your hat too early. The majority of retirees begin collecting Social Security before full retirement age. But doing so cuts the size of your monthly check.

The SSA bases your payments on the 35 years in which you made the most money. Work less than that, and the SSA will average $0 into its

> Divorced? You might be eligible for up to 50% of your ex-spouse's benefits if you were married at least 10 years. To qualify, you must be at least 62 years old and single. Ex-spouses may also qualify for survivor benefits if they haven't remarried before the age of 60.

calculations for the years you weren't employed. The good news is your salary is probably higher later in your career than it was, say, in your early 20s — a sure way to bump up your future benefits.

Wish you didn't start claiming Social Security before your full retirement age? Fortunately, you can withdraw your application. The catch? You've got to do it within a year of filing your claim and pay back the benefits you received.

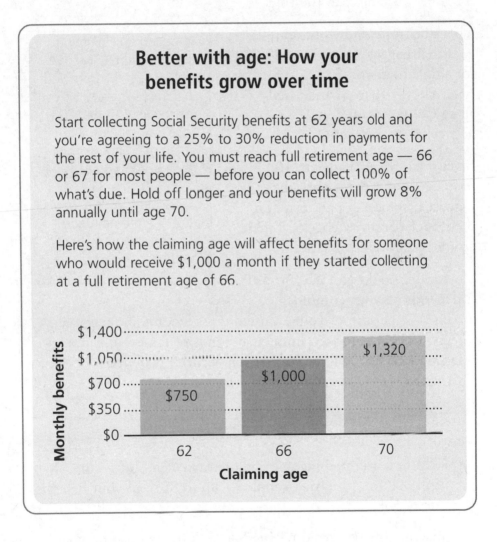

Better with age: How your benefits grow over time

Start collecting Social Security benefits at 62 years old and you're agreeing to a 25% to 30% reduction in payments for the rest of your life. You must reach full retirement age — 66 or 67 for most people — before you can collect 100% of what's due. Hold off longer and your benefits will grow 8% annually until age 70.

Here's how the claiming age will affect benefits for someone who would receive $1,000 a month if they started collecting at a full retirement age of 66.

Maximize your benefits by minimizing taxes

Many seniors are surprised to learn they might have to pay taxes on part of their Social Security payments. Even retirees with modest incomes are subject to the rule.

That's because the income thresholds that trigger the tax — $25,000 for single filers and $32,000 for joint filers — haven't increased since Congress voted in 1983 to levy retirement benefits.

Back then, fewer than 1 in 10 retirees — only those with the highest incomes — paid taxes on their Social Security checks. Today, around half of beneficiaries do.

> Working and claiming benefits early? The SSA will deduct $1 from your benefits for every $2 you earn over $17,640. The year you reach full retirement, it'll knock off $1 for every $3 you earn over $46,920. The SSA will recalculate your benefits at full retirement age to credit you for the withheld benefits.

How much could you have to pay? It depends on your combined income — the sum of your adjusted gross income, nontaxable interest earned from, say, municipal bonds or tax-exempt money market funds, and half of your Social Security benefits.

- If your combined income is between $25,000 and $34,000 — or between $32,000 and $44,000 for a married couple — up to half of your benefits are taxable.

- If your combined income is more than $34,000 — or $44,000 for a married couple — up to 85% of your benefits are taxable.

Fortunately, you can avoid paying Social Security taxes on your benefits. Here's what the government doesn't tell you.

Consider the effects of working. Being on the payroll while collecting Social Security is a surefire way to raise your combined income — and possibly your taxes. But what if you want to keep your job?

If you've reached full retirement age but aren't yet age 70, you can suspend the benefits you've been receiving. By going this route, you'll earn delayed retirement credits that will lock in a higher payment for life.

Form a strategy for other sources of income. Extra wages aren't the only earnings that bump up your combined income. Uncle Sam also includes the money you receive from investments, pensions, and rental property, as well as withdrawals from traditional IRAs and 401(k) accounts. Consider the following ways to tiptoe around the tax issue.

- Save for retirement with a Roth IRA or 401(k). You can withdraw the funds tax-free, and they aren't considered part of your combined income.

- Roll over money from a traditional IRA or 401(k) into a Roth IRA before claiming Social Security. You'll have to pay income taxes in the year of conversion. But you'll avoid having to take required minimum distributions later — those pesky, mandatory withdrawals that can push you into a higher tax bracket and cause your benefits to be taxed.

- Retire to a tax-friendly state. Thirteen states tax Social Security benefits in addition to the federal government, leaving 37 states for you to choose from. Some of the states that tax benefits offer exemptions or deductions based on age or income.

- Keep track of your investments. Capital gains on the sale of stocks and mutual funds, along with dividend distributions, can increase your tax rate and make a larger portion of your benefits taxable. Depending on your circumstances, you might consider moving some of your money in taxable accounts into ones that don't generate as much taxable income.

- Withdraw funds from taxable retirement accounts early in retirement and delay claiming Social Security benefits.

Want to know beforehand if you'll have to pay? Work through the numbers on Page 4 of IRS Publication 915. Or go to *calcxml.com/english.htm* and click the link "How much of my Social Security benefit may be taxed" located under Taxation Calculators.

If you do wind up owing Uncle Sam, you can make quarterly estimated tax payments to the IRS or have federal taxes withheld from your benefits.

Disability denied? Take this step to get what you deserve

You've probably heard how difficult it is to get Social Security disability benefits. It takes a lot of time and effort to prove that a medical condition prevents you from working. In fact, eligibility rules are so strict that 70% of disability claims are denied during the initial application process.

But that doesn't mean you should give up hope. Most folks who appeal eventually get benefits. Here's what you need to do if the Social Security Administration rejects your claim.

- File a request for reconsideration.

- If your claim is denied again, request a hearing before an administrative law judge.

- If the judge rules against you, request an Appeals Council review.

File your appeals online at *ssa.gov/benefits/disability/appeal.html*. You must appeal within 60 days of receiving a denial. If the Appeals Council denies your request, you may file a civil suit in a federal district court.

Fact vs. fiction:
Test your Social Security smarts

Think Social Security will cover all your financial needs? Think again. Benefits replace just 40% of the average worker's wages. Surprised? Quiz yourself to discover how much you really know about Social Security.

Decide whether the following statements are true or false.

1. You need your ex-spouse's permission to claim benefits on their work record.   T ☐   F ☐

2. Benefits won't keep up with rising costs because they aren't adjusted for inflation.   T ☐   F ☐

3. The earliest you can apply for benefits is four months before you want them to begin.   T ☐   F ☐

4. Everyone gets denied the first time they apply for Social Security disability benefits.   T ☐   F ☐

5. Children may be eligible for Social Security benefits based on a parent's work record.   T ☐   F ☐

6. You have to go to your local Social Security office to apply for benefits.   T ☐   F ☐

See answers on the following page.

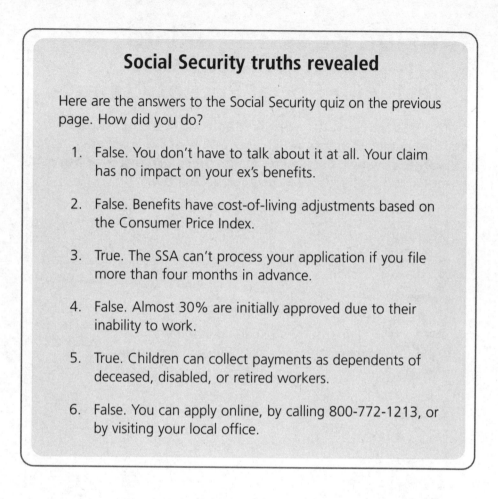

Social Security truths revealed

Here are the answers to the Social Security quiz on the previous page. How did you do?

1. False. You don't have to talk about it at all. Your claim has no impact on your ex's benefits.

2. False. Benefits have cost-of-living adjustments based on the Consumer Price Index.

3. True. The SSA can't process your application if you file more than four months in advance.

4. False. Almost 30% are initially approved due to their inability to work.

5. True. Children can collect payments as dependents of deceased, disabled, or retired workers.

6. False. You can apply online, by calling 800-772-1213, or by visiting your local office.

Pension payout: How to maximize your benefits

Make the most of your golden years with the right payment plan

New guidelines from the U.S. Treasury Department mean more and more seniors are forced to choose between a lump sum payment or monthly pension. And if you're one of them, you know how difficult it is to pick either a one-time windfall or guaranteed lifetime income. So which is better for your retirement?

Follow the 6% rule to decide on your payout. Some experts recommend considering monthly payments if they are worth 6% or more of the lump sum. How do you figure that out? First, take your monthly pension and multiply it by 12. Then divide the result by the total lump sum offer.

For example, Mark was offered a one-time lump sum of $200,000 in exchange for his $1,500 monthly pension. His current plan pays out $18,000 a year, which is 9% of the lump sum. So in this case, it might make more sense for him to stick with his monthly payments.

That's because if he takes the lump sum and invests it, he may need an unrealistic return to make it come out ahead of the monthly payment option. Of course, this is just a starting off point. You'll also want to consider your age, life expectancy, and financial situation.

Weigh your options against your retirement goals. You'll have a steady stream of income throughout your retirement if you stick with monthly payments. The money won't be affected by market fluctuations, and you won't have to manage the funds yourself to make sure they last.

On the other hand, a lump sum provides a cash bonanza, so it could be a better choice if you have debts that need to be paid or expect large medical expenses in the near future. Taking the cash may make sense if your monthly needs are already met with other forms of guaranteed income, like Social Security, and you want more flexibility with investing or passing the funds to your loved ones.

Turn your lump sum into lifelong income

Want to take the lump sum instead of your monthly pension? Use these tips to stretch those dollars through your golden years.

- Consider an annuity. Some experts recommend using part or all of the funds to buy an immediate annuity. That way you'll have a guaranteed source of retirement income. But be careful — you might find that your original plan offered a better monthly payment.

- Stow the cash in a 401(k) or IRA. Your lump sum payday will be treated the same as normal income, which means you have to pay taxes on it. But if you don't need the money anytime soon, rolling some into an IRA or 401(k) could lessen the tax hit.

Before you decide to take the lump sum, consult a financial advisor. Some expert advice could help you avoid major tax mistakes and ensure you make the best decision.

Keep your payments coming with a simple search

Are you one of the 80,000 people missing out on free money? The Pension Benefit Guaranty Corporation (PBGC) — a government agency that helps protect pension payments — says over $400 million in unpaid pensions is waiting to be claimed.

To see if you're entitled to benefits, call 800-400-7242 or go online to *pbgc.gov/search/unclaimed-pensions* and type your name into the search bar.

If your pension is insured by the PBGC, you may be eligible for benefits even if the plan is terminated. Those who start receiving benefits at 66 could get up to $6,169.75 a month, or $74,025 a year. Retire later and you could collect more.

5 steps to protect your pension

Don't make assumptions about your pension. Take these defensive steps against threats that could shrivel your savings.

- Snare paperwork errors. Mistakes can cut a pension amount. Scour your pension benefit statement for accurate years of service, birthdate, and Social Security number. Correct any errors you find.

- Double-check pension calculations. Use the pension formula from the pension's summary plan description. If your results differ from your employer's, ask your plan administrator for a breakdown of the pension calculation.

- Know your stuff. Pension plans can be changed, converted to a different retirement plan, or even terminated. Be prepared.

- File your defense. Store all pension statements, summary annual reports, W-2 forms, tax returns, and your summary plan description in a file. Refer to these if errors or problems occur.

- Confirm information. If you leave a company before retirement, get written confirmation of what your deferred vested pension will be or what you're eligible for. Also verify your address with the plan administrator every few years.

Rock-solid savings: Make the most of your 401(k) and IRA

Withdrawing retirement funds — a fresh look at tax-savvy strategies

"People are nervous about starting to take income out of their retirement savings because they don't want to run out," says James M. Christian, retirement income certified professional and independent financial advisor. "You have a pile of money that you've been accumulating. You've never drawn money out of it, and now it needs to last the rest of your lifetime."

So how do you build a bulletproof strategy that minimizes taxes and ensures your savings will last?

Sidestep pricey penalties by meeting these minimums. You might have heard your traditional 401(k) or IRA described as a tax-deferred retirement account. That means the government hasn't touched the money yet.

Now that you're retired, it's time for Uncle Sam to take his cut. And the IRS won't wait around forever. When you turn 70 1/2, you're required to pull some cash out of your savings every year. This amount, known as the required minimum distribution (RMD), depends on your age and account balance. And if you don't take your RMD? You'll get slapped with a 50% tax penalty on the amount you should have withdrawn.

> Retired? The IRS lets you take penalty-free withdrawals from your 401(k) or IRA after you turn 59 1/2. However, if you're still working at the company that provides the retirement account, you might not be able to access those savings just yet.

Don't fork over additional taxes unnecessarily, Christian says. "That's probably the biggest mistake. It's one thing to be patriotic and pay your fair share, but you don't want to pay more than is required."

To figure out how much you need to withdraw, go online to *irs.gov/pub/irs-tege/uniform_rmd_wksht.pdf*.

Avoid higher taxes with this withdrawal secret. "The common strategy to minimize taxes is knowing where you're going to draw money from," Christian says. "Knowing how that income is going to show up and when it's going to show up on the tax return can help you save easily 10% in unnecessary taxes."

Conventional withdrawal strategies tell you to pull money out of taxable assets — like investment accounts, bank accounts, and money market mutual funds — for the first few years, then traditional 401(k) plans or IRAs, and finally Roth accounts. That way your tax-deferred accounts have more time to grow. But it may not be the smartest strategy.

In one scenario analyzed by Fidelity, withdrawing proportional amounts from each account at the same time cut taxes by almost 40% compared to pulling money from one at a time. How does this strategy work?

Say 20% of your nest egg is in a taxable investment account, 50% is in a traditional 401(k), and the last 30% is saved in a Roth IRA. If you need to draw around $35,000 to cover your expenses, you might pull $7,000 from your investments (20%), $17,500 from your traditional 401(k) (50%), and $10,500 from your Roth IRA (30%).

The only income that will be taxed is the $17,500 from your traditional 401(k). That means you'll stay in the 12% tax bracket your entire retirement.

If you went the traditional route? You'd pay taxes for fewer years, but the hit would be larger. That's because when it was time to withdraw from your tax-deferred retirement account, you'd need to take out more money, which could bump you into a higher bracket.

47

RMD oversights — solve past slip-ups with a few simple steps

Miss your RMD deadline? Don't wait around for the IRS to make the first move. Take action to avoid getting hit with that 50% fine.

- Take the correct amount of money out of your retirement accounts.

- Call the IRS at 800-829-3676 to request Form 5329 or go online to *irs.gov/pub/irs-pdf/f5329.pdf*.

- Haven't filed your taxes yet? Attach Form 5329 to your tax return along with a letter explaining the mistake and what you've done to fix it. Otherwise, mail the form and letter in as soon as possible.

You should hear back from the IRS within a few months.

Foolproof 401(k): The 2 smartest retirement moves you can make

Too many retirees worry that they will run out of savings. Fortunately, with a few smart moves you can grow your money like crazy and put those fears to bed.

Double your nest egg with this simple step. Experts say Americans leave $24 billion on the table each year. How, you might ask, are people missing out on so much money? They don't take advantage of employer-matched 401(k) contributions.

These programs let your employer add money to your retirement account based on the amount of your own annual contribution. So your employer will match a portion of every dollar you save — up to a certain percentage of your salary.

Margaret's company, for example, matches 100% of her contributions up to 5% of her salary. Because she makes $50,000 a year, if she starts saving enough to receive the full employer match, she could get an extra $2,500 in her 401(k) annually.

If she continues to do this over the next 15 years at a 7% rate of return, her retirement savings will balloon to a whopping $130,000. But without her employer's contributions, she'd only have half that much.

Avoid sneaky fees that will break the bank. Do you know the difference a single percent can make? A 1% fee on a 401(k) could cost $590,000 over the course of 40 years, according to an analysis from NerdWallet, a personal finance and information service.

Don't lose a huge fortune to these tiny fees. Dodge those account drainers with a little know-how.

- Watch out for investment fees. You might notice that the mutual fund in your 401(k) takes a 1.5% cut of its earnings each year. That's because the costs of managing the fund are passed on to you. Experts say these fees are easy to fight, though. Simply look for index funds or other low-cost options.

- Ask about money-minded alternatives. Certain charges are built in to your retirement plans, so you can't get around paying them. However, ask if your employer can offer a low-fee option. If your boss has money invested in the company's retirement accounts, he might want a new plan, too.

- Have a backup plan in place. Can't shake those fees? You might want to switch to an IRA. They often have options with lower fees. Crunch the numbers first, though. A generous employer match might cancel out higher fees.

When a traditional retirement account trumps a Roth

Experts often recommend putting your savings into a Roth — or post-tax — IRA or 401(k) instead of a traditional pretax account. The reason? Stowing away money after you've already paid taxes on it lets you access your cash in retirement without giving a cut to Uncle Sam.

Not all savings strategies are one-size-fits-all, though. In cases like these, you might actually be making a big money mistake if you decide to go with a Roth account.

Avoid making the switch if you'll be in a lower tax bracket during retirement. You'll only stand to save money with a Roth retirement account if your tax rates are going to be higher when you've retired. But if it's the other way around?

Melissa thought a Roth IRA would be a guaranteed way to maximize her savings in retirement. She started saving $5,000 in a post-tax account every year after she turned 50. By the time she retired at 65, she had saved up a hefty $134,000.

The only problem? When she was working, she was in the 22% tax bracket, which is higher than her retirement tax rate of 12%. That means a traditional IRA would have actually given her $10,000 more in total savings.

No wiggle room in your budget? A Roth IRA could be a mistake. When you earn a paycheck, the first thing Uncle Sam does is take a bite. Unless you contribute to a traditional retirement account, that is.

Any money you contribute to a traditional IRA will be subtracted from your income before the government takes its cut. And that lowers the taxes on your earnings, which scores you a plumper paycheck compared to if you put the same amount into a Roth account.

Mark found that out the hard way. He put $250 a month into a traditional IRA for years. When he switched to a Roth account? He lost out on the tax break, so even though he was contributing the same amount, his take-home pay dropped by $50 a month.

Like all Roth savers, he'll reap the benefits later when he withdraws the cash tax-free. But if money is tight, many people choose to take advantage of the tax break upfront.

Look before you leap — new law does away with Roth conversion do-overs

In the past, you had the chance to undo your Roth IRA conversion. If you converted a traditional retirement account into a post-tax one, you could decide to change your mind before the tax bill was due.

This strategy — known as recharacterization — was great if you realized the tax savings didn't add up or if you simply changed your mind. But new laws mean Roth conversions are permanent. Make sure you consider all your options before making the switch.

CAUTION

Keep your savings rolling: How to pick the perfect IRA

Mark only worked at his job for a few years before he found a better opportunity. He built up a few thousand dollars in his company's 401(k), but he couldn't bring it with him to his next job. His solution? He rolled over his retirement savings into an IRA.

This gave him more options for his investments. Plus the fees were lower, so he could save more. If you have a 401(k) that doesn't

51

cover your saving needs, you might decide to make the same move.

The first step is to pick out the IRA that best suits your retirement strategy. Unlike a 401(k) — which is established by your employer — you have the freedom to choose your IRA provider. Here's how to get started.

> When you take money out of your 401(k) for the rollover, you have 60 days to put it in your new account. If you miss that deadline, you can get hit with a huge tax penalty. To cut down on costly mistakes, use a direct transfer — which means the money goes right from one account into another.

Decide what type of investor you'll be. Would you rather be more hands-on or would you rather let a pro manage your money?

Some IRA providers will handle your investments — for a price. They take a small slice of your earnings every year as a management fee. However, if you don't want to buy and trade investments on your own, you might decide it's worth the money. Experts say to look for one with a low management fee — 0.4% or less. Shop around to find the best deals.

If you're a more involved investor, consider an account that doesn't come with an annual commission. Some charge fees every time you buy or sell investments, but if you look carefully you can find options without that extra cost.

Choose your investment type to narrow down providers. Not all IRAs will give you the same investment options. For example, an IRA at a brokerage will let you buy mutual funds. And if you go with an insurance company, you could invest in annuities.

Can't make up your mind? Good news. You can have multiple IRAs. You'll have more options for investments, but it can make managing your money more complicated. Remember, you're only allowed to invest an annual combined total of $6,000 — or $7,000 if you're over 55 — in all of your IRAs.

Investment success: Wise ways to help your money grow

Protect your portfolio from these retirement-ruining blunders

Imagine if you put $50 a month in a piggy bank. After 45 years, you'd have $27,000 saved up. Not too shabby right? Think again. If you invested that money instead, you'd be a lot further ahead. Even with a modest 5% rate of return, you'd be looking at nearly $100,000.

Of course, investing isn't a surefire thing. If you make these five mistakes, you could sink your retirement savings. But with a little know-how, anyone can avoid these financial blunders.

Trying to time the market. Think you've spotted the perfect moment to buy and sell your investments? You might want to reconsider acting on price movement predictions. Successfully timing the market is incredibly difficult. Even seasoned professionals can lose big when they use this strategy.

> Not shopping for lone stock? Exchange-traded or mutual funds bundle investments to help you diversify your portfolio. Be sure to research funds carefully. You need to understand the risks and fees involved. And you also want to understand the companies you're investing in.

You should focus on time in the market, instead. Experts say to adopt a long-term investment strategy rather than to pull out of the market based on emotional reactions to price changes.

Not doing your research before you buy. Would you purchase a house without even looking at it? You could find out that the halls are too narrow, the floors are uneven, and the stairs are too steep.

And if you buy investments without researching them first, you might wind up with a similar sense of buyer's remorse.

When you buy stocks, stick with companies that you know and understand. That way you'll have some idea of how the prices will react in the market.

Forgetting to regularly rebalance your portfolio. Chances are, your lifestyle has changed quite a bit since you were in your early 20s. And if your lifestyle is different, your investment options should be, too.

Experts often recommend you begin swapping stocks for safer investments, such as bonds, as you age. So how much should you keep in the market? One method is to subtract your current age from 110. So if you're 65, stocks would make up 45% of your portfolio.

And make sure to check your asset mix and adjust it every year. Since bonds and stocks won't grow at the same rate, you could find yourself with a lopsided portfolio if you just set it and forget it.

Hoarding your investments instead of turning assets into income. You've scrimped and saved for decades to build up an investment portfolio. Now what? Some retirees don't want to cash out their investments, but you need to have money to live on.

If you want security, experts often suggest turning your investments into a guaranteed payday. Look into options like life annuities or treasury-backed bonds. That way you'll always have your expenses covered, even if the stock market has a bad year.

Betting on past performance. Say you flipped a coin three times, and it always came up heads. Does that mean it's going to be heads

> Want to keep more of your cash in the market? Make sure you have a flexible withdrawal plan. A good starting point is to only cash out 4% of your portfolio every year. You might need to change it up, though, depending on how well the market is doing.

the fourth time you flip? Of course not. But some investors make the mistake of betting all their money on the recent past.

Stocks or funds that skyrocketed in value over the past couple of years aren't surefire things. You could lose a lot of money if you put your life savings into a company, only for it to go bust a few years later.

Instead of focusing on recent history, go back and examine long-term trends. Investments that maintain steady growth over 10 or 15 years are a better bet.

Take advantage of this legal account to stock up a quarter-of-a-million dollars

About $280,000. That's the cost of health care throughout retirement for a 65 year-old couple, according to a recent Fidelity survey. You could pay for those costs with traditional retirement funds. Or you could use this investment account and score a triple tax break. Just ask Fred and Fran.

They realized how far their health savings account (HSA) could take them and set aside $7,000 a year in their family plan after Fred turned 44. Their yearly health care costs were low, and their investments grew at 5% every year. That meant by the time they applied for Medicare, their savings had ballooned to over $250,000 — enough to cover almost all of their health expenses in retirement.

Tap your reserves to take care of your medical costs. You can't contribute any more cash to an HSA once you're on Medicare, but you're still able to use those funds. And the best part? The tax advantages.

- Money put into an HSA comes right out of your paycheck before the IRS gets a cut.

- You don't owe taxes on any returns on your investment.

- And if you take the money out of the account to pay for qualified health care expenses? It isn't taxed.

You can use those funds to pay for your insurance premiums. Or you can use them to pay for things that aren't covered under Medicare, like long-term care or dental work.

Need extra income? You don't have to use your HSA for health care. In fact, you can use it for anything you want. If you're 65 or older, you'll avoid the 20% tax penalty, and those funds are treated as a normal retirement account.

That means you can take out money just like you would with a 401(k). All you need to do is pay income taxes. But unlike traditional retirement accounts, HSAs don't have required minimum distributions. Your investments can keep growing until you need the cash.

3 simple precautions to skirt a shady investor

Scammers steal $37 billion from retirees each year. That's more than NASA spent on every single Apollo mission — combined. Use these tips to protect your investments from serial swindlers.

- Avoid the free-lunch trap. Scammers offer free meals and gifts to lure you into high-pressure pitches. Don't do business with someone who won't give you time to mull it over.

- Check licenses. Anyone selling investments needs to have the proper paperwork. Make sure a seller is registered with help from the Securities and Exchange Commission (SEC). Go online to *adviserinfo.sec.gov/ IAPD/ Default.aspx* or call 800-732-0330.

- Review history. Searching for a seller's license at the SEC website will also bring up a list of complaints or issues on his record. Steer clear of traders with a history of personal bankruptcies, customer complaints, or other red flags.

CAUTION

Secure your savings with 4 senior-friendly investments

A twisted ankle was only a temporary setback when you were a teen. Now that you're older, the same injury could do permanent damage. And your investments aren't too different. When you're retired, a risky investment could cripple your savings. Here are some safer options for seniors.

Municipal bonds. Local governments often sell bonds to fund their projects. You give them cash today, and in exchange you'll get a bigger payday a few years down the line. The best part? The money is generally exempt from federal taxes.

That's great news, especially if you're already taking required minimum distributions out of your retirement accounts. You'll get extra income without being bumped up into another tax bracket.

Remember to check out bond ratings before you buy, though. AAA marks the safest bonds, while those with a rating below BBB are riskier.

Treasury inflation-protected securities (TIPS). These are investments you can buy directly from the U.S. government. Unlike bonds, TIPS offer varying interest payment amounts depending on inflation. If inflation goes up, so does the payout on your investment. That means your money will keep up its purchasing power throughout retirement.

And because they're backed by Uncle Sam, TIPS are nearly risk-free. You'll never get a payday that's less than your initial investment. But if deflation occurs, the payout won't be as high.

Certificates of deposit (CDs). Want to flip the script and loan money to the bank? You can with a CD. You give the bank a lump sum, and in a few years you'll get your money back with interest. It's insured by the FDIC, too, so your savings are completely safe.

They offer higher interest rates than savings accounts, but you usually can't take your money out early without getting hit with a pricey penalty.

Dividend-paying funds. Scared of the stock market just because you're retired? Don't be. Stocks may be a riskier investment, but the returns are often higher.

Instead of buying individual shares, consider an index fund made of dividend-paying stocks. Index funds tend to be more stable than individual stock. Plus dividends offer the opportunity for consistent growth while combating inflation.

Sage advice: Choose the right financial planner to dodge DIY uh-ohs

You might think financial advisors will only help people with multimillion dollar portfolios. That couldn't be further from the truth. "There are many advisors serving middle America," says James M. Christian, retirement income certified professional and independent financial advisor.

A financial planner can help you avoid tax blunders or streamline your investment portfolio. You just need to know how to find the right one.

"Call an advisor and ask them, 'How do you get paid?'" says Christian. Look for someone who offers hourly rates or flat fees. That way you can avoid paying long-term management fees or commissions.

And while the upfront costs may seem high, proper planning could save you from major money mistakes in the long run. "Don't be afraid to spend some money for a professional," Christian says. "You're going to get some pearls of wisdom that will save you time, money, and hassle."

Taxes: Refunds and rip-offs you don't want to miss

Senior tax savers to pump up your piggy bank

Did you know the IRS gives free tax advice to seniors age 60 and up through its Tax Counseling for the Elderly Program? It's just one of the ways the federal government tries to help older Americans make ends meet.

Are you one of the millions of retirees on a fixed income? If so, these senior-friendly tax breaks might come in handy.

Credit for the elderly and disabled. If you owe the IRS, this credit — which ranges between $3,750 and $7,500 — could cut your tax liability dollar for dollar. To qualify, you must be 65 or older or have a permanent disability for which you are receiving taxable benefits. Income limits apply.

Want to see if you're eligible? Go to the IRS Interactive Tax Assistant at *irs.gov/help/ita* and click "Do I Qualify for the Credit for the Elderly or Disabled."

Medicare premiums. The IRS considers Medicare premiums — those paid for Medicare parts B and D, Medigap, and Medicare Advantage — deductible medical expenses. To benefit, most seniors who itemize can write off unreimbursed, qualified medical expenses that exceed 10% of their adjusted gross income (AGI).

Let's say, for example, your AGI comes to $20,000. You'd be able to deduct any qualified medical expenses over $2,000.

Long-term care payments. The premiums you pay for qualified long-term care insurance policies are also considered medical expenses.

59

That means you can add them to your Medicare premiums and other qualifying costs when you calculate your itemized deduction.

But be aware that the IRS caps the size of the long-term care deduction, depending on the taxpayer's age. For someone between the ages of 60 and 70, the max is $4,220. Older than 70? You can deduct up to $5,270.

> Looking for a Tax Counseling for the Elderly program near you? Go to *irs.treasury.gov/freetaxprep* or call 800-906-9887. The IRS-certified volunteers who provide free tax counseling often specialize in questions about pensions and retirement-related issues unique to seniors.

Generally, seniors who run their own businesses don't have to itemize or meet the AGI spending threshold to take a medical deduction. But they can't go over the government's limits on deduction amounts.

Qualified charitable donations. Have to take an income-boosting — and taxable — required minimum distribution (RMD) from your IRA? Consider donating the funds to charity. The IRS lets seniors who have reached the age of 70 1/2 directly transfer up to $100,000 from their IRAs to a qualified charity. The gift won't be included in your adjusted gross income, and may help you stay below the cutoffs for taxation of your Social Security benefits.

But don't take the RMD as income before donating, advises Raymond Wilson, a metro Atlanta-based certified public accountant who has prepared taxes for five years. "The check has to be written to the charity, not to the individual who then writes a check to the charity," he says.

Why not? Funds sent to your bank count as taxable income.

Don't owe the IRS? Here's why you should file anyway

Only people whose incomes are above a certain amount have to pay federal taxes. For example, single filers age 65 or older can bring home as much as $13,850 and not have to file a return. That amount increases to $27,000 if the taxpayer is married and filing jointly and both spouses are at least 65.

But you'll want to go ahead and crunch the numbers if you've had taxes withheld and the IRS owes you a refund. Filing a return also starts the clock ticking on the time limits the IRS has in which it can conduct an audit and collect back taxes. And it prevents identity thieves from filing fraudulent returns in your name.

Clearing the clutter — how to store, what to save, and when to shred

It seems to happen every April. Harried taxpayers upturn their homes in a frenzied search for the documents they need to file their taxes — things like mortgage and brokerage statements, W-2s, medical bills, and mileage receipts.

Do you find yourself among them? If so, a little organization will put you on the path to tackling tax season like a pro.

Kick chaos to the curb with three-folder filing. Pick an organizational method that works for you, and file away your tax records as soon as they cross the front doorstep. Some folks find that storing their paperwork with a simple three-folder system helps cut down on tax-time stress. Here's how to label each of the folders.

- Income. It's where you'll keep all records of every penny you earn — salary, interest, dividends, and earnings from the sale of stock. Don't forget about gambling winnings and jury duty payments.

- Deductions. This envelope includes proof of expenses that might qualify as deductions. Examples include medical receipts, statements for mortgage and student loan interest, child care costs, and contributions you made to your health savings account.

- Investments. This is where you'll put contribution and distribution records for tax-deferred IRAs and 401(k) accounts. You'll also want to include contributions to Roth retirement accounts so you don't get taxed twice. And keep paperwork proving the cost basis of your investments — it's what the IRS uses to determine your capital gain.

Time your tax-record tidying to ditch what you don't need.
How long should you keep all those documents? Fortunately, knowing which ones to keep and which to throw out is pretty easy.

The IRS recommends keeping tax records for three years from the date you filed your original return or two years from the date you paid the tax, whichever is later. But keep them for seven years if you claim a loss on debt that you can't collect or stock that has zero value.

Don't begin shredding, the IRS advises, unless you're sure you won't need the paperwork for some other purpose. And keep copies of your income tax returns indefinitely. They'll come

January is when taxpayers begin receiving the forms necessary to complete their returns. Check your mailbox for these documents.
- W-2 to report wages and taxes withheld
- SSA-1099 to report Social Security benefits
- 1099-R for distributions from pensions, annuities, and retirement plans
- 1099-DIV for dividend and capital gain distributions

in handy if you have to fix an earnings error on your Social Security record.

Pare down other paperwork for peace of mind. Tax records aren't the only type of documents you need to manage. Read on for advice on how long to keep other financial paperwork.

- Less than a year. Shred ATM, bank, and credit card receipts after comparing them with your monthly statements.

- More than a year. Keep loan documents until the loan is settled and car titles until you sell the car.

- Indefinitely. Never throw away official documents like Social Security cards, birth and death certificates, marriage licenses, and divorce decrees.

3 things your tax preparer wants you to know about hiring a pro

Form 1040. The federal government first released this infamous income tax document in 1914. Back then, it came with just a single page of instructions. Americans today need a 117-page booklet to make sense of the tax code.

No wonder millions of taxpayers hire someone to help prepare and file their returns. You'll want to follow these tips if you're one of them.

Do your homework. You entrust your tax preparer with the personal information necessary to file an accurate return. That's why it's important to find the right person. The IRS Directory of Federal Tax Return Preparers at *irs.treasury.gov/rpo/rpo.jsf* is a good place to find tax pros with credentials. Check with the Better Business Bureau for complaints, and avoid preparers who base their fees on percentage of your refund.

Once you've found the right person, stick with him, says Raymond Wilson, a metro Atlanta-based certified public accountant. "When you change preparers frequently they don't know your tax history," Wilson says. "Even though you may have a copy of the previous return, there's only so much a preparer can deduce from a few sheets of paper."

Gather up your paperwork. Organizing your tax documents before your appointment can make the process go more smoothly and quickly — which saves you money if you're paying by the hour. At the very least, you'll need to provide identification, a copy of your most recent return, and all income- and expense-related documents.

Don't leave any tax forms at home, Wilson says. "I can't even count the number of returns I've amended because people forget about those one-time distributions they took to buy a car or take a vacation," he says.

But Uncle Sam remembers. That's because the financial institution that distributes the funds, say from an IRA or 401(k), notifies the IRS each time you withdraw money — whether it's taxable or not.

The end result? A nasty letter from the IRS, says Wilson, that prompts panic in clients and return visits to his office. "The moral of the story is, if you get a tax form in the mail, report it," he says.

Ask about withholding.
Everyone, retirees included, must pay tax liabilities throughout the year. If you don't have enough taxes withheld, you could face a surprise year-end tax bill or even a penalty.

That's why seniors need to consider their total income when deciding how much tax

> The IRS issues most tax refunds within 21 days. But what if you need the money sooner? Some tax preparation companies offer refund advances along with their other services. Be aware that some advances require a credit check and come with fees and interest payments. You may be better off waiting.

to withhold from their pensions and Social Security, Wilson says. "A lot of times people will have 10% withheld from their pension," he says. But they fail to account for other sources of income, such as dividends, interest, and required minimum distributions, that could push them into a higher tax bracket.

"If they had considered their total income they would have realized they needed to withhold, maybe, an average of 15% on everything to cover their total liability for the year," he says.

Your tax preparer can help you decide on the percentage of income you need to withhold each year, Wilson says.

Scams 101: How to spot a shifty tax preparer

Scammers posing as tax preparers tend to pop up each filing season in fly-by-night storefronts that advertise big refunds. Once tax season is over, they're gone. And the client is left holding the bag.

That's why you need to steer clear of anyone who operates on a cash-only basis, claims bogus deductions and credits, or directs refunds to an account other than yours. Another red flag? Tax preparers who say they're endorsed by the IRS. The agency doesn't do that.

Always read your return and question anything that doesn't make sense. Never sign an incomplete return, and make sure it includes your preparer's signature and tax identification number. Remember you're responsible for the information on your tax return.

Tax prep checklist:
Dodge the top 4 filing mistakes made by seniors

1 in 4 taxpayers wait until the last minute to file their taxes. But scrambling to meet the deadline increases your likelihood of making costly errors. Use this checklist to avoid common blunders and save big tax dollars.

☐ **Take the higher standard deduction.**

Are you 65+? The IRS lets you increase the standard deduction — $12,200 for singles and $24,400 for married and filing jointly — by $1,650 if you're single or $1,300 for each spouse filing jointly.

☐ **Factor in Social Security benefits.**

Many seniors don't know that Social Security benefits may be taxable. Retirees with extra sources of income could pay taxes on up to 85% of their benefits.

☐ **Include required minimum distributions.**

You generally must begin withdrawing funds from IRA or 401(k) accounts at 70 1/2. If you don't — and fail to include the distribution as taxable income — you'll face a 50% penalty on the amount you should have withdrawn.

☐ **Double-check for accuracy.**

Looking to avoid delayed refunds and penalties? Make sure Social Security numbers, filing status, bank account numbers, and math are correct before filing.

Take stock of your finances to save on capital gains taxes

Most Americans would agree with former Supreme Court Justice Oliver Wendell Holmes Jr. when he said, "Taxes are what we pay for civilized society." In fact, about 9 in 10 taxpayers believe it's a citizen's civic duty to pay his fair share. After all, taxes fund major health programs like Medicare and Medicaid, as well as Social Security.

Any of your investments lose money between the purchase and sale? You can offset your capital gains with those capital losses. Wind up with a net capital loss for the year? You can deduct up to $3,000 of that loss against other income to lower your tax bill. That drops to $1,500 for married couples filing separately.

But that doesn't mean you should hand over a penny more than is necessary. With a little smart planning, you can use IRS rules to minimize — even avoid — capital gains taxes.

What's a capital gain? It's the profit you make from selling assets, like stocks and bonds, that have increased in value. Buy shares of a company for $5,000, sell them for $6,000, and you've got a $1,000 capital gain.

Consider the following before selling an investment that will trigger a capital gain.

Good things often come to those who wait. Think twice before placing a sell order on stock you've owned for less than a year. That's because Uncle Sam rewards long-term investors with a favorable tax rate — 0%, 15%, or 20% — on capital gains from shares you've held for more than 12 months.

Own the investment for less than that and the IRS will take a bigger bite of your profits by taxing them as ordinary income.

Here's an example of just how valuable the tax rate on long-term gains can be. Let's say you're a single filer with taxable income of $30,000. You stand to make a $5,000 profit from the sale of shares in company XYZ. Hold the shares less than a year before selling? You'll pay a $600 tax on the capital gain. A year and a day? There's no tax on the profit.

Selling in lean years can limit taxes. As the following table shows, tax rates on long-term capital gains depend on your filing status and taxable income, including the capital gain. That's why selling an asset when you're not earning much could keep more cash in your pocket.

Tax rate	Single	Married filing jointly	Head of household
0%	$0 to $39,375	$0 to $78,750	$0 to $52,750
15%	$39,376 to $434,550	$78,751 to $488,850	$52,751 to $461,700
20%	$434,551 or more	$488,851 or more	$461,701 or more

Imagine you file as head of household and have a good-paying job that leaves you with $60,000 in taxable income, including a $10,000 long-term gain from the sale of stock. You'll owe $1,500 on the sale.

But you realize that you're going to retire next year, when your taxable income is likely to drop to $50,000, including $10,000 from the sale of stock. How much tax would you owe on the capital gain? Nothing. You'd get to keep all the profit.

Of course, taxes are only one consideration when it comes to investment decisions. Savvy investors consider lots of variables — not just tax consequences — before they sell stock.

Earn extra cash to boost your retirement budget

In your second act? Take a bow and launch an encore career

You've probably noticed that more and more Americans are working well into their golden years. In fact, seniors now make up the fastest-growing segment of the labor pool. The share of older adults in the workforce hasn't been this high since the early 1960s — a time when the average Social Security benefit was much lower and Medicare didn't yet exist.

Are you looking to earn extra cash in retirement? If so, you'll want to check out these great ways to make money.

Abandon the long commute for a virtual ride. Are you an organized person with an administrative background? You can earn money with your computer in the comfort of your own home by becoming a virtual assistant. Duties may include scheduling meetings, entering data, booking travel arrangements, and responding to emails and phone calls. Look for openings on websites like *guru.com* and *flexjobs.com*.

Another option? A remote customer support associate who solves problems and provides information.

> Have a keen eye for detail? Then you could make money as a mystery shopper — someone who poses as a customer and evaluates the service at stores, hotels, and restaurants. But don't get scammed into paying money to get the job. Instead, review the Mystery Shopping Providers Association's list of approved member companies at *mspa-americas.org/member-companies*.

The websites *remote.co* and *weworkremotely.com* are good places to start. And you can find teaching jobs online at *tutor.com*, *vipkid teachers.com*, and *chegg.com*.

Cut back on hours for more free time. Consider transitioning to a part-time basis if you like your current job but want to leave the 40-hour workweek behind. Some companies allow their employees to work reduced hours before easing into retirement. Don't worry, though, if it's not possible. Perfect part-time jobs are out there if you're looking for some extra income.

Building on your strengths is key to success. Seniors with accounting experience might spread the word that they're seeking seasonal work as a tax preparer or bookkeeper. Retirees who love animals can advertise dog walking and pet sitting services at websites like *rover.com* and *wagwalking.com*.

Go into business and be your own boss. Maybe you've always had a unique idea for a new product or service. Now might be the time for a test launch.

But first talk to someone whose judgment you trust. Do some research and investigate similar businesses in your area. Then try to figure out ways you could improve on their sales. Choose a field you like but be careful about investing too much of your nest egg.

You can get the ball rolling by selling and distributing through online platforms like Amazon FBA, Etsy, and Big Cartel.

Senior success story: Tips on staying afloat in the job pool

Sure, you may enjoy kicking off your shoes and taking it easy in retirement. But you also might miss the financial security, socialization, and sense of purpose that comes from a job well done.

If you're interested in returning to work — either full time or part time — the actions you take can increase your chances of being hired, says Carol Fishman Cohen, co-founder of career reentry firm iRelaunch.

"You might suggest a hiring manager test you out in a contract role or special project if they are hesitant to hire you back as an employee right away," says Cohen. In other cases, you might have to update your skills before you land an interview.

Not sure what you'll need to master? "Go online and look at job descriptions and requirements for the type of role you're interested in," Cohen advises. You'll find free training in a wide variety of subjects at the websites *mooc-list.com*, *edx.org*, and *coursera.org*.

Cohen also says senior job seekers should volunteer their services in fields that align with their career goals. The experience is a great thing to include on your resume. Find volunteer opportunities at sites like *idealist.org*, *volunteermatch.org*, and *catchafire.org*.

"And don't shy away from temp jobs," she adds. "They get you in the door."

Cohen says too many people spend their days sending out resumes and researching companies online. It's unlikely that they'll find work that way, she reveals.

"You have to get out of the house," she says. "You have to connect with new people and reconnect with your old contacts."

Do your homework on home work to sidestep these scams

Ever dreamed of making money hand over fist while working in your pajamas? If so, you may have stopped to read those work-at-home advertisements that promise, say, $2,000 a week to stuff envelopes. You just have to pay a one-time, nonrefundable fee — only $49.95 — to get further details on this opportunity of a lifetime. Sounds like a great deal, right?

Wrong. Your fee only pays for a letter instructing you to place an ad touting how easy it is to get rich in the envelope-stuffing business. That's when you realize that any money you make will come from commissions for luring other victims into paying the start-up fee for this scam.

If you come across a job too good to be true, it likely is. Keep an eye out for these other work-from-home scams.

Craft assembly. This hoax promises to pay you high per-piece rates for putting together dolls, toys, and other crafts. But first you have to pay for instructions and supplies. Once you've assembled the product, the company says your work is substandard and refuses to pay.

The end result? You're out of money and stuck with the supplies.

New career. In this scenario, an email alerts you to a waiting job offer. All you have to do is click a link for information. What you don't know is that you'll then be required to enter personal information — including your credit card number — to pay for mandatory training for the job.

Fall for this scam and you'll wind up paying for training and a job that doesn't exist. And the crooks will be able to run up bogus charges on your credit card.

Medical billing. The ad says the health care system urgently needs people who can process claims for doctors and dentists. You're promised all the necessary equipment — software to process claims, training, and support staff — in exchange for an investment of a few thousand dollars. The best part? No experience is necessary.

Work-from-home scammers often seek an upfront investment and promise an absurdly high amount of money. They're also difficult to contact and sketchy on the details of how and when they'll pay you. And don't get fooled by people requesting personal information for a background check. Move on.

The worst part? You'll be out thousands of dollars after paying for fake client lists, software that doesn't work, and a poor support network.

Computer work. In this scam, you're promised a job performing data entry and word processing tasks on your computer. The crooks might even put you through an interview before making an offer.

But there's a catch. You'll need to buy special software that allows you to work on the company's system. Of course, the job disappears once the cheaters have cashed your check.

Land the perfect job with these senior-friendly sites

Looking for full-time or part-time work? You're in luck. Dozens of employers, including the biggest one in the country — the federal government — are eager to hire experienced seniors.

Easily search among companies that show a strong commitment to hiring mature workers and apply directly at *jobs.aarp.org*. You'll find employment opportunities in dozens of categories ranging from accounting and advertising to transportation and warehouse.

Skills a little rusty? The U.S. Department of Labor can give you a leg up. Its Senior Community Service Employment Program pays low-income, unemployed adults age 55 and older as they learn a skill — including using a computer — and work part time at local community groups.

Most seniors move on to a permanent job after six months. Find your local program by visiting *servicelocator.org/older workers* or calling 877-872-5627 toll-free.

Job hunting 101

Ask yourself 6 searching questions to find the right fit

1 Why am I looking for a job?

Knowing your reasons will narrow down your search for your next employer.

2 What did I enjoy most about my old career?

Think about the things you loved and put them at the top of your wish list.

3 What kind of work do I find fulfilling?

Consider your passions and hobbies. Working in a field that interests you adds joy to your life while padding your piggy bank.

4 How flexible am I willing to be?

Don't accept a full-time job if you really want part-time employment. Work close to home if a long commute bothers you.

5 How am I going to manage the hunt?

Use social media and job search websites. Attend networking events and ask friends to inform you of opportunities they run across.

6 What salary am I aiming for?

Research how much people in similar jobs earn. Factor in your experience, education, and related volunteer work.

Returning to work? Give your resume a flattering facelift

Seniors have it hard enough trying to stay competitive in today's job market. Yet many sabotage themselves with outdated resumes that highlight their age instead of their skills.

Want to increase your chances of landing a prized interview? Revamp your resume with these tips.

Avoid ancient history. Your resume's work history should go back only about 10 or 15 years if you've been retired for less than five years, says Carol Fishman Cohen, co-founder of career reentry firm iRelaunch. But, she says, you can highlight earlier experience at the top of your resume if it's particularly relevant to the job you're now seeking.

You don't have to include your graduation date if you're worried it will draw attention to your age. "But if you leave it out, make sure to include the degree earned in addition to the name of the institution so it is clear you graduated," she says.

Watch the formatting. Your resume shouldn't be longer than two pages, Cohen says. And use an 11-point font so the document can easily be read.

Watch the spacing between sentences, she advises.

"One red flag that the person is older is if they leave two spaces after every period," says Cohen. That was the way people learned to type before word processors became the norm. Instead, she says, leave just one space between sentences.

And don't put references at the bottom of your resume. "It makes you look dated," she says.

Omit old-fashioned email addresses. Don't age yourself by putting email addresses that end in aol.com or hotmail.com on your resume. Think about it — those services have gone by the wayside since their launch in the 1990s, making you look less tech savvy. Same goes for landline phone numbers.

Instead, include your cellphone number and a Gmail address. "Don't use something silly like snowbird@gmail.com," Cohen says. "Keep it simple and professional, and make it a variation of your name such as mjsmith0411@gmail.com."

And don't forget about social media. Professional networking site LinkedIn is an absolute must, Cohen says. "There are some managers who won't hire people if they don't have a LinkedIn profile." When preparing your resume, include the link to your profile and other social media accounts if they are relevant.

Forget common skills. It's great that you can type and use a personal computer. But don't include it on your resume. Hiring managers today assume you have these skills. Same goes for experience with common computer programs like Word and Outlook.

"You don't need to include a skill like typing speed unless it's specifically required for the role," Cohen says.

Unclaimed riches — boost your budget without punching the clock

Free money from the U.S. government seems too good to be true. But a windfall might be a mouse click away. The U.S. Department of the Treasury, for example, is holding more than $24 billion in mature savings bonds that haven't been cashed.

Want to find out what your share may be? Go to *treasury direct.gov* and click "Are your Treasury Securities still earning interest?" on the lower left side of the screen.

But don't stop there. The National Association of Unclaimed Property Administrators provides information on unclaimed, state-held funds — money in dormant bank accounts, uncashed dividends and paychecks, and unredeemed life insurance policies, to name a few. Go to *unclaimed.org* or *missingmoney.com* to search by name.

Boost your credit and banking power

Reap the benefits of a better credit score 78

Credit cards: Safe and smart ways to take control of your plastic 86

Beat the bank fee blues 94

Reap the benefits of a better credit score

Living paycheck to paycheck? You can still crank up your credit score

Don't lose hope if you feel trapped between paydays. You aren't alone in this — 78% of U.S. workers are living paycheck to paycheck. Even so, you can still make changes that will improve your credit score.

Start thinking short term. What are some small changes you can make right now to help your credit score down the road?

Build yourself a budget. Try using the Federal Trade Commission's Make a Budget worksheet. You can find it at *consumer.gov/content/make-budget-worksheet*. This resource will reveal how much you're spending each month and where all that money is going.

Once you've taken a close look at your spending habits, you can start modifying them to save money in the future. You may find you can easily cut down on things like your cable package, says Martin Lynch, director of education at Cambridge Credit Counseling.

By trimming your costs, you'll have some cash to spare if you have an emergency, which can keep you out of a credit crisis later on. Plus budgeting puts the lid on overspending and helps you pay your bills on time — moves that can help raise your score.

Read your report. To shore up your score, you need to know what's influencing it right now. That's why you should request a credit report. It will help you spot fraud and pinpoint problems that are bringing down your score.

But beware of scams that hook you into paying for a report. The one sure way to get all three credit reports scot-free is to go on *AnnualCreditReport.com*. This website allows you to get a free report from each of the credit agencies once every 12 months, so try spacing out your requests to track your credit throughout the year.

Free credit monitoring services like *creditkarma.com* and *freecreditscore.com* can help you watch out for unusual changes to your credit report. But not all monitoring services are created equal. Be aware of the limitations and look out for hidden fees.

Keep an eye out for errors. Stay on your toes when you check your credit report so that small, but potentially harmful, errors don't slip past you. A study by the Federal Trade Commission discovered that 26% of participants found at least one error on their credit report that could make lenders view them as a risky candidate.

Always check your report for mistakes in these areas.

- personal information — incorrect Social Security number, address, or name

- accounts — duplicate or unknown accounts

- debts — loan and credit card payments that aren't yours, old debts that should have been removed, debts belonging to a former spouse

If you find a mistake on your report, reach out to both the credit bureau and the organization that supplied the incorrect information to the bureau.

Draw a hard line against hard inquiries. When you're first trying to improve your score, hold off on applying for new credit. Every time a potential lender checks your credit, a hard inquiry is marked on your report. These inquiries will temporarily knock down your score, and the more you have, the more the number drops. You still can, and should, check your own credit. That's a soft inquiry, and it doesn't hurt your score at all.

"The credit landscape changes periodically," Lynch says. And to stay on top of your finances, you need to know how your money moves today affect your options in the future. "Your goal is to keep as much money in your pocket as you can."

Discover the advantages of the VantageScore

You know your FICO score. How about your VantageScore 4.0? It's another scoring system that tells lenders if you're a good loan candidate. Unlike other models, it factors in changes in your borrowing and payment behaviors over time to improve scoring accuracy. Check out these other great features that may boost your number.

- Each credit bureau uses the same algorithm so you'll see more consistent scores across the board.

- Get your score after only a month or two of credit. FICO requires six months of credit history.

- Unpaid medical expenses aren't penalized as harshly as other debts. If the unpaid medical collection is under six months old, it's not included at all.

- Public collection data such as tax liens have less of an impact on scores.

It's easy to check your score for free. Go to *vantagescore.com/ free* to find options from lenders and nonlenders alike.

4 fixes to boost your score over the long haul

Once you've sized up your spending habits, it's time to grapple with the long-term life of your credit score. Remember how your FICO score breaks down into a few main categories? You can bump up your number by focusing on these areas one by one.

Don't be late for your very important dates. Paying all of your bills on time is essential to a good credit score. Are you ready for some shocking news? Late payments will stay on your report as long as some bankruptcies — seven years. Plus the later you are with a payment, the more it hurts your score. Your payment history accounts for 35% of your FICO score, so consistently paying late can really damage your credit.

How to use it without losing it. You may think that as long as you don't hit your credit limit, you're in the clear. But a key way to maintain a good score is to minimize how much of your total available credit you use. Known as the utilization ratio, this accounts for 30% of your score.

So how much should you use? Experts say to keep your use of available credit under 30%. "The lower the better," says Martin Lynch, director of education at Cambridge Credit Counseling.

The easiest way to improve your utilization ratio is to have a record of on-time payments. Your bank may offer you a higher credit limit because of this, which will improve your credit score.

"You just have to ask one question — if I had access to more credit, could I still keep my balance low or could I still pay it off every month?" Lynch says. Otherwise, a higher credit limit could get you in trouble.

Paying down your debt will also lower your utilization ratio, Lynch says. It's a win-win.

Mix it up. Your credit mix shows lenders you can manage different types of loans. This makes up 10% of your credit score. But don't open many lines of credit at once. Lynch says to limit opening a new line of credit to only one or two times in a year. You can let your record of on-time payments build for eight to 10 months and then apply for a different type of credit to diversify your credit report.

Are you and your credit old friends? The length of your credit history counts for 15% of your FICO score and is a factor that may come as a surprise to some people, according to Lynch. So think twice before closing an old credit account because of a high interest rate.

"It's often much better to leave that account open and transfer the balance or pay it down," Lynch says.

Never miss a bill with these 2 tips

Say goodbye to late fees and hello to a better credit score when you get your bill payment schedule down pat.

Take the easy route and never miss a bill again. Automatic payments let you settle your recurring bills with regular, scheduled transfers from your bank account. Some lenders may even offer you a lower interest rate if you auto pay your loans.

But don't let easy get you lazy. Keep track of your account information so you don't overdraw or get billed incorrectly. You have the right to stop automatic payment at any time.

Worried about overdraft fees? Set up reminders instead. Check with your bank to see if they offer email and text reminders, or sign up for a bill tracking app like Mint to get alerts for low funds and upcoming due dates. This way, you stay on track with your bills without giving up any control.

Top 4 benefits of a
HIGH CREDIT SCORE

Earn lower interest rates

Receive better interest rates on credit cards and loans with a good credit score. You'll also get the negotiating power to try for an even better rate than you're offered. Plus when you shell out less in interest you can pay off debt faster.

Slash housing costs

Some landlords screen rental applicants by credit score, so you have a leg up with a good number. You may also avoid paying a security deposit for utilities.

Spend less on car insurance

People with bad credit tend to make more auto claims, according to insurance companies. Insurers may reward a high score with a better rate.

Score better phone plans

Having a high credit score shows you're reliable, so you can often skip security deposits and access better plans. And providers may offer discounts on the latest phones when you sign your contract.

Transform your score with these new tricks

Feel like you've tried everything to boost your score without any success? Do you bank responsibly and regularly pay your utilities on time? Then you may be a good candidate to try the new Experian Boost service or look into UltraFICO scoring.

Get rewarded for your money management skills with Experian Boost. With Experian's new service, you can improve your FICO score by adding your utility and cellphone bills to your credit report. The best part? Experian Boost will only consider your on-time payments.

In the past, utilities only showed up on your credit report if you defaulted on your payments. But now, even if you slip one month, you don't have to worry about your score going down.

If your FICO score is between 580 and 669, you're among those most likely to benefit. Experian says 3 out of 4 people with a FICO score under 680 saw an improvement in their number after adding utility info.

And 10% of folks who didn't have enough credit information to have a traditional score were able to get scores by using the new Experian Boost.

Here's what you need to know.

- This free service is optional. Sign up before you apply for credit — it only takes five minutes.

- You must have online banking and grant Experian access to your account information. Then you confirm what extras you want to add to your report.

- The boost to your credit score will happen immediately.

- You can revoke access at any time if you want to stop using the service.

- The lender you're seeking must use Experian to see your boosted score. Your credit report at the other major credit bureaus, Equifax and TransUnion, will not be impacted and neither will scores based on those reports.

Your banking habits take on a special role with UltraFICO. If your FICO score is just below the cutoff for getting a loan, an UltraFICO score may be what you need. This new scoring system available for Experian-based scores takes into account your banking activity. You get to pick which accounts you want to link.

This will show lenders the age of your accounts, bank transaction frequency and recency, evidence of money on hand, and your history of positive balances.

This scoring could improve your number even if you already have a good one, and it may be particularly helpful if you have a score in the high 500s or low 600s.

According to experts at FICO, 7 in 10 Americans with cash consistently in their account boosted their score with UltraFICO. Just under half of people with new credit benefitted by 20 points or more.

Here's the lowdown on this brand new service.

- You must opt in and share the additional information to get your score. A system is in place to protect your data.

- Your job, income, and how you spend money aren't considered.

- If you keep at least $400 in your savings account and haven't overdrawn your accounts in the past three months, you'll likely get a boost.

- The UltraFICO score doesn't replace your normal FICO score. But if the traditional score makes you ineligible for a credit line, a lender may offer to recalculate with the new scoring system.

Credit cards: Safe and smart ways to take control of your plastic

Dig yourself out of debt and never fall down the hole again

Americans over the age of 60 owe about 30% of the nation's credit card debt. Are you part of this market? High balances and growing interest can seem daunting, but they become worse if you wait. Focus on budgeting and putting spare cash to work so you can proudly make your way back to financial freedom.

How to melt away a snowstorm of debt. Pay the minimum on all your bills. Then figure up how much extra you can put toward your tab, and pick one of the following methods.

- The snowball method. Settle your smallest balance first and get motivated by your accomplishment. Then put that money into the next smallest balance and so on.

- The avalanche method. Clear the balance with the highest interest first. Then put that freed up money toward the balance with the next highest interest. Keep going until they're all paid off. This method may be faster and save you more money if you can stick to it.

- The blizzard method. Try a combination of the other two. First square up your smallest balance, then pay the rest in order of highest interest rate.

And keep an eye out for "snowflakes." These are small, unbudgeted amounts of income like rebates and tax cuts. Instead of spending the money, put it toward your debts.

Dance the two-step strategy and get biweekly benefits. Want to pay the minimum and still save hundreds in interest charges? Try paying your credit card bill every two weeks. You'll end up making 26 half payments in a year — that's 13 full payments compared to 12 on a monthly schedule. You won't have to shell out more money each month, but you'll get a load of benefits.

- That extra payment each year helps you wipe out your balance faster.

- Since your interest is calculated daily, if you make payments more frequently, you'll rack up less interest each time.

- You may also improve your credit score by lowering your utilization ratio and keeping your payments on time.

Set up an emergency fund to stave off a debt disaster. Even if you don't have a lot of spare cash, setting aside for an emergency could be essential to staying out of the red in the future. If you put aside $20 a week, you'll save over $1,000 after a year. Stash away enough for at least one month's worth of expenses and aim for more. Add to it with your "snowflakes" when you've paid off your debt.

How to freeze out debt with the blizzard method

Julie has the nation's average $6,354 in credit card debt. She's resolved to pay off all four of her cards using the blizzard method. She'll start with the smallest debt and when that's paid off she'll begin paying in order of highest interest rate, also known as annual percentage rate (APR). She's scrounged up an extra $125 each month, so she'll add that to the minimum of her first debt and roll it over to the others as she pays them off.

For example, the card with the lowest balance has a minimum payment of $25, so she'll first add the $125 to that payment for a total of $150 each month. When she clears that balance in six months, she'll add the $150 to the $51 minimum payment on the card with a 23% APR.

She'll continue this for the rest of the debts, always adding the total monthly payment of the previous debt to the minimum of the next. Here's a chart of how her progress will look.

After two years and seven months with no new charges, Julie is able to pay off all four of her debts. Find the best method for you with a debt calculator like one at *budgetworksheets.org/debt-payoff*.

Credit card details		Starting amount	Month 6	Month 21	Month 25	Month 31
APR	Minimum payment					
5%	$25	$750	$0	$0	$0	$0
23%	$51	$2,524	$2,507.49	$0	$0	$0
15%	$25	$1,050	$976.49	$766.84	$0	$0
9%	$41	$2,030	$1,872.42	$1,446.13	$1,324.15	$0
Total debt		$6,354	$5,356.40	$2,212.97	$1,324.15	$0

Denied credit? 4 quick fixes to get you back in the game

Rejection never feels good in any part of your life, but when it comes to credit cards, a "no" now doesn't have to be a no forever. Here's what to do after you've been denied.

Figure out why you were rejected. If you were denied because of information on your credit report, you'll receive an adverse action notice with a specific reason for your rejection. For instance, it may be because you have too much debt or had late payments.

Use this setback as an opportunity to check your credit report for errors and ways to improve your score. You have 60 days from rejection to request a free copy of your report from the bureau that provided your information.

Find stability in a secured card. Like regular credit cards, secured credit cards help build your credit history. The difference is you put down a deposit as collateral — this amount is typically your credit limit. Just be sure the issuer reports to the three major credit bureaus, otherwise your hard work won't be recorded where it matters.

If you decide to close your account, the deposit you paid will be refunded to you. Interested? Check *bankrate.com/credit-cards/secured* to find a card, but keep a lookout for fees.

Pay ahead with a debit card. If you're worried about overspending, a prepaid debit card may be your best route. Unlike secured cards, they don't build credit. But you don't have to worry about spending more than you can afford. Fill it only with your monthly budget to stay on track.

Keep an eye out for fees you might not think of. Signature and PIN transactions can cost $1 to $2 each.

Jump onto a friend's shoulders to reach your goal faster. Piggybacking isn't just for kids — with credit cards you can piggyback onto a close friend or family member's account as an authorized user.

Make sure they have a good credit history because your score is improved when their payment history appears on your report. Although you aren't required to spend, you have the bonus of being able to use their card.

Even if you both spend wisely, piggybacking may not improve your score. Not all credit card companies report account activity on the authorized user's credit report. So call the credit card provider in advance to make sure it does.

Stop credit card junk mail and protect your wallet

Preapproval for credit cards may seem like a reward for good behavior, but be cautious when you receive offers in the mail. Not only can all this junk mail be flat-out annoying, it can also tempt you to open new lines of credit that may have high fees and APRs hidden behind confusing language.

You can sidestep this temptation by opting out of prescreened credit offers.

• Go online to *OptOutPrescreen.com* to block these offers for five years, or call 888-567-8688 toll-free.

• You can stop the offers permanently, too. Along with the online form, you'll need to sign and mail in the "Permanent Opt-Out Election" form. You can print it off their site.

• You can opt back in at the same website and number.

Opting out won't hurt your credit score, and even though they ask, you aren't required to give your Social Security number.

Plastic surgery: Nip excess and tuck bonuses into your pocket

Don't botch your savings or credit by leaping at credit card bonuses that seem too good to be true. Get the inside scoop, and then decide whether to sign on the dotted line.

Keep cash-back cards simple and reap the rewards. Who wouldn't be excited to get a few dollars back on a purchase they'd make anyway? But the devil's in the details, so watch out for cash-back blunders.

- Aim for a card without annual fees, which can range from just $1 to over $150.

- Avoid overspending to break even with a fee.

- Pick a card that offers at least 1.5% cash back.

- See if the bank that issued your card offers a bonus if you deposit your cash-back rewards into one of their accounts.

- Pay off your bill every month. Don't get stuck paying interest greater than your cash-back amount.

- Cards with a flat cash-back rate are easier to keep track of than ones with bonuses that change every month.

Don't lose out on rewards with poor planning. When you're earning points or miles instead of cash back, what you lose in flexibility, you often get back in better redemption value. Make sure travel rewards cards fit your lifestyle, though.

- Be realistic about what rewards you'll use. A travel card isn't worth much if you're not going to redeem the points you earn.

- Research airlines before redeeming your points. You can score a better deal with certain airlines.

Get out your magnifying glass and read the small print. You want your APR as low as possible, especially if you carry charges month to month. Also look out for fees, and be sure you have a grace period. Without one you might be charged interest starting on your purchase date.

- Don't put off redemption too long. Miles may lose value or expire in the future.

- Pick points if you can. They tend to be more flexible than miles.

- Don't pay a fee greater than your rewards.

Stay away from the store-card stranglehold. A 20% discount at your favorite store for signing up for the store card seems like a deal. But make sure the potential drawbacks don't outweigh the savings.

- Store credit cards often have very high APRs, so if you're not paying off your bill at the end of the month your discount could be getting destroyed by the average 23% interest rate.

- Getting a store card is easy even if you have a low credit score. Be cautious and pay on time to slowly improve your score.

- These cards often offer a lower credit limit. Don't accidentally hurt your utilization ratio and credit score by overspending.

- Don't apply for multiple cards and damage your score with hard inquiries.

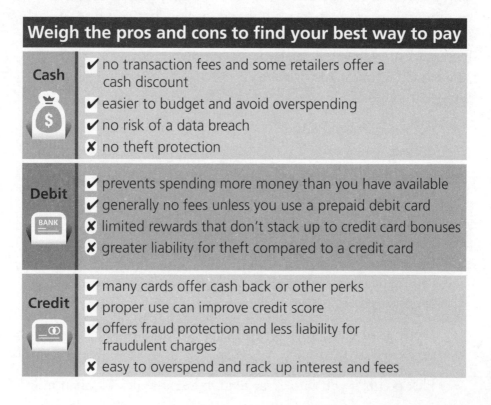

Weigh the pros and cons to find your best way to pay

Cash

- ✔ no transaction fees and some retailers offer a cash discount
- ✔ easier to budget and avoid overspending
- ✔ no risk of a data breach
- ✘ no theft protection

Debit

- ✔ prevents spending more money than you have available
- ✔ generally no fees unless you use a prepaid debit card
- ✘ limited rewards that don't stack up to credit card bonuses
- ✘ greater liability for theft compared to a credit card

Credit

- ✔ many cards offer cash back or other perks
- ✔ proper use can improve credit score
- ✔ offers fraud protection and less liability for fraudulent charges
- ✘ easy to overspend and rack up interest and fees

Safety in (virtual) numbers: Secure your credit card when shopping online

Your credit card number can't get stolen — if you don't have one. That's the beauty of a "virtual" credit card. A new number is generated for every online store you shop at, so your account information is one step further away from any potential fraudsters. Look into these options to get started.

- Bank programs. Big banks like Bank of America, Capital One, and Citi offer online tools that generate unique credit card numbers for you to use instead of your real number when you shop on the internet. They may also allow you to set up spending limits and expiration dates for each virtual account.

- Apps. Hook an existing credit card to free apps like Token and Privacy and get new numbers for your online purchases. Neither will share your information, and Token doesn't even store it.

Put your pennies to work for easy savings

These money-saving apps will round up your total purchase and sweep the extra cents into investments or savings.

- Acorns. After it rounds up, Acorns invests the rolled over money for you. The basic level costs $1 a month. Find more at *acorns.com*.

- Qapital. This app lets you create your own savings rules to feed your checking account. Basic plans cost $3 a month. Discover your options at *qapital.com*.

Beat the bank fee blues

3 costly banking mistakes you want to avoid

From bad handwriting to a forgotten account balance, banking slip-ups cost you money and make it easy to fall off the savings wagon. Here are some common missteps you should avoid.

Don't let overdrafts be your balance reminder. Your checking account could go over the limit because of a small error. But just because your mistake is small doesn't mean the consequences will be. Overdraft fees average $32.53, although they're typically a few dollars less at online banks. Fend them off with the ideas below.

- Dodge the overdraft by keeping tabs on your account balance and payment schedule. An easy way is to download the bank's app to your smartphone. Then you can check whenever it's convenient.

- Don't take the bank's overdraft coverage. Instead, enroll in something called overdraft protection transfer. If you go below your balance, the extra money is pulled from an account you've linked rather than the bank. You'll still be charged a fee, but it's only around $10.

- If your overdraft is a first offense, see if your bank will waive the fee.

Control your transfer trigger finger to keep fees away.
Government regulations limit you to six transfers and withdrawals from your savings and money market accounts each month. If you go over, you may be charged a $2 to $15 fee. Or your account may be converted into a checking account.

A few exceptions to the transaction limit are withdrawals made in person at a bank or ATM. If you can, make the most of your transfers by moving large sums at a time.

Don't pile up unnecessary paper costs. It's time to buy new checks and you almost choke when the bank tells you it will cost $27 per box. Instead of buying them from your bank, check online for other sellers or even your local warehouse club or Walmart. You'll keep an extra $15 in your pocket if you order a box of 150 for 8 cents per check instead of 18 cents. And it's possible to save even more than that.

You may like to keep a physical record of your monthly bank statements, but switching to a digital archive could save you some serious cash. Some banks charge $6 per printed statement. If you go paperless, that's an extra $72 in your wallet every year.

Find out if you qualify for free checks and paper statements. TD Bank offers them to customers over 60 if they keep $250 in their account.

Joint accounts: How your backup can backfire

Adding your child to your bank account may seem like a smart safety precaution, but it could actually make matters worse in the long run.

If your child survives you, he might have to pay a federal gift tax on an account worth over $15,000. But you could be the one taxed if you outlive him. Half of the joint account could be included in his estate, so you could face state inheritance tax on it when it transfers back to you.

Don't let tricky laws tax you on your own money. Instead of adding a joint owner to your account, set it up to transfer on death. By adding a beneficiary, you avoid both taxes. Since your child doesn't have account access until after your death, the transfer cannot be considered a gift or part of his estate.

CAUTION

Get your bank to pay you more

Whether you're switching banks or want to get more out of one you already use, bring up these seven questions your bank hopes you won't ask to snag your best deal.

What fees will I have to pay? You should check your statement for fees anyway, but it doesn't hurt to ask upfront about any sneaky extras you may encounter. Three major categories you should care about are maintenance fees, ATM fees, and overdraft fees.

How long before I can draw on deposits made to my account? Typically, deposits of cash and checks under $200 are available the next day and larger deposits after two to nine days But if your account is new, less than 30 days old, banks can put a longer hold on your money.

What's the penalty for falling below the minimum balance? These fees, also called monthly maintenance fees, average around $13.58. The charge will often be waived if you meet the minimum account balance or directly deposit a specified amount of money each month.

What interest-bearing accounts are available? Look at your options for savings, checking, and money market accounts. Make sure they fit your needs before deciding.

Which accounts carry your highest interest rates? Interest rates will vary by bank and account. Explore your options to get the best rate for your lifestyle. Money market accounts typically have higher interest rates than savings and checking accounts. Online banks often offer better rates than big brick-and-mortars across the board.

Will you reduce my loan rate if I have automatic payments made? Discounted rates commonly run 0.25% lower. That means on a $10,000 loan you could save $68 on interest over five years. Even if you don't plan to take out a loan right now, you may need one in the future, so it doesn't hurt to ask.

Is there a sign-up bonus? Banks often use these to lure in new customers, so snap one up when you can. You may score a couple hundred dollars in bonus cash. Keep a sharp eye for limitations and expiration dates, though. High minimums and fees could outweigh the benefit.

Apps make on-the-go banking easy

Many banks offer apps to help you manage your account. Here are some of the useful features to look for.

Check your credit score.

View and redeem credit card rewards.

Pay bills, transfer money, and view account statements.

Bank App

Take pictures of checks with your phone to deposit directly into your account.

Make investments and track their progress.

Smart banking moves: When to pay, negotiate, or walk away

Tired of high bank fees and low interest rates? It may be time to switch banks. But before you do, consider fighting back.

Challenge frustrating fees and save your cash. It might only take a call to wipe out fees drawing down your account. Monthly maintenance fees could cost you over $160 every year. Banks will often waive the fee if you meet the minimum balance on the account. But if yours is particularly high, you may want to look into other account options.

Pay attention to interest rates and get more bang from your bank. The average interest rate for a savings account is 0.09% APY, but big banks are often closer to 0.01%. Checking account interest rates are typically lower than savings accounts and average around 0.01%. Ask your bank if there are alternatives to your current account that may have a higher interest rate.

Switch your money to a bank with better deals. If your bank lacks competitive rates and won't waive fees, it may be time to wave goodbye. Two great alternatives to big brick-and-mortar banks are credit unions and online banks.

- Credit unions are non-profit institutions, so they often boast higher interest rates and lower fees than big banks, along with better customer service. Some of the best rates for high-yield savings accounts are up around 3%, with one credit union offering an amazing 6.17% rate. However, these accounts often have strict, low-balance limits. Ask if the credit union participates in shared branching. That would let you use some ATMs outside your network for free.

> Want a bigger bang for your savings buck? Try a certificate of deposit (CD). Commit to one year and get a rate around 2.8%. That's better than an online savings account. You can get an even higher rate with a longer commitment, but if you withdraw early you'll be penalized.

- Online banks usually give you the best interest rates, especially for savings accounts. You'll find rates regularly at 2% or more without heavy restrictions. And without the overhead costs of maintaining a physical location, they usually have lower fees.

Love the convenience of ATMs? Online banks often charge only 11 cents per transaction and may even reimburse the fee. Others participate in ATM networks so you won't have any transaction fees. See the next story to learn more about online banking.

Simplify your bank switch

Avoid bank split-up stress when you follow these steps before closing your old account.

- Check to see if the bank you're considering offers a switch kit to make the transition easier.

- Open an account at your desired new institution.

- Stop automatic payments from your old account, and switch them as needed to your new one.

- Leave enough balance to cover any checks or payments waiting to clear.

- Switch direct deposits to your new account.

- After remaining bills connected to your old bank have been fulfilled, you should feel comfortable closing your old account.

How savvy savers put more money in their pocket

You have a nest egg tucked safely away at your brick-and-mortar bank. But advertisements for online savings accounts have you wondering if you could be earning more interest.

So do you switch? Well, consider that accepting a below-average interest rate is like giving yourself an extra fee. The common 0.01% rate at brick-and-mortars doesn't even keep up with inflation.

Imagine you deposit $5,000 in savings online with an interest rate of 2%. After five years you'll earn $520.40 in compounded interest. If you do the same at 0.01% interest, you'll earn just $2.50 in interest. And the difference becomes more significant the longer you leave it in.

That definitely gives you a motive to switch. Here are more reasons you may want to take the plunge and open an online savings account.

Leave behind wall-to-wall fees. Online banks pass on their overhead cost savings to their customers by imposing fewer fees. The majority don't have a monthly maintenance fee. Those that do often have lower ones, saving you between $57 and $163 every year.

You can be sure your bank is secure. You want easy access to your money without the risk of someone else slipping in. Luckily, verifying an online bank is simple — just check the FDIC BankFind page online at *research.fdic.gov/bankfind*. You can feel protected when you know your institution is insured by the government.

Feel safe and sound with stellar safeguards. When looking for an online bank, make sure it offers strong security measures to protect your personal information. Look for features like multi-step verification, which requires more than a password to log in. The extra security could be a fingerprint or code sent to your phone.

You can help keep your information safe with these easy steps.

- Use secured Wi-Fi networks.

- Change your passwords regularly.

- Get text alerts for large transactions.

Help is available whenever you need it. Don't forget to make use of your internet banking customer service. Assistance is typically available by phone call and either online or through their app — some round the clock.

Estate planning to secure your family's future

Life insurance: The right
protection at the right price 102

Wills and trusts: Expert advice to
safeguard your money 108

Bid farewell to the high
cost of funerals 118

Life insurance: The right protection at the right price

Want to cash out early? Make sure you'll get your money's worth

Mark bought whole life insurance when he was in his 30s. Now he has been paying into it for almost 40 years, so he's built up a fair bit of cash value in his policy. When the market took a downturn and Mark's 401(k) took a hit, his financial advisor suggested tapping into his insurance to let his portfolio recover.

If you're in a similar situation or need money to cover an emergency expense, you might think about doing the same. Here's what you should consider before cashing in on your life insurance.

Tap into your reserves to help pay your bills. Over the years, you've paid thousands of dollars into your life insurance policy. If you'd put that same money in a bank account or an IRA, you'd be able to call on the cash when you need it. Fortunately, some life insurance policies let you do just that.

Whole life insurance policy holders can withdraw money from their plan, provided they have had it long enough. And the best part? Cash value withdrawals are usually tax-free up to your policy basis, the amount you've paid in premiums.

That said, think ahead to avoid unintended consequences.

- Withdrawing money reduces how much your plan is worth, so experts often advise against this method if you want to maximize total benefits. If you're counting on your life insurance to pay a large sum to your spouse or children, consider different options.

- Pulling out too much cash could also increase your premiums if you want to maintain the same death benefits.

Don't need your insurance anymore? Trade it away for a payday. Say your kids are grown up and you've decided you don't need life insurance anymore. You might consider cashing out your plan entirely, a move known as surrendering the policy. In exchange for giving up your coverage, you receive the cash value your policy has accumulated.

Some contracts may charge fees if you surrender your policy too early. And the gain on the policy — the amount you receive minus the premiums you've paid — is taxed as well. The cash windfall could bump you into a higher tax bracket.

Swap your future benefits for cash upfront. When you're thinking of cashing in on your policy, you could opt for a life settlement. Essentially somebody buys the policy from you, but keeps paying the premiums. When you die, they get the benefits that would have gone to your beneficiaries.

Often, you'll get more money for a life settlement than you would if you simply surrendered your policy. However, experts say it can be tricky to know if you're getting a fair deal. Plus you have to share your medical records with the new policy owner.

The taxes from these sales can be complicated. Talk to a tax specialist or financial advisor if you're considering this option.

Borrowing trouble: Calculate the true cost of a life insurance loan

Tempted to take a loan out on your life insurance policy? You've heard that you don't have to pay anything back and that the money is tax-free as long as you don't borrow more than the amount you've paid in premiums. If you need quick cash, this sounds like a great option. But these loans could cost you a lot more than you originally bargained for.

For example, if your loan balance winds up higher than the cash value of your policy, you'll have to start making payments to cover the difference. That's because you're not actually borrowing from your own policy. The loan comes from the life insurance company, and your benefits are used as collateral.

Look at Julia's situation. Over the years, she'd paid about $100,000 in premiums into her life insurance account. After factoring in interest and investments, her policy was worth $150,000 in cash value. She decided to take out a loan for $135,000 to cover the costs of her knee replacement surgery and recovery.

> Policy loans can be costly, but experts say they aren't always a bad idea. If you can't afford your premiums, you can use the loan money to keep up with payments. You might decide you're better off settling for a smaller payday than losing your policy.

- Her insurance company charged a 5% annual interest rate on that loan. She decided not to pay back the interest each year, so her insurers added it to the loan balance. After five years, she owed about $173,000.

- The policy's cash value continued to grow, too — but at a slower rate. Five years later, it was only worth $165,500.

- Because the cost of the loan was more than the insurance policy's cash value, the company came to collect the difference. But Julia had spent most of the money, so she couldn't pay the bill. That meant the loan balance, minus the $100,000 she paid in premiums, was reported as income to the IRS. So she must pay taxes on about $73,000. Ouch.

And here's another problem. If Julia passes away with an outstanding loan, the insurance company will subtract the loan balance from her death benefits. That means her beneficiaries would get a much smaller payout.

Before you decide to borrow from your life insurance policy, talk to an expert to evaluate your options and determine the best move for you and your loved ones.

Secret to slashing your premiums by hundreds each year

Diet and exercise will help you live a longer, healthier life. And if you have life insurance, that means you'll end up paying more in premiums over the years.

Putting in the hard work only to wind up spending more money might not seem fair. Fortunately, some insurance companies offer discounts for healthy lifestyles.

You have to report your exercise and diet habits to your insurance company, and in exchange you can get up to 15% off your premiums. So if you're paying $125 every month, you might swipe a $225 yearly discount.

Talk to your insurance company to see if they offer any policies that would let you save by making healthier choices.

Track down lost policies to claim forgotten cash

Life insurance policies provide cash that could help your heirs pay for a funeral, memorial service, or probate fees. However, these plans are often forgotten, and the benefits are never redeemed. In fact, experts estimate that over $2 billion remain unclaimed. Here's how to make sure that money doesn't go uncollected.

- Take advantage of policy locators. The National Association of Insurance Commissioners provides a free website where you can search to see if your loved one had a life insurance plan that you might not have known about. Go to *https://eapps.naic.org/life-policy-locator/* to use the policy finder tool.

- Search through old paperwork. If you comb through financial files and forms, you might find a policy letter or insurance application that tips you off to a previously unnoticed plan.

- Contact past employers or professional organizations. People occasionally get life insurance benefits through work or other groups they're a part of. If you suspect that your loved one had a policy but you can't find any information, reach out to see if the organizations they belonged to can aid your search.

- Check for unclaimed properties. Life insurance companies are supposed to reach out to beneficiaries when the policy holder dies. But sometimes they can't track down the right people. After a while, the company will turn the benefits over to the state's unclaimed property program. Go online to *unclaimed.org* to start your search.

Life lessons — dodge these blunders to protect your savings

You're counting on your life insurance policy to protect your loved ones after you pass away. But if you make the wrong moves, your savings could dry up before the plan pays out. Don't make these common — and costly — mistakes.

Paying your premiums monthly. When you shop at the grocery store, you might notice a single-serving box of cereal costs $1. But a big box that contains 20 servings costs only $5. So when you pay a bit more upfront, you get more bang for your buck.

The same idea holds true for life insurance. If you pay your premiums in one big annual fee instead of monthly installments, you can get a discount as high as 8%. That means if your current premiums add up to $2,500 a year, you could put $200 back in your pocket.

Not shopping for the best rates. Would you buy a car for full price if you knew that another dealership sold it for half off? What about life insurance?

Unless you shop around for the best prices, you might miss a great deal. Experts have found that the same coverage can vary by hundreds of dollars depending on which company sells you a plan.

Waiting too long to buy a policy. It's tempting to put off unpleasant tasks as long as you can. But the longer you wait to buy life insurance, the more you'll have to pay.

If you buy a policy at 60, you might pay around $3,000 annually in premiums. Wait just five years, and you can expect a policy to cost at least $2,000 more each year.

Tap into your benefits to cover the cost of care

Terminal and chronic illnesses can cause considerable financial stress. And passing on the costs to your loved ones only complicates the situation. Fortunately, life insurance policies could let you get your benefits early to help you afford the care you need.

These accelerated death benefits can be used to pay for nursing homes, hospice care, and even in-home caregivers. Check with your insurance company to see if this option is included in your policy. If it isn't, you may be able to add it to an existing policy. However, those benefits might come with higher premiums.

Wills and trusts: Expert advice to safeguard your money

Don't make these beneficiary blunders when you plan your estate

Estate planning errors often go unnoticed for years. After all, who wants to spend time reviewing what will happen after you pass away?

By the time your will is read, any mistakes you've made can't be fixed. And that means your loved ones could have to deal with expensive, complicated legal hurdles. Avoid these common pitfalls to spare your friends and family.

Leaning on your will to pass on your savings could cost your family thousands. Believe it or not, your will isn't an ironclad way to transfer your money after death. Beneficiary designations on your retirement accounts, like your 401(k) or IRA, trump all other legal documents.

Take it from Deborah. After her divorce, she changed her will so her ex-husband wouldn't get her retirement savings.

The only problem? She forgot to change the beneficiary designations on her IRA. So when she died, her ex got all the money she wanted to pass on to her children.

Expect long legal battles if you choose the wrong beneficiary. You might be tempted to name your estate as your beneficiary to avoid the hassle of updating your accounts.

But it might surprise you to find out just how expensive that mistake could be. When you leave your accounts to your estate, that money becomes subject to probate. That means it could take months — or even years — before your heirs can claim their cash. Plus they will likely have to pay thousands in legal fees.

A plan with no backup might come back to haunt your loved ones. "The most common mistake I encounter in estate planning is failing to consider all of the 'what ifs' that need to be addressed in a well-developed, comprehensive estate plan," says Certified Elder Law Attorney Michael Delaney.

Take, for example, a senior who wants to leave his entire estate to his only child so that she can look after her disabled son. "But what if something happens to his daughter, and she is not around when the senior passes?" asks Delaney.

Without a secondary beneficiary in place, the man's retirement funds will go through probate, and his grandson might not get all of the intended inheritance.

The tax trick that could come back to haunt you

Bought a piece of land that's skyrocketed in value? You might be tempted to sell it to a relative for a nominal fee instead of willing it away.

The idea of selling off your property to loved ones for a mere $1 may sound good in theory. You could lower the tax burden of your estate significantly, right?

Wrong. That's because if property is sold for less than market value, the IRS treats it as a gift.

So say your house was valued at $275,000 when you sold it to your grandson for $1. If he sells it for market value, he'll have to pay taxes on the $274,999 gain. However, if you'd just left it in your will, your grandson may not have a tax bill to worry about.

Where there's a will there's a way to save hundreds on legal fees

Why let lawyers and legal fees siphon off your hard-earned cash after you've worked so hard to build up your savings? With a little know-how, you can slash the cost of estate planning and leave more to your loved ones.

Looking to go it alone? A do-it-yourself will can cut your costs. If you have a simple estate, check with your state laws to see if a handwritten — also known as a holographic — will is legal. You could save time and money if you go this route. Plus you may not need a witness to sign the document.

But unless you're on your deathbed, experts recommend going the more formal route and creating a typed and witnessed will. That's because it is often difficult to prove the validity of handwritten wills. And if you don't have witnesses, the document might not hold up to the scrutiny of probate court.

You can find a low-cost alternative on the internet. Free online templates or advanced software can help guide you through the process. Some of the higher-end programs can cost as much as $80, though. Plus you might have to track down witnesses and pay a notary fee, depending on your states laws.

However, that's still cheaper than the hundreds or thousands you will spend for a lawyer to write a will from scratch.

Get discounted legal advice to create a will that holds up in court. One way to avoid problems and still save on legal fees is to simply write the will yourself and hire a lawyer to review the document.

This may be your best option. After all, many lawyers start with a basic template when they write wills for clients. But online forms don't always take state laws into account, so legal experts can ensure you've met all the requirements.

You can also look for a lawyer who offers free or reduced cost work. Some states or law firms offer free or discounted legal services for low-income seniors. To see if you have that option, reach out to your state bar association.

A will is a complex legal document. If you're not careful, you could create problems that cost hundreds — if not thousands — in legal fees when it's time to execute the will.

If you have a complicated estate or worry that someone will contest your will, hiring a lawyer to write the whole document from scratch could save your heirs in the long run. Weigh your options carefully before deciding the right move for you.

Debt after death: Be sure your heirs know what they owe

Do you know what happens if you still owe money to your credit card company when you die? Will your family have to pay your debts? Happily, no.

Unless you share the debt or live in a community property state, any money you owe will be paid out of your estate. Chances are, your spouse and heirs won't have to worry about those balances.

However, collectors may reach out to executors, spouses, or children who are authorized to pay your debts with your assets. If debtors begin to harass them, your loved ones can send a written letter forbidding further contact.

Let your loved ones know that the state attorney general's office can help file complaints against aggressive debt collectors. To find your local office, go online to *naag.org*.

A will is not enough:
4 more documents you need
to protect yourself

Revocable living trust
Probate is time-consuming and expensive. If you want to spare your heirs, put your property into a trust.

Advance directive
Your living will ensures you get the health care you want when you can't speak for yourself. Include your preferences on life-sustaining treatment, nourishment, and pain relief.

Health care proxy
This form appoints someone to make sure your advance directive is followed. Don't forget to fill out a HIPAA release so your proxy can access your medical records.

Durable power of attorney for finances
Who pays your taxes or handles your assets while you're at the hospital? This document names someone to manage your money if you become incapacitated.

This hassle-free hack can save time (and money) on your will

Mary wanted to make sure her favorite family heirlooms went to the people who would appreciate them the most. She planned to leave her antique sewing machine to her daughter. And she decided to give her father's watch to her grandson.

Before she knew it, Mary's will was impossibly long and complicated. That meant her lawyer charged her thousands to write up a draft. And if she ever wanted to change it? That would be a few hundred more. Instead of putting all these little gifts in her will, Mary could have saved time and money by writing a personal property memorandum.

This document lets you give tangible personal property away without the hassle of adding instructions to a will. They're easy to write yourself, and you can even use a free online template to get started.

Making a change is easy, too. All you need to do is write up a new list and attach it to your will. No lawyers or notaries required. However, you do need to make sure your will mentions that you have a personal property memorandum.

These documents aren't accepted in every state. To see if you could include one in your estate plan, reach out to a lawyer or research your local state laws.

'Trusty' tip to protect your savings from the soaring cost of care

Long-term care costs can be impossible to afford, even if you have a nest egg stowed away. That's why 2 out of 3 seniors in nursing homes turn to Medicaid to pick up the bill.

The only problem? You can't qualify for Medicaid if you have too much money. So you're faced with a dilemma. Do you drain your bank account to pay for care or do you put your needs on the back burner so you can pass on savings to your loved ones? Fortunately, there is a middle ground.

Turn to trusts to pass on your cash. Irrevocable trusts, when used correctly, can help you qualify for Medicaid without breaking the bank and leaving your heirs with nothing.

A trust transfers ownership of the assets to someone else. And Medicaid won't count those funds against the asset limit — which varies from state to state — when deciding on whether or not you qualify for benefits.

The downside? Irrevocable trusts are out of your hands. You lose all rights to control that money, so make sure you select a trustee you can count on.

If you do go this route, you need to know about the Medicaid look-back period. Putting money into a trust is considered giving away your assets. Do that within five years of applying for Medicaid, and as a penalty, you'll have to wait months before you get assistance.

Add an investment tool to minimize the penalty. You can slash the length of the waiting period and still give your heirs a portion of your savings by pairing the trust with an annuity. Take Joan for example.

- She lives in Florida, where Medicaid estimates a nursing home stay costs $8,000 a month. Medicaid determines the length of the penalty period by dividing the amount of the gift by the average cost of monthly care. If Joan put $80,000 into a trust, she would have to wait 10 months before getting benefits.

- Instead she put $40,000 in a trust and used the other $40,000 to buy a private annuity. Because Medicaid doesn't view buying an annuity as giving away money, she'll shorten the length of the waiting period by five months. Plus the income from the annuity, along with Social Security and other income, can be used to pay for long-term care until Medicaid kicks in.

- This strategy allowed her to protect and pass on half of her savings to her loved ones.

This is a complex, sophisticated legal process, though. "How trusts are treated when applying for Medicaid varies from state to state. The margin for error is very small, and a mistake can be very costly," warns Certified Elder Law Attorney Michael Delaney. "An experienced, knowledgeable attorney can assist you through the complicated process of qualifying for Medicaid if you or a loved one need long-term care."

POA ploys — stop scammers from skimming off of your savings

Appointing a power of attorney (POA) is a great way to ensure your money will be handled properly if you aren't able to do it yourself. Of course, putting your trust in the wrong hands can have catastrophic results. Watch out for these surefire signs of a scam.

- Somebody is asking for more control than they need. Say you appoint a temporary power of attorney so someone can renew your car registration. Why should he need your bank account information, too?

- Offers that seem too convenient. For example, a long-lost relative suddenly shows interest in caring for you. Is this the same nephew who wants to increase your retirement savings with a suspicious no-risk investment opportunity? He might not have your best interests in mind.

The best way to avoid these scams? Put your trust in the hands of people you know well. Contact a lawyer immediately if you ever suspect someone is taking advantage of you.

CAUTION

Tackle your own trust to put thousands back in your pocket

"Deciding whether or not to include a living trust in your estate plan is a little bit like deciding whether or not to get insurance," says Certified Elder Law Attorney Michael Delaney. "If you buy automobile insurance but never get in an accident, you might look at the insurance premiums as a waste of money. But if you get in an accident with no insurance, you will wish you would have paid the premiums."

Compared to a will, a revocable living trust is a better way to protect your heirs from the complications and expenses of probate. Unfortunately, setting up a trust could cost you thousands in attorney fees.

There is a surprisingly simple workaround, though. Simply write the trust yourself. Plenty of people go this route. All you need to do is draw up the paperwork and then get it notarized. Here's how to get started.

> Looking for a lawyer to help with your estate plans? Consider an elder law attorney, someone who specializes in the laws and regulations that affect seniors most. To find one near you, go online to the National Elder Law Foundation's website at *nelf.org* and click on the button labeled "Find an attorney."

- Figure out what you want to put in the trust. Gather any paperwork — like deeds and titles — that goes along with your assets.

- Choose your beneficiaries. Just like with a will, you'll need to decide who gets what after you die.

- Pick a trustee to take over. You'll be in control of the living trust until you die, but afterward somebody has to take charge. They'll handle your assets, pay your debts, and distribute property per your instructions, so make sure you put your faith in someone reliable.

Now you're ready to write out the trust. You can use free templates online or purchase software that will help you through the process.

Or if you still need a little bit more help, do most of the legwork yourself and then consult a lawyer. Preparation helps shave down those hourly fees.

Outline your online life to manage your digital legacy

You have a plan for your cash, your car, and all your property. Think you're done with your estate planning? Think again. Chances are you have email accounts, social media pages, and even online bank accounts. That means you need to come up with a plan for your online life, too.

- Provide passwords for your virtual finances. Your executor needs access to all of your online bank accounts. If you don't write down the passwords, it could take a while before your last wishes are carried out.

- Leave instructions for social media pages. You might want your executor to delete the account. Or maybe you'd rather have him post a final farewell for your friends.

- Family photos or videos stored online? Make sure to leave the account details so your loved ones can download a copy.

Don't put usernames and passwords in your will — it will become public after your death. Instead, leave a list for your executor.

Bid farewell to the high cost of funerals

Why you should never prepay (and what to do instead)

Paying ahead for your funeral has all the makings of a good idea — put the money down now so your loved ones don't have to worry about it later. It's great in theory, but experts say it may not be the smartest move for your family or your finances. Prepaying your funeral comes with a host of potential problems.

- Funeral homes can go out of business, taking your money with them.

- You may not receive a refund if you move or if you cancel or change your plan.

- Funeral costs may change, leaving your family to pay additional money.

- If your survivors don't know you prepaid, they could end up paying again at a different funeral home.

You could buy an insurance policy to cover the cost of the funeral, but the payout may not be as high as the total you paid toward premiums. A pay-on-death account may make more sense. You can set one up at your bank and deposit enough money in it to pay future funeral expenses. The money is still yours until you die. After that, it will go directly to your beneficiary. If you wish, you can even designate the funeral home as the beneficiary of this account.

Whatever you choose to do, research your options, compare prices at different funeral homes, and let a trusted family member know your plans.

Sidestep swindlers that target grieving family members

When a businessman showed up to Maxine's husband's funeral and told her that her late husband owed him money, she wasn't sure how to react. Stunned, she wrote a check for thousands of dollars right there and then. Unfortunately, Maxine fell straight into a scammer's trap.

"They'll scan obituaries to see if there are any local funerals," says National Council on Aging Senior Program Manager Genevieve Waterman. "They'll go and try to get in with the family and say, 'This person owes me money, and I need it by such and such date.'"

Don't be pressured into handing over a check or cash. Ask for written proof to verify the debts are real, but never pay them off with your own money or give them any personal information. Most debts need to be paid out of the estate, not your pockets.

CAUTION

Graceful goodbyes don't have to cost a fortune

The average funeral costs a whopping $8,000, and that's not including the price for a cemetery plot. But with these tips, you can lower the bill by thousands and still provide a personalized memorial service for your loved one.

Take charge to cut down on fees. Many people turn to a funeral director to help them buy a coffin, arrange a ceremony, and handle the burial. But in most states you can take care of these things yourself.

For example, Tom saved $2,000 by building a casket for his late sister, Joan. And he saved another $250 when his wife volunteered to do Joan's hair and makeup.

But you don't have to take on everything. You can trim your bill by using some funeral home services while taking care of other

119

tasks yourself. Simply arranging transportation instead of using the funeral home's hearse could save you $300 or more.

Check your local laws before you opt to tackle any elements of funeral planning, though. You might need to arrange for permits.

Free memorials allow for more personal services. Holding the service at a funeral home may be convenient, but it's costly. You'll have to pay for the staff and facilities. And that can cost upwards of $500.

For a more intimate option, hold a memorial at your church or home. Not only will you save hundreds of dollars, but you can ensure the memorial will be led by someone who knew and cared for your loved one.

Natural burials: A surprising way to save some green

The soaring costs of traditional burials could be a burden on your family. After all, a basic casket costs about $2,000. And if you want to upgrade? You could be looking at $10,000 or more — not including the cost of embalming, a burial vault, and other fees.

That's why more people are turning to green funerals. Not only are natural burials better for the environment, they're cheaper, too. A green burial costs about $5,000 less than a traditional funeral.

You'll find nearly 100 green cemeteries scattered throughout the country. But even if you don't live near one, you can still arrange to have an environmentally friendly burial. Simply ask your family to forgo embalming and purchase a cheaper, biodegradable casket.

Ask the cemetery where you plan to be buried if you can omit the concrete vault or grave liner, too. That can shave hundreds — if not more — off the price.

Top-notch defense against financial fraud

ID theft: Lock down your data to protect your privacy 122

Clever tricks to scam-proof your wallet 133

ID theft: Lock down your data to protect your privacy

Flagging fraud: Signs too important to ignore

The problem with identity theft — a fraudster's use of your Social Security number or other personal information for financial gain — is that you might be a victim and not know it. Months could pass before you notice, making it increasingly difficult to fix the damage.

That's why you should be on the lookout for these four surefire clues that someone has stolen your identity.

Credit mix ups. Something fishy might be going on if you see an unexplained drop in your credit score, are denied a loan, or receive bills and statements for accounts you don't recognize.

Review your credit report to see if anything is out of the ordinary — an incorrect address, a loan or credit card you never opened, or an inquiry from an unfamiliar lender. Go to *AnnualCreditReport.com* or call 877-322-8228 for a free report from each of the three major agencies every 12 months.

Be sure to close all accounts the identity thief opened or used fraudulently to help save your credit rating.

Health insurance woes. In this scenario, your health insurer notifies you that you've reached your coverage limit — even though you've hardly used your insurance. It could mean an identity thief has stolen your information to obtain medical treatment. If that's the case, you might not have coverage when you need it.

Signs of medical identity theft include getting bills for health services you didn't receive and calls from debt collectors for medical bills you don't owe. If this happens to you, notify your insurer and health providers, get copies of your medical files, and make sure they're corrected.

Missing mail. Your mailbox is a treasure-trove of personal information. And identity thieves know it. They look through the mail and steal information from credit card and bank statements, along with names, addresses, and phone numbers. So be sure to keep an eye out for missing mail.

> The Federal Trade Commission (FTC) encourages victims of identity theft to call 877-382-4357 and file a complaint. Notifying the FTC won't guarantee that your problem will be resolved, but it can help the commission and other agencies investigate and take action.

If you notice that a specific piece of correspondence isn't getting to you, contact the company whose mail you're missing to verify that it was sent out. You can also ask if someone requested a change of address on your account. Identity thieves sometimes do this so you won't notice unauthorized charges on your bill.

Pick your mail up as soon as it arrives and, if possible, give your outgoing letters and bills to your carrier or take them to a post office box.

Government notification. An identity thief may use your Social Security number to file a tax return in your name. Why? So he can claim a fraudulent refund. Unfortunately, you may not find this out until you try to file and the IRS says it already has your return. Get around this problem by filing your taxes as early as possible.

Another red flag? Your Social Security account lists income that you didn't earn. That means someone may have used your number to get a job. Go to *ssa.gov* to sign up for a "my Social Security" account so you can monitor your Social Security statement.

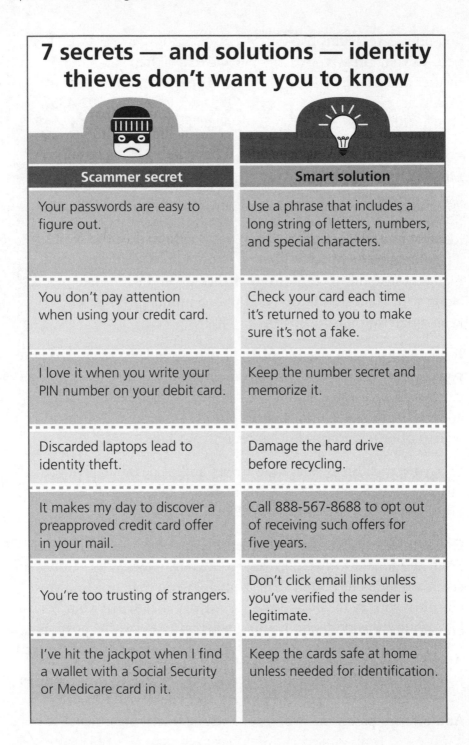

7 secrets — and solutions — identity thieves don't want you to know

Scammer secret	Smart solution
Your passwords are easy to figure out.	Use a phrase that includes a long string of letters, numbers, and special characters.
You don't pay attention when using your credit card.	Check your card each time it's returned to you to make sure it's not a fake.
I love it when you write your PIN number on your debit card.	Keep the number secret and memorize it.
Discarded laptops lead to identity theft.	Damage the hard drive before recycling.
It makes my day to discover a preapproved credit card offer in your mail.	Call 888-567-8688 to opt out of receiving such offers for five years.
You're too trusting of strangers.	Don't click email links unless you've verified the sender is legitimate.
I've hit the jackpot when I find a wallet with a Social Security or Medicare card in it.	Keep the cards safe at home unless needed for identification.

Smart swiping — dodge the downsides of debit

Debit or credit? It's a question you hear whenever you pay with plastic. But you might be surprised to learn that it's best to plot your spending strategy before you're at the register. Why? Because a debit card leaves your piggy bank much more vulnerable.

Unlike credit cards, debit cards are linked to the cash in your checking account. If a scammer hacks your card information, he can empty your account within minutes. That could leave you with bounced checks and no money during the 10 business days banks are permitted to investigate claims of fraud. And the amount the bank reimburses you depends on when you report the crime — the sooner the better.

Things are different, though, when a thief steals your credit card information. Your liability tops out at $50, and you only have to report the fraud and get the charge reversed.

CAUTION

3 tips for staying afloat in the sea of ID theft

Last year, more than 14 million Americans fell victim to identity theft — that's more than the populations of New York City, Chicago, and Houston combined. Following these simple steps will go a long way in making sure you don't join them.

Create a secure password. Don't make a hacker's job easy by creating weak and common passwords like "123456" or "qwerty." It's the online equivalent of handing over your house keys to a burglar. Use a long password — at least 12 characters if you can — and mix it up with uppercase and lowercase letters, numbers, and symbols.

And create separate passwords for each account. This way, if thieves hack into one account they won't have access to all of them.

125

Having trouble remembering all your passwords? Try using an online password manager to create and store the sensitive information.

Protect your online presence. Be careful if you shop over the internet — scammers sometimes hack retail websites to steal payment information. That's why you should never store your credit card info on a website. Instead, take an extra minute to enter your data each time you fill your virtual shopping cart.

For extra protection, use two-factor authentication when logging into an account. Along with your username and password, you'll need an additional code — which is sent to your cellphone or email address — to complete the login. This helps keep hackers out of your accounts, even if they've stolen your password.

Watch what's in your wallet. An identity thief can do a lot of damage quickly if he picks your pocket and finds a wallet full of credit cards. It's best to carry just one and leave the rest in a safe place at home. The same goes for identification cards — don't carry your Social Security and Medicare cards unless you'll need them.

It's also a good idea to ask your bank and credit card company to send you an email or text message any time a transaction goes through on your credit and debit card. This way you'll know immediately if anyone accesses your account.

Finally, check the expiration date on your cards and note when your bank will mail out a replacement card. Contact your financial institution if the replacement is late — it may have been stolen.

Start shredding the news: A simple way to keep your details safe

The old saying "one man's trash is another man's treasure" rings especially true for scammers. In fact, dumpster diving — rummaging through the garbage — is one of the preferred ways identity thieves steal sensitive personal information.

Fortunately, you can help protect your identity and money by shredding these five types of documents before tossing.

Financial documents. Con artists love to find mortgage and student loan records, pay stubs, and stock trade confirmations in the trash. Be sure to shred bank statements, too, unless you need them for tax purposes. It's also a good idea to cut expired credit and debit cards into tiny pieces so the information can't be reassembled.

Health care paperwork. Be extra vigilant when it comes to destroying your medical records. They contain a gold mine of information, including names, telephone and Social Security numbers, email addresses, and insurance numbers. And don't forget about prescription labels — whether on the bottle or stapled to the bag. Crooks may use them to refill prescriptions on your dime.

Bills and receipts. Shred credit card, utility, cable, and phone bills after paying them. The same goes for ATM receipts, which feature your account number and at least part of your debit card number. You also need to shred credit card receipts. They contain the last four digits of your card number, and often your signature as well.

Junk mail. Go on the defensive when it comes to mail from lenders — particularly those who send preapproved offers to open a credit card. And those offers of credit that come in the form of convenience checks? They're particularly juicy bait for identity thieves, so shred them before they fall into the wrong hands.

Travel documents. Boarded an airplane recently? Con artists can decipher the barcode at the bottom of your boarding pass and get your phone number, travel plans, and frequent flyer number.

You also might want to shred your expired passport if you've already replaced it. That's because it contains your name, date of birth, and place of birth — along with your photo and signature. Such information could be used to open fraudulent accounts in your name.

Don't let check writing be hazardous to your wealth

Are you one of the millions of seniors who prefer to pay bills the "old-fashioned" way instead of over the computer? If so, you still have to keep your guard up. After all, financial fraud isn't always a high-tech crime.

So watch out — never write checks with a ballpoint pen if you plan to mail them. Identity thieves might steal the check, use common household cleaners to wash off the ink, and then rewrite the check to themselves for any amount. Instead, use a gel-based pen. The ink is much more difficult to wash off.

Consider these other ways to prevent identity theft and protect your life savings.

- Never put your credit card or Social Security number on a check.

- Mail bills from the post office.

- Review bank statements for check fraud.

- Never leave your checkbook in the car.

CAUTION

Information lockdown: Slam the door on social media fraud

Facebook and Twitter aren't just for the kids anymore. Nearly 40% of Americans 65 and older are using social media sites, up from just 3% in 2005. And why shouldn't they? After all, it's a convenient and inexpensive way to keep in touch with long-distance family and reconnect with long-lost friends.

Identity thieves, of course, have taken note of the increase and turned social networking sites into prime hunting grounds. Once they find the information they need, the scammers can ruin your credit and even leave you with a criminal history.

Keep your details in the dark. Never feature the following on your social media account.

- Everybody loves getting "happy birthday" messages on social media. But a crook will use your birthdate, along with your Social Security number, to steal your identity. And don't disclose where you were born, either. It's a common security question that, if answered correctly, can be used to reset your passwords.

- Hackers troll social media accounts for photos and updates on pets. So don't disclose any details about Fido, particularly if you use his name in a password. A fraudster might also gain access to your online accounts if he knows how to answer the security question "what's your pet's name?"

- Con artists posing as a trustworthy institution — your bank or the Social Security Administration — will try to contact you after trolling social media for your phone number and address. If you respond, they'll try to trick you into giving out personal information. Same goes for your email address, which in many cases serves double duty as a username.

Be wise when you're being social. Review the security settings on your social media accounts and make them as private as possible. Be careful about accepting friend requests. They could be from a crook posing as someone you know.

And avoid taking silly online quizzes, playing games, and filling out surveys online. Many are data mining schemes that ask for information on, say, your first car or your favorite color. You may be giving away answers to security questions that will unlock access to your accounts.

Guard your card and fend off thieves the smart way

Identity theft comes in many forms. Someone pretending to be you might wipe out your bank account, get a loan, or claim your tax refund. It's no surprise that having your identity stolen can destroy your life.

The Federal Trade Commission says credit card fraud is the No. 1 source of identity theft. Fortunately, you have a way to put the kibosh on ID thieves before they open a card in your name.

Call up the three major credit bureaus and tell them to freeze your credit. This shuts off access to your report from anyone but you, preventing fraudsters from opening accounts or borrowing money in your name. There's no charge for the service, but be prepared to answer some questions to verify your identity.

You'll need to temporarily lift the freeze if you apply for a loan or credit card.

- Equifax — 800-685-1111

- TransUnion — 888-909-8872

- Experian — 888-397-3742

Something smell 'phishy' to you? Don't let scammers reel you in

Ever hear of a keylogger? No, it's not a south Florida lumberjack. It's a dangerous — and hidden — software that identity thieves use to record every keystroke you make at the computer. The program captures your credit card numbers, logins and passwords, PINs, and the websites you visit.

And it's super easy to install. All the scammers have to do is send you an email with a link or attachment. Click it open — oops! — and the keylogger begins to silently record every letter and number you press.

"Identity thieves are getting better and better at this," says Howard Dvorkin, who has written extensively about cybersecurity. "What's going on out there is really horrible, so you've got to be very, very careful."

He says a healthy amount of suspicion will help keep your internet identity safe from hackers. You just have to know what to look for.

For example, Dvorkin says, fraudsters often send emails that appear to come from your bank. When you open it, you're likely to see a message telling you there's an urgent problem with your account. You'll then be directed to click a link.

Don't do it. The con artists — called phishers — want you to provide the personal information they need to access your account.

Look for these other signs that an email is "phishy."

- nosy requests for sensitive information

- poor spelling

- the sender's address doesn't match that of your bank or has a public domain like gmail.com or hotmail.com

- you're not addressed by name, but as a "valued customer"

Your best bet? Call your bank to find out if there really is a problem, advises Dvorkin, who is also chairman of the consumer education company Debt.com.

You can do more to keep your identity safe from hackers.

"Install and update your anti-virus software," Dvorkin says. "Viruses change daily, and last week's fix might not work on this week's problem." Make sure your Wi-Fi is password protected and that your computer firewall updates automatically.

Unfortunately, Dvorkin says, there is no 100% foolproof method to prevent hacking. But you can minimize the damage.

The key, he says, is to act immediately after learning that your information has been compromised. Here's what to do.

- Change the passwords on all your accounts.

- Contact your financial institution and dispute the fraudulent charges.

- Lock down your account and put a fraud alert on your credit report, which lets lenders know you've been hacked and prompts them to take extra steps to verify your identity.

- Review your credit reports for fraudulent accounts.

- Consider signing up for a credit monitoring service.

4 tactics to protect your plastic from card skimmers

Ever hear of skimmers? They're illegal devices identity thieves attach to payment terminals — like ATMs or gas pumps — that record your debit or credit card information. Follow these guidelines to protect your info.

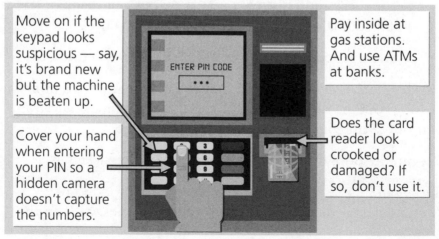

Move on if the keypad looks suspicious — say, it's brand new but the machine is beaten up.

ENTER PIN CODE
***

Pay inside at gas stations. And use ATMs at banks.

Cover your hand when entering your PIN so a hidden camera doesn't capture the numbers.

Does the card reader look crooked or damaged? If so, don't use it.

Clever tricks to scam-proof your wallet

Swindlers and seniors: Look out for alarm-ringing hoaxes that target the older set

Older folks lose a staggering $2.9 billion each year to financial scams, according to a recent report from the U.S. Senate Special Committee on Aging. That's enough money for 10,000 people — roughly the entire population of Sedona, Arizona — to each build a new 2,000-square-foot home. With numbers like that, it should come as no surprise that over half of documented fraud victims are seniors.

Why do criminals target men and women in their golden years? Retirees tend to have a regular stream of income. And they're likely to have a financial nest egg. They're also more prone to developing health problems or dementia — factors that make them vulnerable to fraud.

And, says National Council on Aging Senior Program Manager Genevieve Waterman, they're less suspicious than younger generations.

"They're more trusting and friendly and want to talk to people, especially if they're lonely," she says.

Plus, Waterman adds, older Americans tend to feel ashamed if they've been scammed. That means they're less likely to report the crime to police. Stop swindlers in their tracks before it comes to that by learning how they go after golden agers.

Beware of bandits hiding in plain sight. Scammers present themselves in a number of ways to gain your trust and fly under the radar. Look out for these common con artists.

133

- computer hackers who single out less tech-savvy seniors to gain access to personal data

- caregivers who steal money and misuse legal documents

- fraudsters who pose as financial advisors to gain access to your retirement fund

Keep an ear out for signs of the grandparent scam. Waterman says one of the top ways fraudsters contact retirees is over the phone. A common scenario looks like this.

An impostor calls, claiming to be your grandchild. He says he's been arrested and needs you to immediately wire money to post bail. Crying, he begs you not to upset his parents with the terrible news.

Don't think you'd fall for it? Think again. Con artists go to great lengths to fool their victims, including trolling social media sites to learn the names of family members. The swindle is so successful that 1 out of 4 targeted seniors over age 70 pay up.

"The scammers are really just tugging at the heart of the situation," Waterman says.

Fortunately, though, you and your family don't have to fall prey. First of all, don't panic and send money right away.

Waterman advises that you hang up the phone and then call a relative who can shed light on the situation. Or call your grandchild at a number you trust — not the number on your caller ID, which could be fake.

Fend off fraudsters who say the government is calling. Waterman says seniors need to be wary of calls coming from crooks claiming to represent Uncle Sam. Some try to charge a fee for new Medicare cards, for example, while others attempt to coax you into giving them personal information so they can steal your identity and commit fraud.

Waterman recommends screening your calls. Don't pick up unless you recognize the phone number. If the scammer leaves a message, don't call back.

"Typically, government agencies don't call you," Waterman says. Instead, she says, their first contact is usually through the U.S. mail.

Simple steps to recover from a scam

What should you do if you become the victim of a scam? It's important to act quickly to minimize your financial losses. Immediately contact the police. Let your financial institutions know that your accounts have been compromised and see whether they can stop any fraudulent payments.

You should also contact Adult Protective Services so they can assess the situation and determine the best course of action. To find the agency closest to you, call the Eldercare Locator at 800-677-1116. Or go to *napsa-now.org*, click the link under the heading "Help in Your Area," and select your state.

Reach out to a trusted friend or family member if you've been scammed. Don't be afraid or embarrassed to tell them your story — you're not alone, and they can help you recover. And you'll be doing them a favor by warning them about potential swindles.

Expert tips help you spot the telltale clues of a con

Criminals constantly put troubling new twists on old scams. It's the only way they can stay in business. But identity theft expert Carrie Kerskie says you can recognize a hoax by looking for telltale signs. If you notice any of these red flags in your contact with someone — a sense of urgency, severe consequences, and specific demands — you've been targeted for fraud, she says.

For example, a scammer pretending to be from the IRS might tell you the only way to avoid being arrested for tax evasion is to pay a fine in gift cards. Or a dishonest broker might say you'll miss a once-in-a-lifetime investment opportunity if you don't wire him money right now.

Crooks often use the following tactics when targeting seniors.

- pressure you into making an uninformed decision with words like "last chance" and "limited offer"

- call, text, or email constantly to build up trust

- pretend to be your friend so you'll agree to suggestions

- say they work for the government to gain authority and credibility

- isolate you from loved ones to deter outside influences

Scammers want you to make decisions in a hurry. They might even threaten you. Don't engage — slow down, be skeptical, check out the story, and talk to someone you trust.

And if a stranger offers you something that sounds too good to be true, it probably is. After all, the likelihood that you've won a free trip to Paris in a contest you don't remember entering is pretty slim.

Think twice when the voice on the other end of the line asks for your Social Security number or credit card information to verify your identity or hold your fake reservation.

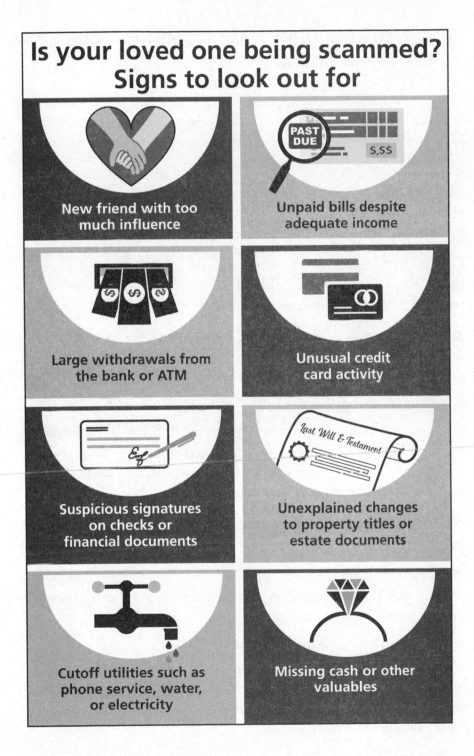

Is your loved one being scammed? Signs to look out for

New friend with too much influence

Unpaid bills despite adequate income

Large withdrawals from the bank or ATM

Unusual credit card activity

Suspicious signatures on checks or financial documents

Unexplained changes to property titles or estate documents

Cutoff utilities such as phone service, water, or electricity

Missing cash or other valuables

Dodge the double cross — don't get slammed by the latest shams

Want to buy the Brooklyn Bridge? Maybe not. But naive investors in the late 1800s thought it was a good idea after scammer extraordinaire George Parker convinced them they'd make a fortune collecting tolls on the newly constructed bridge.

And the marks who lost their life savings? Many only discovered they had been conned when police stopped them from building toll booths high above the East River.

Of course, fraudsters have gotten a lot more sophisticated since then. Watch out for these subtle and creative ways scammers try to steal your identity and drain your bank account.

Tech trickery. Oh no — your computer screen has frozen. But wait. A message, supposedly from a tech support company, pops up offering to fix the problem and protect your computer from viruses. All you have to do is give the sender remote access to your computer.

Don't do it. Because next thing you know, he'll install malware — a damaging type of software — on your computer to scan your files for personal data. Of course, the crook will also request your credit card information so you can pay for the phony service.

Never give control of your computer to someone who contacts you out of the blue.

Romance robbery. Millions of people use online dating services to find a mate. But scoundrels scour these websites for an opportunity to steal your heart and savings.

These con artists create fake profiles to get in touch with you, and when the time is right, profess their love. Then they'll claim they need cash for, say, a medical emergency or airfare to visit you. They'll take your money — usually via a wire transfer or gift cards — but there's no surgery or trip.

138

How can you avoid getting scammed? Talk to a close friend or relative about your new love interest and pay attention if they're concerned. And don't send money to someone you haven't met in person.

Pretend prizes. So a letter turns up that says you've won a million dollars. Who wouldn't be happy? It sounds like easy money. But there's a catch.

The sweepstakes host says you need to wire some money to cover taxes and fees before you claim your winnings. A few days after you pay, the other shoe drops. You find out it's a phony prize and the money you wired is gone.

Never pay a fee to claim a prize you've supposedly won or to improve your chances of winning.

Left-handed lawsuits. The thought of being behind bars sends shivers up most people's spines. Con artists know this and, pretending to be law enforcement officers, call to tell you a warrant has been issued for your arrest. The charge? Failure to report for jury duty.

Other times, scammers posing as debt collectors say you're about to be sued for nonpayment. In both cases, the huckster offers a way to solve the matter — either send cash or provide personal information.

Remember, U.S. courts never demand payment or sensitive data over the phone. And legitimate debt collectors are required to provide you with a written validation notice featuring the amount of debt and the name of the creditor.

Dial down the danger: How to hang up on phone fraud

Does your cellphone ring once and then cut off? Think twice before returning the call. The number you dial might connect you to an international phone line with sky-high rates and connection fees. And the longer you stay on the line — expect rambling messages or complaints of a bad connection to keep you there — the more money you lose to scammers.

This single-ring swindle is just one of the many ways con artists use the phone to target potential victims. Be sure to keep your eyes peeled for these other phone schemes.

The "benefits" bluff. Is somebody on the line claiming to be from the Social Security Administration? Stop right there if the caller says the agency's computers aren't working or that you're due a cost-of-living increase.

Next thing you know the trickster will ask you to verify data — your Social Security number, date of birth, mother's maiden name, or bank account information. He'll use this info to change your direct deposit accounts and steal your benefits.

Your best bet? Hang up.

The "disaster" deceit. Whether it's California wildfires or Florida floods, lots of people open their hearts and pocketbooks after a natural disaster.

Unfortunately, crooks consider this prime time for setting up fake charities. So it's wise to assume phone requests for donations are a scam if you've never previously pledged money to the organization or provided it with your contact information.

If you want to find and donate to a legitimate charity, look into its credentials at the Better Business Bureau's Wise Giving Alliance at *Give.org* or at similar sites like *CharityWatch.org* and *CharityNavigator.org*.

The "helpful" hoax. In this latest twist on an old IRS scam, criminals send out automated phone messages that request a call back. They'll even spoof an IRS caller ID number to make it look like the organization's Taxpayer Advocate Service (TAS) has left the message.

Once you return the call, the con artist sets to work trying to get as much personal information as possible. Remember — the TAS, which helps taxpayers resolve problems with the IRS, won't call you unless you initiated contact with the agency.

No. 1 way to combat relentless robocalls

It's not just you. Everybody is flooded with robocalls — those automated, prerecorded messages delivered to your phone. Nearly 48 billion robocalls were made in the U.S. last year. That adds up to 12 calls per person each month, although some people get lots more.

Of course, robocalls can be valuable — think notifications of school closures or flight cancellations. But the majority are from scammers and telemarketers who might, for example, claim that you owe the IRS money or offer you a "free" cruise that really comes with a high price.

You can cut down the number of legitimate sales calls you receive by registering your phone number with the National Do Not Call Registry. Call 888-382-1222 or visit *donotcall.gov*.

But that won't stop illegal robocallers from trying to contact you. So don't pick up calls from numbers you don't recognize. Let them go to voicemail. If you mistakenly answer a robocall, don't give out any personal information.

Don't let door-to-door stings come a-knocking

Beware anyone knocking on your door with a good deal. That's because door-to-door scams are one of the top ways criminals coax seniors into parting with their money. After all, retirees are more likely to be home during the day and think it impolite to give an immediate "no" to someone at their door.

That's why you need to be on the lookout for these potential swindles.

Fake magazine sales. Students are often unaware that they've been hired to sell cheap magazine subscriptions that will never arrive.

Protect yourself by asking to see a copy of the seller's license along with a contact card or pamphlet. This way you can do some research before deciding if it's wise to purchase a subscription.

Bogus home contractors. Beware asphalt pavers who claim they have material left over from a recent job in your neighborhood. You could end up losing thousands on substandard work and materials. Same goes for contractors who say your roof needs major repairs.

Avoid losing your shirt by researching the contractor at *bbb.org* to see what consumers' experiences have been. And never invite one of these sales people into your home.

Alarm system "upgrades." Con artists claiming to work for your security company will say they need to upgrade your alarm system. Instead, they'll disconnect your system and install another one from a different company that has an extended contract and bloated cancellation fees.

> Lots of door-to-door scammers require immediate and upfront payment for services they'll never provide. Avoid falling for this ruse by not responding to unsolicited offers. If you need repairs done on your home, schedule an appointment with a reliable company so you know that the person at your doorstep is legitimate.

Your best course of action? Turn the person away or call your security company to verify the visit.

Fraudulent census surveyors. In this scam, someone claiming to be from the U.S. Census Bureau asks for your Social Security number, bank account number, or mother's maiden name. That's your first clue you're dealing with a fraud — the bureau never asks for such information.

If someone knocks on your door wanting to complete a survey, ask to see a U.S. Census Bureau ID badge and call the regional office in your state to verify the survey taker is legitimate.

Battle the high cost of health care

Medicare and more: Quality coverage
without spending a fortune 144

Rx essentials: Stop paying too
much for meds .154

Vitamins, minerals, and herbs: Spend
your supplement dollars wisely 162

Doctor visits: Get more, pay less 167

Take a bite out of dental costs 172

Loud and clear savings for
your eyes and ears 176

Simple cures for soaring hospital bills . .180

Long-term care: Affordable solutions
for your retirement years 184

Medicare and more: Quality coverage without spending a fortune

Plug the holes in your coverage to shore up your savings

Betsy thought Medicare would take care of all her medical costs. So when she wound up getting slapped with a huge bill for doctor visits and outpatient services, she was shocked.

After you meet your deductible, Part B still doesn't cover 20% of your bill. And because there's no cap for out-of-pocket costs, the charges can pile up quickly. Betsy's X-rays, consultations, and treatments added up to tens of thousands of dollars.

You don't want to get caught off guard by sky-high health care costs. That's why many seniors choose to fill the holes in their coverage with Medigap or Medicare Advantage. But which option is best for you?

Take advantage of these plans to slash your premiums.
Medicare Advantage plans, also known as Part C, replace your traditional coverage. Offered by private companies, they come with the same benefits as original Medicare, but many go above and beyond and include services Medicare doesn't cover, like dental, vision, and even wellness programs.

These plans are often regional, so availability and your network of doctors will be limited based on where you live. If you lodge in more than one state throughout the year or travel frequently, you could find yourself without access to doctors.

You still have to pay Part B premiums if you enroll in Medicare Advantage. But some plans will reimburse you for part, or all, of those payments. The catch? These low-premium plans often come with higher deductibles. That means if you need to see the doctor, you'll pay more out of pocket before coverage kicks in.

So who stands to benefit most from an Advantage plan? Experts say seniors who are in good health and want the lowest possible premiums are ideal candidates. Research all available plans before you commit to one.

Bridge the Medicare gap with add-on benefits. Like Medicare Advantage, Medigap comes from a private insurance company. But there's one key difference. These plans supplement your coverage instead of replacing it.

You'll have to pay another premium on top of the amount you spend on parts A, B, and D. The upfront costs are often higher, but the lower out-of-pocket costs make these plans great for people who take frequent trips to the doctor.

And if you travel often or need to see a variety of doctors, you won't have to worry about network coverage limits, like with HMOs and PPOs. Your insurance will be accepted by any physician who takes Medicare.

Not all Medigap plans are the same, though. You'll choose from a number of plans, each with different coverage or premiums. Shop around and compare benefits to get the best deal.

Use these time-tested tactics to avoid enrollment errors

What do 18, 40, 50, and 65 have in common? They're all milestone birthdays. But none of the others change your health care strategy quite as much as turning 65 — when it's time to enroll in Medicare. Do it wrong, and you'll wind up overpaying by thousands. Follow these tips to enroll the right way and protect your nest egg.

Sign up on time to avoid hefty penalties. Your seven-month initial open enrollment period starts three months before the month you turn 65, and ends three months after the month you turn 65.

Carefully select your coverage during this period. If you don't sign up for Part B on time, you could be slapped with a late enrollment penalty. For every year you put it off, your premiums go up 10%.

Mark, for example, forgot to enroll in Part B. He waited two full years before he signed up. Had he done it on time, his monthly payments would have been $135.50. But because he missed the deadline? He had to pay an extra $325 every year.

Consider coverage early to save down the line. Original Medicare often doesn't cover all your needs. "One of the biggest decisions you need to take into account is whether or not to pursue something beyond basic Medicare parts A and B," says Jim Blankenship, certified financial planner and author of A Medicare Owner's Manual: Your Guide to Medicare Benefits.

And the earlier you start thinking about it, the better. When you first sign up for supplemental coverage, you're guaranteed the best possible rates. If you miss the open enrollment window, you might be subject to medical underwriting.

That means insurers can charge you more — or even deny you coverage — based on your health, age, or preexisting conditions.

Don't let changes take your wallet by surprise. Supplemental plans can change from year to year, says Blankenship. And if you're not paying attention, that could cost you a pretty penny. Your preferred prescriptions might not be covered, or you could find your favorite doctor is no longer in your network.

Blankenship suggests taking the time to review your plan at least once a year. You can make changes during the open enrollment period from Oct. 15 to Dec. 7.

Need a little help? Your local State Health Insurance Assistance Program (SHIP) can help you understand your benefits and options. Track down your state's program by going online to *medicare.gov/contacts*.

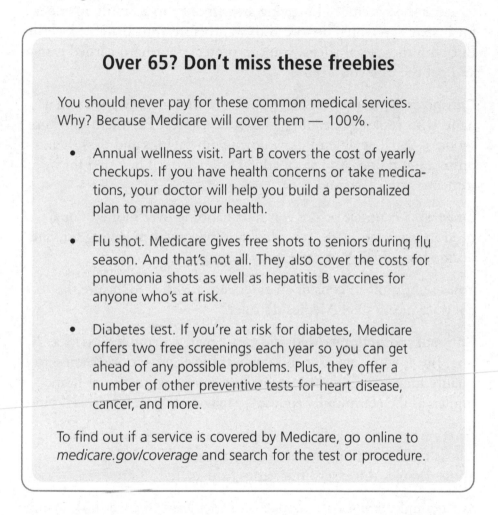

Over 65? Don't miss these freebies

You should never pay for these common medical services. Why? Because Medicare will cover them — 100%.

- Annual wellness visit. Part B covers the cost of yearly checkups. If you have health concerns or take medications, your doctor will help you build a personalized plan to manage your health.

- Flu shot. Medicare gives free shots to seniors during flu season. And that's not all. They also cover the costs for pneumonia shots as well as hepatitis B vaccines for anyone who's at risk.

- Diabetes test. If you're at risk for diabetes, Medicare offers two free screenings each year so you can get ahead of any possible problems. Plus, they offer a number of other preventive tests for heart disease, cancer, and more.

To find out if a service is covered by Medicare, go online to *medicare.gov/coverage* and search for the test or procedure.

3 tricks to protect your cash and still qualify for Medicaid

Medicaid will foot the bill for costly procedures and expensive nursing homes, but there's a catch. If you have too much money, you have to pay out of pocket first. That means people are often forced to spend down their assets — often to less than $2,000 — before they can qualify for benefits.

Keep in mind, though, the government looks back at all your financial activity for the past five years. And if you're caught trying to game the system — by giving away money to a family member, for instance — you'll be forced to wait before your benefits kick in. But with these legal tricks, you can protect your hard-earned cash and get the care you need.

Caregiver agreements. Have a relative who already gives you a hand with cooking, cleaning, and other chores? Pay them for those services. You'll be able to draw down your savings and pass them on to a loved one. And as an added bonus, you'll be cared for by someone you know and trust.

Draw up a contract before you start handing over money. You'll need to pay a fair wage, record what services you're paying for, and decide how often your caregiver will work.

You might want to consult an elder care attorney to ensure the contract meets all of Medicaid's rules.

Spousal protections. Medicaid treats married couples' assets as one. But if you have to spend down those assets for one spouse to qualify for nursing home benefits, the spouse who stays at home — known as the community spouse — may end up in a financial bind.

That's where Medicaid's spousal protections come in. The law allows the community spouse to keep as much as $126,420 in assets, though the exact limit varies from state to state.

For example, when Larry applied for Medicaid to cover his nursing home costs, he and his wife, Maxine, had combined assets totaling $65,000 — well over their state's limit of $2,000. But because of spousal protections, Maxine got to keep the resources without affecting Larry's eligibility.

Before you spend down your assets, check your local laws and speak with an expert. You might find you can keep more than you thought.

Private annuities and trusts. Want to leave money to your heirs and minimize the waiting period? Some experts recommend pairing an irrevocable trust with a private annuity.

The trust lets you gift cash to your loved ones while the annuity helps you cover the cost of care during the waiting period. To read more about this tactic, check out *'Trusty' tip to protect your savings from the soaring cost of care* in the chapter *Wills and trusts: Expert advice to safeguard your money.*

Hang up on Medicare card scams to protect your ID

Medicare recently finished sending out new ID cards with randomly generated codes. These 11-character codes replaced your Social Security number to better protect your identity from scammers.

Unfortunately, some fraudsters are using the changes to take advantage of seniors. They pose as government workers and call you up to tell you there's a problem with your new ID. They say you can sort it out by giving them your personal info. And you'll have to pay them to ship out a new card.

But wait — Medicare workers won't call you unless you've reached out to them first. Don't give out any personal information or money to unsolicited callers.

CAUTION

Dodge Medicaid delays with this application advice

Ready to apply for Medicaid benefits? You'll need to jump through hoops to prove you're in need of care. Get your ducks in a row to help the process go smoothly. Here's how.

Gather up your paperwork to get it right the first time. Many people miss out on benefits because they don't give enough information with their applications. Make sure you have these documents on hand before you apply.

- birth certificate or driver's license

- proof of citizenship

- documentation of assets and income

- copies of utility bills, mortgage payments, or rent receipts to verify your address

- medical records if you have a disability

- records of your Medicare or other health insurance coverage

Check with your state to see if they require other documents.

Kick-start your application. If you have a home computer, you can get started online. Go to *HealthCare.gov*, choose See Topics from the menu bar, and select Medicaid & CHIP. You can apply through the Health Insurance Marketplace portal or choose the option to contact your state Medicaid agency and apply directly to them.

Not tech savvy? Don't worry. You can apply in person at your local Medicaid office. To find the one closest to you, call the Centers for Medicare & Medicaid Services at 877-267-2323.

Follow up to finalize your paperwork. The government has 45 days to respond to your application. If you don't hear anything by then, get in touch with Medicaid to find out more information.

You can appeal denied coverage, too. You should receive a letter with details about why you were turned down and how to request a hearing. Hang on to any medical bills you've received since you originally applied. If your appeal is successful, you might be reimbursed for the expenses.

Medicare vs. Medicaid

End the confusion with this program snapshot

Can't remember all the differences between Medicare and Medicaid? Both will help you afford care, but that's about all they have in common. Here's how to tell them apart.

Medicare	Medicaid
What is it?	
Health care program run by the federal government.	Health care program designed by the federal government and administered by states.
Who can use it?	
Most people age 65 and over, and younger individuals who are disabled or have kidney disease.	People with low incomes, though eligibility varies by state and is based on factors like age and disability status.
How can it help?	
Part A provides hospital insurance, Part B pays for outpatient services like doctor visits, and Part D covers prescription drugs.	Pays for medical services such as long-term care and doctor and hospital visits. Some states offer additional benefits like prescription drug coverage.
What does it cost?	
Most people pay about $135 a month in Part B premiums and $33 a month in drug coverage, though it varies by income. You'll also pay coinsurance and yearly deductibles.	You may have to pay a deductible, coinsurance, copay, or similar charge. The amount varies by income and state.

Fend off fraud to earn extra cash

Think a health care provider is committing Medicare fraud? Take action and you could be in for a payday. Medicare is writing checks to the good guys who help them recover funds. Here's how to claim yours.

Call Medicare at 800-633-4227 to report fraud. Before you call, gather all the information you can. You'll need to give them your name and Medicare number, the provider's name, the reason you suspect fraud, and details about the service or item in question.

It will take time for your tip to get processed, so don't worry if you don't hear back from Medicare right away. If your tip does help them catch a scammer? You could get up to $1,000 in reward money.

Medical tourism: Should you take a trip to escape sky-high health bills?

The average cost of a hip replacement in the U.S. is a whopping $29,000, according to a price report from the International Federation of Health Plans. In Spain, that same surgery costs about $6,750.

For the kind of cash you'd spend in the U.S., you could buy plane tickets to Madrid, book a hotel for a few weeks, get the surgery, and still have money left over. And that's just what some people do. Experts estimate that almost 2 million people traveled overseas to save on health care last year. Here's what you need to know before you try it yourself.

Consider the risks before you splash the cash. Traveling overseas isn't without risks. If you don't feel comfortable speaking the language, you could run into problems at foreign hospitals.

Plus, flying can increase the likelihood of blood clots. So taking a trip back right after your surgery could cause problems.

If you are considering traveling to another country for a medical procedure, consult an expert first. They'll help you understand the risks involved and how to avoid them.

To find a physician who specializes in travel medicine, reach out to the International Society of Travel Medicine. You can call them at 404-373-8282 or use their online directory at *istm.org/AF_CstmClinic Directory.asp*.

Confirm credentials before you travel overseas. You want to make sure your chosen hospital is safe, but researching foreign clinics isn't easy. Fortunately, respected international agencies will help you determine if the facilities are up to snuff.

Check out *worldhospitalsearch.org* or *patientsbeyondborders.com* to find out more about the quality of care you can expect from specific hospitals around the world.

How to pay no more than $8.50 for your meds

Are prescriptions taking a big bite out of your income? Medicare might be able to lend a hand.

The Extra Help program offers reduced-price drugs for seniors who are struggling to afford their meds. Prices are capped at $3.40 for generics and $8.50 for brand names.

To be eligible for the program, you must be enrolled in a Medicare prescription drug plan. Annual income limits are set at $18,735 for individuals and $25,365 for married couples. Your assets must also be below the limits. Exceptions apply if you live in certain states or have dependents.

Some people are automatically enrolled in this program. If you haven't received a letter about automatic enrollment and want to apply or see if you qualify, go online to *socialsecurity.gov/ i1020* or call 800-772-1213.

Rx essentials: Stop paying too much for meds

Get your meds filled for free to keep cash in your pocket

More than half of seniors take at least four medications every day. Those costs can really add up. But believe it or not, you can get free prescription drugs. You just need to know where to look.

Ask around at the grocery store to save hundreds. Next time you swing by the market for milk and eggs, pick up your prescriptions, too. Why? Your pharmacist might not have told you, but you can get free medicine at some grocery chains like Publix, Price Chopper, and Meijer.

At one supermarket pharmacy, for example, you may not have to pay a cent for a 90-day supply of diabetes medication that might cost you $20 somewhere else. And next time you need that $27 antibiotic? It could be free, too.

Of course, the offers vary depending on your grocery store. Simply ask them what sort of deals they have next time you need to refill a prescription.

Get a little extra help from drug manufacturers. Having trouble affording your pills? Some pharmaceutical companies offer free medicine to low-income people who don't have health insurance. Go online to *rxassist.org/patients* to search for patient assistance programs run by manufacturers. Or ask your pharmacist for the manufacturer's phone number and contact them directly to see if you're eligible for free meds.

And if you have Medicare, you can go online to *medicare.gov/pharmaceutical-assistance-program* and search for your prescriptions to find assistance programs.

154

Want to curb your spending? Ask about free samples. Your doctor might have just the thing you need to slash prescription prices. Simply ask her for a few free samples next time she writes a prescription.

If you're lucky, you might go home with medicine, free of charge. And that could wind up saving you hundreds of dollars. For more details, read *Track down free samples to save thousands on prescriptions* in *Calendar of savings*.

Clip coupons to save money on meds

Did you know coupons and rebates are available for some prescription drugs? Most folks don't.

To find them, talk to your doctor or reach out to the drug manufacturer. They might set you up with discount cards or send you coupons. You can also use third-party websites, like *goodrx.com* or *needymeds.org*, to find more offers.

Remember, if you have Medicare Part D, you can't use coupons with your insurance. That's because the government says they violate federal kickback rules.

You're not out of luck, though. If you buy the drugs with cash, you can still take advantage of those coupons. Talk to your pharmacist and see if the coupon price is better than your insurance copay.

Use these tricks to cut your Rx costs by more than half

Don't let menacing medicine costs weigh your wallet down. Use these six tips to save a bundle.

Go generic to lower your bills. You can shave up to 85% off your prescription prices by switching to generic drugs. These meds are just as effective as name brands, but they're much easier on the pocketbook. All you have to do is ask your doctor or pharmacist if your medicine has a cheaper alternative.

Keep in mind, your doctor may not want to change your prescription. Certain types of drugs, such as blood thinners, need to be taken in very specific doses. Swapping them out for a different brand, which will have a different formulation, could have dangerous consequences.

Shop around to score the best bargains. The same prescription might cost $90 at one store but only $9 at another. So how can you find out where you should buy your medications?

Comparison shopping is the only way to get the absolute best price. So instead of picking a single pharmacy for all your meds, consider asking around about prices. You can also use online tools, such as *goodrx.com* or *webmd.com/rx*, to compare drug costs at various pharmacies.

> Consider shopping for drugs at big-box stores, like Costco or Sam's Club. Even if you aren't a member, you might be able to fill prescriptions at their pharmacies. And that could save you up to 80% on your meds.

To help avoid dangerous drug interactions, let each pharmacist know about other medications you're taking.

Sign up for discount programs to slash prescription prices. Grocery stores and drugstores are always trying to get more customers in the door. Some have even started offering pharmacy discounts. If you're a savvy shopper, these loyalty programs can help you save hundreds on your meds.

You might have to pay a small annual membership fee, but in return you'll get the lowest prices on medications.

Make sure you know exactly what the programs offer before you sign up. And check to see if they'll actually help you save money.

The program may not offer discounts on every medication, or you might not be able to use them if you have Medicare Part D.

Think bigger and you'll save more. You might have noticed that the giant box of cereal actually costs less per ounce than the single-serving ones. The same often holds true for prescriptions, too.

You can buy some meds in a 90-day supply instead of a 30-day supply, which winds up saving you money over the long run. But only do this with medicines you take every month. If you just need to take something for 15 days, don't waste your cash on three months' worth of pills.

The doughnut hole is closing — what it means for your wallet

Medicare Part D beneficiaries know the dreaded "doughnut hole" all too well. For most plans, once your total drug expenses reach $3,820, your out-of-pocket costs skyrocket. And your insurance doesn't kick back in until you hit a total of $5,100 for the year, when catastrophic coverage begins.

Congress is finally closing the doughnut hole. But that doesn't mean you're completely out of the woods. In the past, you had to pay your own way while you were in the coverage gap. Starting in 2019 for brand-name drugs and 2020 for generics, you're only responsible for 25% of the costs.

CAUTION

Split your pills to slash your costs. This clever — and perfectly legal — trick can cut your medicine cost in half. Simply buy higher-dose drugs and cut them even-steven.

Of course, you can't do this with any old pill. If your medication is a capsule, contains a hard outer coat, or is labeled as extended release, it shouldn't be cut in two. Check with your doctor first. He will let you know if you can switch to an extra-strength prescription that's safe to split.

Talk to your doc to avoid bigger bills. Doctors don't often think about prices when they write prescriptions. But if you simply stop and ask, you might find out about cheaper treatments.

Your physician could recommend less expensive drugs, help you decide which medications you no longer need to take, or suggest therapeutic treatments instead of pills.

Call on charities to dodge the crushing costs of care

"A Medicare patient who is taking drugs for cancer could easily end up spending $8,000 to $12,000 a year," says Dan Klein, president and CEO of the Patient Access Network (PAN) Foundation. That's because Part D doesn't have an out-of-pocket limit, so those costs add up. "And the median income for Medicare beneficiaries is right around $26,000 a year. Obviously you can't square that circle."

Fortunately, you can get help from private charities like PAN. These organizations were created so seniors could get financial aid without violating the federal anti-kickback laws that stop Medicare beneficiaries from using drug coupons and participating in copay assistance programs. And over the years, they've provided billions of dollars in financial assistance to people who can't afford medicine and treatment.

So how can you get some of that cash? Klein recommends you start by going online to *panfoundation.org* or calling them at 866-316-7263. You'll find a list of disease-specific programs and grants designed to help you with coinsurance payments, prescription costs, and other medical bills.

The whole process will only take about 10 or 15 minutes. And you'll know right away if you've received financial aid. "We have patients who call us from the pharmacy and enroll right there and then," Klein says.

Tech savvy? Sign up for the FundFinder app at *https://fundfinder.pan foundation.org*. It provides a list of grants and financial assistance programs from several charities. And if any new ones pop up, you'll get notifications sent directly to your phone or computer.

Chasing convenience? Consider mail-order meds

The U.S. Postal Service delivers a mind-blowing 187.8 million pieces of mail every day. And your prescriptions could soon be among them. More and more insurance plans are offering mail-order pharmacy benefits. So instead of driving to the store to pick up your pills, you can get them in your mailbox — often for a lower price tag. Here's how to know if it's the best option for you.

- Do you take a prescription regularly for a chronic illness? Do you often forget to refill prescriptions? Then you might be an ideal candidate for mail-order meds. They're often set to automatically refill and ship out, so you never miss a dose.

- Need a customized compounded medicine? Want to talk to your pharmacist face to face? Have to take a prescription immediately? Stick with a brick-and-mortar pharmacy. They offer more personalized services without the snail mail wait time.

Think twice before you splash cash on foreign drugs

Skyrocketing insulin prices have left people looking for all sorts of ways to save. Some have even taken to traveling across the border, where medicine costs can be a tenth of what they are in the U.S. You need to know a few things before you pack up your bags and decide to venture out of the country, though.

Moving meds across borders could land you in legal trouble. The Food and Drug Administration (FDA) only allows you to import prescription meds under certain circumstances. But even then you can't just mail insulin or other prescriptions to the United States or bring them back in person willy-nilly.

Among other requirements, you have to verify that the drugs are for personal use. You'll need a doctor's note or prescription, and you can't import more than a three-month supply.

Ordering online? You might not be getting what you think. Web-based pharmacies that operate out of other countries offer low-cost medicines for traveling Americans. Sounds great, right?

Wrong. The vast majority of Canadian online pharmacies, for example, sell drugs that aren't approved by Health Canada, the government organization in charge of health care and drug safety. In fact, a recent study found that 96% of these online pharmacies were illegal operations.

You could wind up getting expired medications or fake pills. Or you might have your identity stolen by scammers. Experts recommend avoiding these online pharmacies all together. If you do plan to get meds from Canada, stick to trusted brick-and-mortar stores.

Play it safe when buying drugs abroad. Different countries have different safety regulations for prescriptions. That means drugs manufactured in other nations won't always meet FDA standards.

To find quality medicines when you're out of the country, the Centers for Disease Control and Prevention (CDC) recommends you contact the nearest U.S. embassy or consulate. They should be able to put you in touch with reliable doctors and pharmacies.

Crunch the numbers to confirm you're really getting the best deal. If you do decide to purchase drugs from another country, make sure you understand all the other fees involved.

First, you'll need to factor in the plane tickets or price of gas. A supply of insulin may be cheaper in Canada, but does that still hold true after you add up the costs of getting there?

And you need to remember that prices aren't listed in U.S. dollars. You can use an online currency converter, like the one at *travelex.com/currency-converter*, to see what the actual price will be.

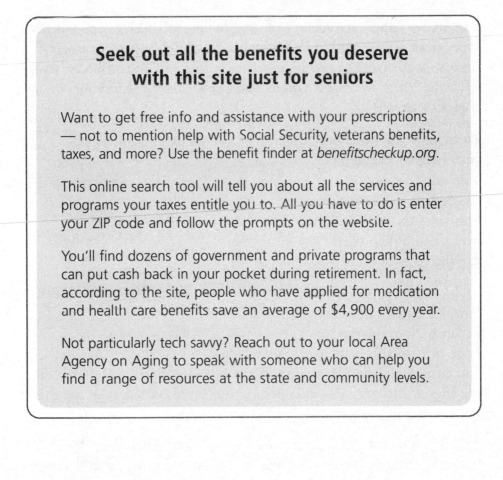

Seek out all the benefits you deserve with this site just for seniors

Want to get free info and assistance with your prescriptions — not to mention help with Social Security, veterans benefits, taxes, and more? Use the benefit finder at *benefitscheckup.org*.

This online search tool will tell you about all the services and programs your taxes entitle you to. All you have to do is enter your ZIP code and follow the prompts on the website.

You'll find dozens of government and private programs that can put cash back in your pocket during retirement. In fact, according to the site, people who have applied for medication and health care benefits save an average of $4,900 every year.

Not particularly tech savvy? Reach out to your local Area Agency on Aging to speak with someone who can help you find a range of resources at the state and community levels.

Vitamins, minerals, and herbs: Spend your supplement dollars wisely

Slash your costs with these simple shopping strategies

Experts say Americans spend over $32 billion on dietary supplements every year. With that kind of money, you could buy every single person in the world a mouthwatering veggie sub and still have cash left over. Yikes. Wouldn't you like to know how to trim your spending down?

Treat your vitamins like your meds to save big. The same shopping strategies you use to save hundreds on prescription drugs could help you cut the costs of your vitamins, too.

Simple things, like buying in bulk or opting for store brands, can help

> Can you use your health savings account (HSA) or flexible spending account (FSA) to buy vitamins and minerals? Maybe. But you'll need a letter of medical necessity or a prescription from your doctor to prove the supplement is for treating a specific medical condition. Check with your HSA or FSA provider first to double-check your plan's rules.

you trim your costs. If you do go for generics, check to see that all the ingredients and amounts per serving listed on the label are the same as the brand names you're comparing them to.

And if you own a pill splitter, you can use it on tablets that don't have a special coating or time-release formula. Cutting extra-strength vitamins in half could be cheaper than buying more lower-dose pills.

Lend a hand to crack down on tainted vitamins

The only thing worse than wasting your dollars is harming your health. Luckily, the FDA protects both your wallet and well-being by acting fast to pull dangerous supplements from stores. They need a bit of help from consumers, though. So what can you do?

Be on the lookout for serious reactions that pop up after you start taking a new vitamin or mineral. Anything from itching to loss of appetite could be cause for alarm.

Stop taking supplements immediately after you notice anything unusual. Reach out to the FDA as soon as possible by filling out a report online through the Safety Reporting Portal at www.safetyreporting.hhs.gov.

CAUTION

Go for a single pill to pare down your supplement bill. Are you taking a vitamin D supplement, a calcium chew, fish oil, and vitamin B12? You might want to consider multivitamins or combination supplements. Instead of buying half a dozen products, you'll only need to pick up one.

Of course, make sure you're only taking a combination supplement or multivitamin if you need all those nutrients. Otherwise, you might just be shelling out extra money. Talk to your doctor to see if she recommends a multivitamin for you.

Compare costs to get the most bang for your buck. Would you buy a car without checking to see if you can get it cheaper anywhere else first? So why do the same with supplements.

It's not as simple as going from dealership to dealership, though. Because supplements don't need approval from the Food and Drug Administration (FDA), you could wind up paying for a pill that doesn't have all the advertised ingredients.

Third-party websites, like *consumerlab.com* and *labdoor.com*, test supplements to see how different brands measure up. You can use them to find the best products, compare costs per dose, and find certified retailers.

Be on the lookout — use these tactics to dodge dangerous supplements

Found a product that claims it can boost your immune system, improve your mood, and trim your waistline? It might not measure up to those promises. Supplement manufacturers are legally allowed to make all sorts of miracle claims about their products, even if there's not a shred of scientific evidence to back it up.

And what's worse? Some supplements can be dangerous, too. The FDA has even found potentially harmful prescription drugs mixed into them. So how can you steer clear of these risky health products?

Look for seals of approval. Prescription drugs have to go through years of rigorous tests before the FDA approves them for sale. The same isn't true for supplements, though. Fortunately, a few independent organizations test supplements so you can be sure you're only getting what's listed on the label.

Look for seals of approval from reputable foundations such as the U.S. Pharmacopeia (USP) and NSF International. Be sure to examine the labels closely. Some scammers will put similar seals on their supplements to trick you into buying a second-rate product.

And remember, these certifications don't necessarily mean what you're buying will live up to its advertising. They just let you know the listed ingredients and amounts are actually in the bottle.

Comb the labels to spot suspicious additives. Carefully read all the ingredients to make sure you know what you're taking. You want to know what is actually in the supplement, and the amount you should take.

Need a little help comparing products and interpreting the labels? Check out the National Institutes of Health's Dietary Supplement Label Database. Go online to *dsld.nlm.nih.gov*, and you can search for supplements by name, manufacturer, or ingredient. You'll find a complete list of ingredients in almost 76,000 supplements.

If you have any questions about certain ingredients, ask your doctor or pharmacist for more information. They'll help you steer clear of harmful additives and ingredients.

Avoid dicey additives with a little help from the FDA

How could you possibly know that anhaline, eremursine, and peyocactine are all names for the same ingredient under investigation by the FDA? Shoppers can't be expected to memorize every potentially harmful additive.

That's where the FDA's new webpage can help. The Dietary Supplement Ingredient Advisory List gives you a lineup of ingredients — and their common synonyms — currently being evaluated. You'll also find a link to ingredients the FDA has already taken action on or has issued statements about.

To find the list, go online to *fda.gov* and type "dietary supplement ingredient advisory" into the search bar. If you're not tech savvy, you can call the FDA at 888-463-6332 for more info.

Warranted or wasted: 2 ways to tell if you need extra nutrients

Feeling blue? Your favorite health blog said adding B12 to your pillbox would improve your mood. And that online ad said ginkgo extract is exactly what you need to fix your slipping memory. Before you know it, you've got a vitamin, herb, or mineral for every ailment. But do you actually feel any better?

A recent survey found that 70% of seniors take some kind of supplement. But those products might not all be worth the money. Use these tips to make sure you don't waste hard-earned dollars on supplements you don't need.

Find the gaps in your diet before you shell out for supplements. Experts say most of your vitamins and minerals should come from food. But as you age, that can get harder. Waning appetites, costly foods, and even trouble chewing can cause you to miss out on essential nutrients. And that's when you should consider taking a supplement.

So how do you know if you're lacking nutrients? First, take a look at your own eating habits. You can use an online tool, like the calculator at *fnic.nal.usda.gov/fnic/dri-calculator*. All you need to do is enter your age, height, weight, and activity level. The website will crunch the numbers and give you details about the amount of nutrients your body needs.

Get some expert advice to help you make the most of your money. You may have heard that seniors often have trouble absorbing calcium. But that doesn't mean you need to go out and buy a box of calcium chews. After all, wouldn't you hate to waste $60 on calcium supplements every year, only to find out your body doesn't need any extra help?

Your doctor can run tests and make recommendations based on your needs. And she can help you be sure you're taking supplements safely. Certain ingredients could blunt the effectiveness of your prescription medications or even cause dangerous interactions with over-the-counter meds.

Doctor visits: Get more, pay less

Find a physician who fits your lifestyle — and pocketbook

Have you ever longed for the "good old days" when doctors made house calls? Your waiting is over — they are here again. For an annual fee, a concierge doctor will be available to you round the clock by phone, text, email, or in person.

If you're searching for a new doctor and want personalized care, a concierge doctor might be a good choice for you. This type of primary care doctor may have a patient load of just 350 people, which means he has the time to see you whenever you need him — and he'll even come to your home. Because he emphasizes preventive care, he is more likely to order additional diagnostic tests to make sure all the bases are covered.

An ounce of preventive health care may not always be worth a pound of cure, but it might keep you out of the hospital, according to recent studies on primary care relationships. And adults who have a primary care doctor rack up 33% lower health-related costs and have better patient experiences.

It all sounds great, doesn't it? The downside is it could cost you a pretty penny. Annual fees range from $100 to $2,500, depending on how many patients are in the practice and where it is located. And you may still pay a copay for your visits. But yearly wellness tests are usually covered by the annual fee, and most practices accept insurance, including Medicare.

Don't want to pay the hefty fee? Look for other types of primary care doctors that may better suit your needs — and your pocketbook. Here are some other options.

167

Direct primary care physicians. Some doctors are embracing a version of concierge care, but without the administrative burdens of dealing with the government or accepting insurance. Called direct primary care, this arrangement lets doctors focus on the quality of care rather than quantity of patients. Their practices are usually limited to between 500 and 1,000 patients.

Like concierge doctors they collect a fee, but it's usually much less — often $50 to $100 a month. They don't accept insurance, but the fee gives patients access to deeply discounted services, same- or next-day appointments, and very short wait times. If you're uninsured, this could be a good choice for you.

> When you're really sick you may instinctively look to the emergency room for help, but try to avoid it unless your condition is life-threatening. Instead, seek out an urgent care where a visit averages between $50 and $150. It's cheaper than the hospital where you could easily pay hundreds or even thousands more.

Traditional primary care physicians. You're probably most familiar with the fee-for-service model, where you pay separately for each visit, treatment, and procedure. These practices treat many patients — often more than 2,000 — so they sometimes work in teams. This increases your chances of seeing a nurse practitioner, physician assistant, or other health care worker instead of the doctor himself.

If a strong doctor-patient relationship is important to you, you may be disappointed with a traditional practice because you won't have much time with the doctor. That is, when you finally do get to see him, because the wait time for appointments is often a few weeks.

On the plus side, these practices all accept insurance so most people can get their medical needs met for a reasonable price.

The bottom line is your time, money, and health are all very important. Choose a primary care doctor that satisfies your needs in all three of these areas.

Do-it-yourself medical tests for less

There it is, that unmistakable burning irritation when you visit the restroom. You think it could be a urinary tract infection (UTI). But you hate to waste a copay on a doctor visit if it's not.

Consider picking up a UTI test at your local drugstore. Simply follow the instructions and wait for the results. Then call your doctor to discuss what to do next. If your test is positive, some doctors will call in an antibiotic for you.

At-home medical tests are affordable, quick, and fairly simple to use. You can find many types of helpful tests at the pharmacy and online, including allergy, strep, cholesterol, thyroid, vitamin D, and more.

These tests are not foolproof. Be sure to use FDA-regulated tests and new test strips. And always follow up with a doctor.

Get 24-hour access to your doc at the touch of a button

It's Saturday night and you ache all over. In the past, you'd be stuck waiting it out or going to the emergency room. But now, you can simply pull out your smartphone and log in to your virtual doctor's office.

If you've ever video chatted with your grandkids, then you're ready for telemedicine. Using similar technology, a real physician meets you online via webcam on your laptop, phone, or tablet for a consultation about your health.

How do you find a teledoctor? Your private insurance or Medicare policy may tell you which virtual clinics are available for your plan. Or search online for "virtual doctor" and your insurer's name. If you're not insured, search for telemedicine providers like Amwell, Doctor On Demand, MDLIVE, and LiveHealth Online. Always choose a practice with board-certified physicians.

169

What's it going to set you back? Many experts recommend telehealth services to supplement your primary care. Options are also available for behavioral and mental health, chronic disease management, post-operative surgical care, and specialty consultations. And visits range in price from $35 to $230, depending on the service. A single virtual visit can save $100 on average, or it may be free with insurance.

How does it work? First, download the app for the clinic you have chosen and set up an account. Next, create a profile with the same basic information you would give any doctor's office. Finally, enter insurance and payment, if needed.

Once the account is set up, answer a few questions about your medical concerns.

> Telemedicine delivers specialized care to patients who have trouble accessing it. Whether you are looking for someone to help you manage a disease like diabetes, understand a life change like menopause, deal with a skin condition, or cope with an emotional challenge, you can now find affordable specialists online.

You may be able to select a doctor from a list of profiles. You'll then be moved to a virtual waiting room or the doctor will be with you right away. One clinic reports an average wait time of only five minutes, and services are available 24 hours a day, seven days a week.

Access help for your health at free medical clinics

When you don't have enough insurance, it's tempting to wait out an illness and hope for the best. But it can be more costly if you develop complications down the road.

If you spend more than 5% to 10% of your income on out-of-pocket health care costs each year — even with insurance — then you're probably underinsured. Still, putting off your health for fear of the cost is not the solution. Help is available.

- Federal health center programs offer primary care, health education, and transportation to appointments. These services are provided on a sliding fee scale. Find a local health center at *findahealthcenter.hrsa.gov*.

- *Freeclinics.com* maintains a list of nationwide medical centers that offer services at little or no cost, depending on your income.

- Charity health clinics also provide free or low-cost services for people who are uninsured or underinsured. Find one near you by searching the National Association of Free & Charitable Clinics directory online at *nafcclinics.org/find-clinic*.

Partner up to pare down medical costs

Following Carol's unexpected diagnosis, the doctor appointments and treatments began to stack up. Soon, paying off her mounting balance and keeping track of everything became too much for her. That's when a friend recommended a patient advocate.

The advocate helped her decipher her benefit options, challenge claim denials from insurance companies, negotiate her balances, review her bills, and organize all the paperwork. He made the process much easier and saved Carol thousands of dollars.

Professional advocates offer fee-based services and charge either an hourly rate or a commission of 25% to 35% of the amount they save on your bills. Need help with your health care situation? Locate advocates through groups like these.

- National Association of Healthcare Advocacy Consultants at *www.nahac.com*

- AdvoConnection at *advoconnection.com*

- Alliance of Claims Assistance Professionals at *claims.org*

- Patient Advocate Foundation at *patientadvocate.org*

Take a bite out of dental costs

Bristling at the high cost of care? Sink your teeth into deep discounts

It's no surprise that seniors need regular dental care — even those with false teeth. Yet more than half of older Americans say they haven't been to the dentist in the past year. Why? The cost. Most health insurance plans, including original Medicare, don't cover routine dental care.

But that's no reason to forego a healthy mouth. Here's how to get discounted dental work, even if insurance and Medicare won't cover it.

Take a seat in the classroom. Most schools accredited by the American Dental Association have clinics where closely supervised students provide care at reduced costs. It's a win-win situation, as the students gain valuable experience and you get a discount. Looking to find an accredited school in your area? Go to *ada.org/en/coda/find-a-program*.

Some dental hygiene schools provide preventive care — cleanings and fluoride treatments, for example — as part of student training. Find accredited dental hygiene schools at *adha.org/dental-hygiene-programs*.

Try bargain hunting. Lots of dentists advertise their services. So keep an eye out for postcards in your mailbox offering free or reduced-price exams and cleanings. If you already have a dentist, ask about no-interest payment plans and discounts for seniors or longtime patients.

And you'll want to comparison shop if you need a costly implant or root canal. Look up average prices in your area at *fairhealth consumer.org* or call local dentists for price quotes. If your dentist charges significantly more than others, ask why.

Drive the discount-card route. Have you heard of dental savings plans? They work much like warehouse clubs, but your annual fee pays for discounts on dental services instead of bulk items. You can save up to 60% on checkups, cleanings, root canals, crowns, and bridges. Expect to pay between $80 and $200 a year for individual coverage.

And there's no annual limit on expenses or a waiting period before benefits kick in. Ask your dentist if he is a participating member of a savings plan.

Log on for helpful information. The Health Resources and Services Administration works with federally funded health centers to offer free or reduced-cost medical services to people who can't afford it. Locate dental care at more than 1,000 clinics across the country by going to *findahealthcenter.hrsa.gov*.

> The American Dental Association says you should replace your toothbrush — those with soft bristles are best — every three to four months. But don't spend your hard-earned money on a new toothbrush from the grocery store. Instead, stock up on free toothbrushes the next time you visit the dentist.

The nonprofit Dental Lifeline Network also provides free dental care to individuals who can't afford to pay. To qualify, you must be 65 or older, disabled, or medically fragile. Visit *dentallifeline.org* and click on State Programs for information. In addition, United Way and your state or local health departments may know of area programs that offer free or reduced-cost treatment.

Size up coverage options to see if insurance is right for your wallet

Should you buy dental insurance? Maybe, maybe not. Most policies pay for cleanings and checkups every six months, along with an annual set of X-rays. Basic procedures — fillings and extractions, for example — are generally 80% covered. And major treatments? Insurers will usually pay half the cost of root canals, dentures, and implants.

You'll want to weigh your dental needs against the cost of a policy's premium to find out if insurance is right for you. Ask yourself these questions to see if an alternative might be less expensive.

- What procedures will I need this year? Review prices with and without insurance.

- What is the policy's maximum benefit? You're responsible for any costs above that limit — often capped at $1,500 a year.

- When do I need the treatment? After you purchase the plan, many insurers make you wait months before they'll cover a filling or root canal.

- Will I be more proactive about dental care if I have coverage? People with insurance tend to get more preventive care and save on big expenses down the road.

Whether or not you decide to invest in a policy, it's best to set aside funds for the unexpected. Adding pretax dollars to a flexible spending account or a health savings account is a cost-effective way to start.

Another option? Dental savings plans offer significantly reduced rates in exchange for an annual fee. And that fee is often hundreds of dollars lower than the cost of an insurance policy.

Is arthritis making it difficult to grasp a toothbrush? For a low-cost solution, try wrapping tennis racket grip tape around the handle. Or you could slide a foam tube over the bottom end. Another option? Invest in an electric toothbrush. They have chunkier handles that are easier to grab and hold.

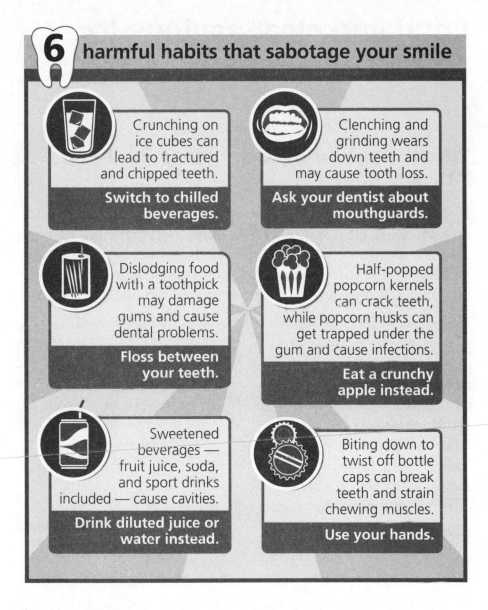

6 harmful habits that sabotage your smile

Crunching on ice cubes can lead to fractured and chipped teeth.

Switch to chilled beverages.

Clenching and grinding wears down teeth and may cause tooth loss.

Ask your dentist about mouthguards.

Dislodging food with a toothpick may damage gums and cause dental problems.

Floss between your teeth.

Half-popped popcorn kernels can crack teeth, while popcorn husks can get trapped under the gum and cause infections.

Eat a crunchy apple instead.

Sweetened beverages — fruit juice, soda, and sport drinks included — cause cavities.

Drink diluted juice or water instead.

Biting down to twist off bottle caps can break teeth and strain chewing muscles.

Use your hands.

Loud and clear savings for your eyes and ears

Vision loss: Low-cost strategies for living independently

By the age of 65, some 1 in 3 Americans is affected by an age-related eye disease like glaucoma, cataracts, macular degeneration, or diabetic retinopathy. Vision loss among seniors is a major health care problem — one that can prevent you from completing simple tasks like cooking a meal and managing your medications.

"Some people are lucky enough to have a sighted spouse who can help," says Audrey Demmitt, a peer advisor for VisionAware, an organization that helps adults with vision loss stay independent. "But too often there are visually impaired seniors living alone in pretty unsafe circumstances."

For some, she says, the fear of falling keeps them from moving around their own homes.

EyeCare America connects seniors with eye exams and follow-up care, often with no out-of-pocket expense. Learn if you qualify at *aao.org/eye care-america*. And Lions Clubs International offers financial assistance for eye care through local clubs. For information, go to *lions clubs.org* and click "Find a Club" at the top of the page.

So what's the first thing you should do after being diagnosed with a vision impairment? Call a local low-vision clinic, Demmitt advises. They'll provide training and devices — high-intensity lamps, magnifiers, needle threaders, and clocks with large numbers, for example — to make the best use of your limited eyesight.

Demmitt says you'll also need to contact a vision rehabilitation agency. Specialists will teach you new ways to carry out daily activities, including reading and writing, moving about safely, using the telephone, organizing your household, preparing meals, and caring for your personal needs.

Some vision rehabilitation professionals will work with you in your home, while others provide training in an agency setting.

Think all that help is financially out of reach? Think again.

"A lot of times seniors tell me they can't afford low-vision services," Demmitt says. She tells them they can. That's because Uncle Sam gives grants to each state in an effort to boost independent living among visually impaired individuals 55 years or older. Those funds go toward low-vision screenings, support groups, transportation, adaptive aids, and training.

Your state vocational rehabilitation agency can help you locate programs that offer the grants. Or you can ask your local low-vision professionals for information. For a list of state agencies, low-vision services, and consumer organizations in your area, go to *vision aware.org/GSdirectory* and type in your state.

Eye out for a bargain? Spend less on specs

Buying prescription eyeglasses could easily set you back hundreds of dollars. But you can get a brand-new pair for far less. And it doesn't matter where you live because you'll find great deals online. Visit websites like *voogueme.com, goggles4U.com,* and *zennioptical.com* to browse among hundreds of frames.

Overwhelmed by all the options? Each site offers instructions on how to order and provides tools to narrow your search by shape, material, and size. Some sites even allow you to "try on" frames virtually to see if they suit your face. Prices start at less than $8.

To order, all you'll need is a prescription from your eye doctor. It should include the distance in millimeters between your pupils to ensure a proper focus. And don't pay more by adding a scratch-resistant coating — plastic lenses already have it.

Hearing aids — big savings to keep you smiling from ear to ear

Around 1 in 3 seniors between the ages of 65 and 74 suffers from hearing loss — a medical condition that, if left untreated, can lead to depression and social isolation. Yet only 20% of people who could benefit from hearing aids use them.

A major reason? Sticker shock. A single hearing aid, on average, fetches $2,400. That's close to $5,000 a pair. And original Medicare won't cover the cost. So what's a senior on a limited income to do?

Government programs take the burden off. Have you served in the U.S. military? If so, you may be eligible for free hearing aids through the Veterans Administration (VA). Call your nearest VA and ask for the Veterans Service Center to find out if you qualify.

Current and retired federal employees may get hearing aid coverage through insurance plans in the Federal Employees Health Benefits Program. Qualified Blue Cross Blue Shield beneficiaries, for example, are eligible for up to $2,500 in hearing-related services every three years — more than enough for a new hearing aid.

> Unsure if you're losing your hearing? Lots of hearing aid manufacturers — Miracle-Ear, Phonak, Oticon, and Signia, to name a few — offer free online assessments. Just remember you should have a professional check your hearing each year if you're age 60 or older.

In addition, some Medicare Advantage plans offer extra benefits — including hearing aids. Check with your plan administrator if you have an Advantage plan.

Some states cover hearing services for adults under their Medicaid programs. Find your state's Medicaid office contact info at *medicaid.gov/about-us/contact-us/contact-state-page.html*.

Private organizations lend a helping hand. Many local Lions Clubs offer affordable hearing aids to individuals based on their income. Go to *lionsclubs.org* and click the "Find a Club" button to locate your nearest club and get an application. Here are other organizations that can assist you.

- The Starkey Hearing Foundation supplies hearing aids to people who otherwise can't afford them. Visit *starkeyhearingfoundation.org/hear-now* or call 800-328-8602 to speak with a consultant about the Hear Now program.

- The nonprofit AUDIENT assists low-income seniors in finding hearing aids and related treatments at deep discounts. Call 866-956-5400, ext. 2 to speak with a representative.

- Visit Hearing Charities of America at *hearingaiddonations.org/resources* for local and national resources.

Listen up: Sound advice on living with hearing loss

Have a hard time holding up your end of a conversation? Do loved ones complain that your television is too loud? Maybe you wish everybody would just stop mumbling.

Contact your physician right away if you suspect an age-related hearing problem. After all, Medicare Part B covers diagnostic hearing tests if your doctor orders them. In the meantime, these no-cost ideas will make you more comfortable.

- Let people know you're having difficulty understanding what they're saying.

- Find a quiet location to talk, and pay attention to expressions and gestures.

- Ask others to face you as they speak slowly and clearly.

In addition, state programs provide free or low-cost phone equipment to accommodate hearing loss. For information on what your state offers, visit the Telecommunications Equipment Distribution Program Association at *tedpa.org* and click "State Program Map" at the bottom of the page.

Simple cures for soaring hospital bills

Worried sick over hospital rates? 3 practical ways to control costs

Being stuck in a hospital bed can be scary and expensive. In fact, the average three-day hospital stay costs around $30,000 without insurance. That's the annual salary of a preschool teacher earning $15 an hour. No wonder 7 in 10 Americans say reducing health care costs should be a top government priority.

> Hospitals often give discounts — up to 20% — to patients who pay their bills in advance. Why? It's a way of ensuring payment. While the practice won't help you in an emergency, with a little planning you can save on diagnostic tests, lab work, and even elective surgery.

Remember these tips if you don't want to find a surprise hospital bill in your mailbox.

Do research and stay in network. The first step to keeping costs under control? Comparison shop. Call your area hospitals for estimates — you'll find varying prices for the same procedure. For a ballpark figure of how much a test or surgery should cost, go to *healthcarebluebook.com*, *guroo.com*, or *newchoicehealth.com*.

You can often log in to your insurer's website to compare out-of-pocket expenses at area hospitals. Once you've chosen a facility, request in-network providers — those who have contracted with your insurer, resulting in lower prices.

Check your status as a patient. Medicare beneficiaries need to find out if the hospital considers them an inpatient or outpatient. That's because Medicare Part A, which pays all hospital charges for the first 60 days after a $1,364 deductible, covers inpatient costs only.

If you're considered an outpatient, you'll be billed under Medicare Part B. That means you might wind up spending a lot more — a $185 deductible and 20% of the hospital bill, no matter how high.

And if you need rehabilitation after your hospital stay? Medicare will pay for physical and occupational therapy in a skilled nursing facility only if you've been a hospital inpatient for at least three days.

Take advantage of no-cost facilities. Are you one of the millions of Americans without insurance? You don't have to go without health care. In fact, you can get treatment for free if your income is at or below federal poverty guidelines. Reduced-cost care may be available for those who earn more. To find the hospitals and public health centers that offer such assistance, go to *hrsa.gov*, search for "Hill-Burton Facilities Obligated," and choose the first result.

But don't stop there. Nonprofit hospitals are required to provide "medically necessary" care — including hospital stays and emergency room treatment — for free or at a discount to people who can't afford it. Find out if you're eligible for charity care by speaking with a financial counselor at your local hospital.

Urgent care clinics: Avoid facility fees to keep costs in check

Urgent care centers seem to be popping up everywhere these days. In fact, the number of clinics in the U.S. grew to 8,800 in 2018 — up nearly 45% from five years earlier.

So what's driving the increase? Convenience, for one. Most urgent care centers are open in the evening and on weekends. Wait times are usually less than 30 minutes. And patients tend to spend far less than they would in an emergency room.

Still, you'll want to take action before a non-life-threatening condition — the flu, a fractured toe, a skin rash, for example — has you headed to the nearest urgent care center. That's because some hospital-owned urgent care clinics charge a "facility fee" to offset high operational costs.

The fee, which can be hundreds of dollars, is in addition to the cost of the office visit. While seniors on Medicare no longer have to worry about the surcharge, many other insurers won't cover the fee or will pay just a portion of it.

Fortunately, you can avoid the surcharge by comparing prices. Call local clinics, preferably before you need to visit, and ask if they impose a facility fee. If a receptionist is unsure, speak with the billing department.

To find urgent care centers near you, go to *solvhealth.com/urgent-care* and type in your location.

Art of the deal: The fastest way to lower your medical bills

Hospital bills sure add up fast. Fortunately, just about everyone who negotiates pays less.

It's best to haggle before you receive treatment. But even if you don't, you may still save. Call the billing department and ask for a reduction based on financial need. Don't give up if your request is denied.

Instead, ask to speak with a manager and, if necessary, continue up the chain of command. Be polite but persistent. You'll need to collect documentation — pay stubs and tax returns, for example — proving you can't afford to pay.

Another option? If you can cover part of the bill, offer to pay that amount in cash. You might be able to settle for less than half the total amount.

Can't lower the balance? Don't ignore it. Doing so could ruin your credit score. Instead, ask the hospital about paying off your bill in interest-free monthly installments.

Look out for these common billing errors to keep more of what's yours

Billing bloopers are more common than you think. And as you'll see in the following scenarios, the mistakes can really add up. If you find these errors on your itemized bill, demand they be removed. You'll bump up your savings by hanging on to more of your money.

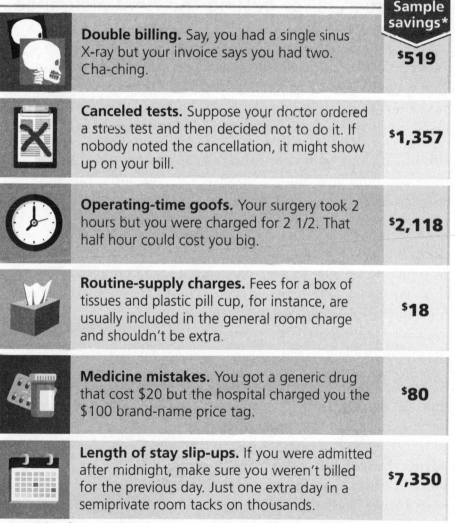

	Sample savings*
Double billing. Say, you had a single sinus X-ray but your invoice says you had two. Cha-ching.	**$519**
Canceled tests. Suppose your doctor ordered a stress test and then decided not to do it. If nobody noted the cancellation, it might show up on your bill.	**$1,357**
Operating-time goofs. Your surgery took 2 hours but you were charged for 2 1/2. That half hour could cost you big.	**$2,118**
Routine-supply charges. Fees for a box of tissues and plastic pill cup, for instance, are usually included in the general room charge and shouldn't be extra.	**$18**
Medicine mistakes. You got a generic drug that cost $20 but the hospital charged you the $100 brand-name price tag.	**$80**
Length of stay slip-ups. If you were admitted after midnight, make sure you weren't billed for the previous day. Just one extra day in a semiprivate room tacks on thousands.	**$7,350**

*Taken from standard charges at a New York hospital. Actual prices will vary.

Long-term care: Affordable solutions for your retirement years

Savvy secrets for getting the right insurance coverage for you

Some 325,000 Americans bought long-term care insurance last year. One reason? Very few can afford to pay $7,400 a month for a semiprivate room in a nursing home or $4,000 a month for care in assisted living. Medicare won't cover home care or visits to adult day care either.

But buying long-term care insurance can be confusing. So consider these tips from Jesse Slome, executive director of the American Association for Long-Term Care Insurance, before signing on the bottom line.

Shop around for savings. Slome says you shouldn't get scared off by high prices. "Often agents start with a Cadillac product because that's what they believe in," he says. "That's OK if you can afford it, but most people can't." So what usually happens next? The customer decides not to buy insurance.

That's the wrong thing to do, Slome says. "With long-term care insurance, some coverage is always going to be better than no coverage," he advises. Instead, ask about plans you can afford — perhaps a policy with a lower coverage amount and less protection against inflation.

Looking to connect with nearby family caregiving resources? Contact the Family Caregiver Alliance at 800-445-8106, or go to *caregiver.org* and click your state on the Family Care Navigator map. You'll find loads of information on local services, programs, and resources.

Find the right agent. Seek out a professional who can wade through lengthy contracts and help you understand the nuances of a policy, suggests Slome. Otherwise you risk not getting the proper coverage.

He says the language in a contract can make an enormous difference to the policyholder.

"It's the details of the contract that spell out how and when claims are paid and how much is paid," he says.

Ask the following to sift through potential agents.

- How long have you been selling long-term care insurance? Slome says a specialist will generally have at least three to five years of experience.

- How many insurance companies are you "appointed" with? Being appointed means the insurer has authorized the agent to sell its products. The more the better for comparison shopping purposes, he says.

Planning for the long haul — 4 moves to keep your story in your hands

Nobody likes to think about long-term care. Yet 2 in 3 seniors will eventually require help with daily tasks like getting dressed, working around the house, paying bills, and preparing meals.

Of course, you never know for sure if you'll need such assistance. But having a plan in place goes a long way toward ensuring you get quality care while shielding your savings. You can start with these tips.

Narrow down housing options. Most older adults want to stay in their homes as long as possible. If you're among them, look around your house and think about how well it will accommodate your future needs. Maybe a few changes would make it safer to live in. Also think about your neighborhood and if you'll be able to get to stores and doctor appointments if you can no longer drive.

Find that staying in your home won't be feasible? You might decide that a senior living community would best suit your future needs. Study the available options so you'll be ready to move at the appropriate time.

Paint a financial picture. Make sure a trusted family member or friend can pay your bills — mortgage, insurance premiums, utilities — in case you're temporarily unable to do so. Tell them about your monthly expenses and if you pay through automatic debit or by check.

> One preventable reason why seniors go into nursing homes? They become too physically frail to care for themselves. But you can keep your independence for years to come. Combining regular physical activity with a healthy diet is the No. 1 thing you can do to stay strong, mentally sharp, and self-sufficient for life.

You can make the payment process easier by consolidating several bank accounts into a single location. And don't forget to introduce them to your accountant, banker, and other financial professionals.

Have a talk with family. You have lots of options for long-term care — whether it's occasional assistance a few days a month or as often as every day. Tell your family about your wishes and what you would want to do if your preferred setting could no longer meet your needs.

Filling them in on your financial situation will give them a leg up on obtaining the services you might need. Tell them about your assets, including the location of safe deposit boxes, pensions, retirement savings, and annuities. They'll also need to know about any long-term care or disability insurance you might have.

Line up your documents. Your family can't legally handle your personal business unless you set up a durable power of attorney — a document that gives someone the power to act on your behalf if you're unable to make decisions on your own.

You'll need one for your finances and another for health care. Without the paperwork, your loved ones will have to go to court to gain approval — an often time-consuming and expensive process.

It's also a good idea to check with your bank to see if it requires you to sign its own power of attorney form. Many financial institutions do this to lower the risk of fraudulent activity.

2 tactics for paying your family caregiver when you're strapped for cash

Family caregivers spend, on average, 24 hours a week assisting loved ones with tasks like grooming, dressing, cooking, and house-keeping. And if they live with the person requiring help? They put in about 40 hours a week — the same schedule as a full-time employee. Yet the vast majority of these caregivers don't get paid.

Have a family member who is helping you age in place? Read on for ways Uncle Sam might help you compensate them.

Medicaid may put your aide on the payroll. If you're receiving financial assistance from Medicaid, you might be eligible for funds to pay a family member — adult child, grandchild, even ex-spouse — to lend you a helping hand. Benefits vary by state, but in most cases the money would either go to you directly or to a management company that would pay your caregiver's salary.

The application process for caretaker payments includes an assessment to determine the level of support you need. Contact your local Medicaid office to see if you qualify.

Boost your home care budget with help from the VA. U.S. military veterans at risk of being placed in a nursing home qualify for monetary assistance to help them remain at home. They must be enrolled in the Veterans Health Administration's standard medical benefits package to receive payment for health-related goods and services, including caregiving from relatives.

In addition, the U.S. Department of Veterans Affairs (VA) provides benefits to family caregivers of veterans injured in the line of duty on or after Sept. 11, 2001. The program is slated to expand over the next few years to include veterans injured in previous years. Call the VA's Caregiver Support Line toll-free at 855-260-3274 to learn more.

Need a helping hand? Look no further for free government benefits

States offer a wide range of support services — from adult day care and home repair to legal assistance and meal delivery — to adults 60 years of age and older. But how do you sort through all those government programs for seniors?

Get what you deserve by going to the federal government's Eldercare Locator at *eldercare.acl.gov*. Just enter your ZIP code or city and state at the top of the page to find the agencies that connect older adults with community-based services.

Don't have a computer? No worries. One phone call will connect you with the same resources — many of which offer free services. Call the Eldercare Locator at 800-677-1116 to speak with an information specialist.

You can also dial 211 to get help finding local resources for things like home health care, transportation, and homemaker services.

Real estate secrets help you buy, sell, or rent like a pro

Your mortgage road map: Navigate
home loans with ease 190

Ready, set, sell: Cash in on
your home's value 194

Stretch your home-buying dollars 199

Keys to a smart move for less 205

Home sweet home: Open the door
to better insurance rates 211

Property taxes: How to save on
the homefront .216

Unlock the value of rental properties . . .219

Your mortgage road map: Navigate home loans with ease

2 smart ways to put more money in your pocket each month

If mortgage payments are eating up your savings, changing your monthly rate may help you manage your money. See if one of these two methods could save you a bundle.

Get a do-over with refinancing. Are you paying massive amounts of interest on your mortgage? Consider refinancing. Here are some of the benefits.

- Refinancing will replace your current loan with a new one, hopefully with a lower interest rate. That means you'll save money over the life of your loan.

- Since you've already paid off some of your house, you should also get a lower monthly payment.

- If you have an adjustable-rate mortgage (ARM), refinancing gives you the opportunity to switch to the security of a fixed rate. Unlike an ARM, a fixed-rate loan allows you to pay the same monthly payment throughout the length of the loan. That safety costs more upfront, though, because ARM rates are initially lower.

Be aware that your loan length may also change, which could hurt your savings in the long run. For instance, you may end up paying more interest if you extend your loan by another 30 years even if your rate is lower.

From appraisal fees to closing costs, you'll likely pay thousands to refinance. Test your options with a loan amortization calculator like the one at *amortization-calc.com* to make sure you'll still come out ahead.

Borrowers beware — nonprime loans could put you in a bind

Nonprime loans are just subprime loans by another name. Remember those? They helped cause the 2000s housing market crash because so many people couldn't repay them. These tricky loans — offered to people who don't qualify for the best rates — are making a comeback as lenders take on riskier mortgages. But does that mean it's prime time to go for a nonprime loan?

Maybe not. Experts say to apply for a prime mortgage first to see if you qualify because it will have better terms. If a nonprime loan is your only option, be extra cautious. You'll probably have to pay a higher interest rate that may be adjustable, which could increase your likelihood of defaulting on the loan.

To improve your credit and work your way toward becoming a prime borrower, read the chapter *Reap the benefits of a better credit score.*

CAUTION

Reel in lower payments with a mortgage recast. Good terms on your mortgage are a boon for your bank account, so you don't want to lose them. Look into a mortgage recast to lower your monthly payments without changing your terms. Here's what that would mean.

- You'd pay a lump sum to lower your loan balance. Then your monthly payments would be recalculated based on the new amount, resulting in a lower bill.

- This will save you on interest without shortening your loan term.

- Since you're not getting a new loan, you probably won't need a credit check.

- You won't have to pay closing costs, so fees often stay as low as $250.

Recasting is particularly beneficial if you move to a new home before selling the old one. You can use any profit you make when you sell your old place to pay the lump sum required to recast the mortgage on the new house.

Keep in mind that many lenders require a lump sum of at least $5,000 before recasting, which ties up more money in your house. So before you put extra cash toward your mortgage, make sure you have savings put aside for emergencies or large future expenses.

> Not all mortgages can be recast. You may have the option if yours is backed by Fannie Mae or Freddie Mac, but those backed by Veterans Affairs and the Federal Housing Administration generally can't be recast. Lenders may have different requirements, so check with yours first.

How to turn your home into a cash cow

Need extra cash for daily expenses or a home renovation? You can tap into your home's money pot to help you out, but be careful not to lose in the process.

Review reverse mortgage risks and rewards. You may be interested in a reverse mortgage if you've invested in your home but need some return now. Still, you'll only be eligible for one if you're over the age of 62 and have paid off over 50% of your house. That's because your home equity is the collateral for the loan. You can get around 60% of the equity as a lump sum, monthly payment, or line of credit.

It sounds great to have your lender pay you for a change, but remember you're also taking money out of your house. The longer you have the reverse mortgage, the more your loan goes up and your home equity does down.

If you decide to move to assisted living, you'll probably have to sell your house to pay off the loan. Why? If the home isn't your primary residence for more than 12 months, the loan must be paid back.

But before any of that can happen, you'll have to spend several thousand dollars in fees to arrange the reverse mortgage. The exact amount will vary based on your home's value but will include loan origination, closing, and service fees.

Use a cash-out refinance without getting kicked. Like with any refinance, this option replaces your current mortgage with a new loan, so watch for changing interest rates.

In this case, though, the new loan is greater than the amount you currently owe on your house. And you keep the difference between the new loan and what you owe. For example, if you currently owe $80,000 on your house and need a loan for $30,000, your new mortgage would be $110,000.

Your house is the collateral for the mortgage, so using the loan for home improvements is a good choice because you're adding value back into your house.

Typically, you need at least 20% equity in your property to refinance this way, and you're usually limited to cashing out 80% to 90% of that equity. You can only receive this payout as a lump sum. Closing costs range from 3% to 6% of the mortgage, so be prepared to spend a few thousand dollars before getting any back.

When you shouldn't pay off your mortgage early

Retiring mortgage-free is a tempting prospect. But before you take that weight off your shoulders, consider these reasons you may want to bear the burden a little longer.

- You have debts with higher interest rates.
- You don't have an emergency fund built up yet.
- You'll tie up your assets and won't have liquid money for emergencies.
- You'd have to dip into your retirement funds.
- You're saving for big purchases like a home renovation or wedding.
- You still can take a mortgage deduction on your taxes.
- You might move in the next few years.
- You have experience investing and could use your money to earn more.

Ready, set, sell: Cash in on your home's value

Make small home improvements to build a big return

Minor improvements can have a major impact on your sale price. Find out how to eke all you can out of your house when you sell.

Cash in when you clean and declutter. A professional organizer can cost up to $2,500, so maximize savings by handling tasks yourself. For a potential 3% to 5% bump in your selling price, cheap decluttering and cleaning fixes are no-brainers.

- Take down most of your personal photos so buyers can imagine themselves living in your home.

- In the kitchen, tuck away towels and move small appliances off the counter into the cabinets.

- Skip the costly bathroom remodel — it will only have a 70% return. Instead, do some easy sprucing up. Attack grime by attaching a scrub brush to your drill to power wash your bathtub. Soak shower heads in vinegar overnight using a plastic bag and rubber band, and watch mineral buildup disappear.

Save old floors and prosper. Instead of getting new flooring, consider putting fresh life into the one you already have.

- Adding new wood floors would cost about $5,500, but simply refinishing ones you have drops the cost to $3,000. You can expect a full return on your investment, so if you're afraid you'll damage the wood yourself, hire a professional. The update may even snag you a closing deal. Plus your shiny, durable floors could help contribute to an extra 3% to 5% bump in your sales price.

- For carpeted rooms, rent a deep-clean vacuum. They cost $40 for a 48-hour rental compared to a $4,000+ replacement expense.

Keep paint plain and pocket the change. Neutral colors are your best bet for attracting buyers because they have a broad appeal. Focus on high-traffic rooms to get the biggest bang for your buck.

- Try rolling on a light taupe in your living room and pale periwinkle in the bath. These room color combinations could bring in an extra $2,793 and $2,786 respectively, according to an analysis by Zillow, an online real estate company.

- The kitchen is a key room. Instead of painting the walls, consider rejuvenating the cabinets. If you go for a tuxedo style — the top cabinets a different color than the bottom — you'll not only make the cabinets look new but also potentially gain another $1,547 in sale value.

Is a 'smart' house a smart move?

A recent survey of home buyers found that more than half preferred a house with high-tech capabilities over one without. But that doesn't mean you should rush to install all the latest "smart" gadgets in the hopes of selling your home faster or getting a better price.

Large-scale updates may not pay off because technology changes so quickly. Plus they could deter buyers who aren't interested in having wireless technology throughout their house.

Rather than spend thousands you may not get back, find the middle ground with small updates. A smart thermostat is a good choice. Options include The Nest and Honeywell, which both offer models under $250. A video doorbell is also affordable at $100 and up. According to *Consumer Reports*, these fairly inexpensive upgrades could shorten your home's time on the market.

CAUTION

Staging secret: Earn more with proper decor

Give your house a facelift without spending a fortune. Staging makes it easier for buyers to visualize themselves in your space. By restyling your home and boosting its appeal you may reap the benefits of a shorter time on the market or even a 1% to 5% price increase.

Susan Patterson, who owns the business Standout Staging, says you should stage before you put the house on the market. "Staging is always less expensive than your first price reduction," she says. Attractive listing photos will increase foot traffic and help you sell faster.

Stage for success without overspending. A pro-stager is an asset if you've already vacated your house. But if you still live there and want to do it yourself, Patterson suggests some key actions you should take.

- Look at houses online on the Multiple Listing Service (MLS). Compare yours to pictures of homes that stand out. With fresh eyes, you can see if your home is crowded or needs paint, then make those changes.

> Last minute touches can have a lasting effect on potential buyers. Patterson's day-of tip is to make sure the house smells great. Try baking cookies, or open the doors to let in fresh air an hour ahead. And be sure to put away personal items like clothing and makeup.

- Planning to buy furniture for your new house? Buy it now to use for staging.

- "Edit" your house. Take out unnecessary furniture, and improve room flow with what's left.

- If you only have time to do one thing, focus on decluttering.

Want a little help? Look for a stager with a redesign service. They'll rearrange your furniture and decor for you. It's often cheaper than full staging, around $400 to $1,000, and is finished in a day.

Turn up the highlights in your home. If you're not planning to stage your whole house, focus on key rooms like the living room and kitchen. Patterson encourages using lamplight over fluorescents to make the rooms more inviting.

And make sure you stage those tricky spaces. You never want a buyer wondering what they would do with a room, Patterson says. "If there's any room in the house that's just super awkward ... that's a room I would stage because that's the one people are going to focus on."

"Every home has imperfections, no matter how new it is," Patterson says. "Staging to me really highlights the positives of the house and definitely helps to downplay any perceived negatives and make them less noticeable."

iBuying makes home selling easy — but is it worth the cost?

How would you like to sell your house without ever sticking a "For Sale" sign in your yard? Consider selling to an online real estate company. Called iBuying, it's one of the latest innovations in the housing industry. Companies like Zillow, Offerpad, and Opendoor offer to buy your house. Say yes, and your house is sold. No fuss, no muss.

So what's the catch? You might end up paying a whole lot more for the convenience. Take a look at how it works, and decide for yourself.

iBuying is as easy as one, two, three. Follow these steps and you can close on your house sale in as little as a week or up to three months. You have the flexibility to choose.

- Request a free offer. Just answer a few questions and, in some cases, submit pictures.

- Receive an offer after two days, maybe less. You'll have around five days to accept or reject it. But don't expect to negotiate a better price. Unlike a normal buyer, counteroffers aren't typically accepted.

- Accept the offer. After that the iBuyer's team will assess your house. If it needs repairs, you can complete them or let the iBuyer do it. They'll cover their repair costs by dropping your sale value. If you're uncomfortable with the lower price, you can still cancel your contract at this point. If both parties agree to the adjusted price, the sale can be finalized.

Weigh the pros and cons before you decide. Selling with an iBuyer can be a great option if you're on a strict deadline, want to reduce moving stress, or haven't been able to sell the traditional way.

But you most likely will be offered less for your home than you would on the open market. And expect a high fee when you close with an iBuyer — 6% to 13%.

Opendoor's fee includes costs you'd pay anyway like the buyer's agent fee and listing costs. It adds a 1% convenience charge as well. Expect to pay 1% to 3% for closing costs on top of that. As great as it may sound, you'll need to think carefully about whether the convenience is worth the extra costs.

Sell it yourself: When to spend extra to earn a little more

- Set the right price by looking at "comps" — the sale price for similar houses near you. Having trouble? Look into an appraisal. It will cost around $340 but can help you accurately price your home.

- Hiring a real estate lawyer to set up the contract is a wise move. Consider setting aside $500 for one.

- List your property on free sites like Zillow or Trulia, but consider paying for placement on a Multiple Listing Service. Expect to pay the provider around $400 for the extra exposure.

Stretch your home-buying dollars

Buy your next home mortgage-free

Don't you wish you could buy your dream retirement house without worrying about mortgage payments? You can, if you use the housing market's best-kept secret — a program called HECM (pronounced heck-um) for purchase.

You may have heard of a standard HECM (Home Equity Conversion Mortgage), which is a government-backed reverse mortgage. Instead of using the equity in your current home for income, a HECM for purchase allows you to buy a new home and finance part of it through a reverse mortgage. To be eligible for the program:

- you must be 62 or older.

- the new house must meet the program's standards. Certain houses like cooperative units and manufactured homes built before 1976 aren't allowed.

- the house must be your primary residence.

Discover how a HECM can help you. "There are many benefits to using the HECM for purchase program," a spokesperson from the Federal Housing Administration (FHA) says.

For example, its flexible repayment plan gives you the option to not make any monthly mortgage payments. And you'll only have one set of closing costs between the combined reverse mortgage and home purchase. Plus you have the option to pay off the loan if you want to. That will put equity into the house for your heirs.

Many older adults want to downsize to a smaller home, move to a house with less maintenance, or relocate closer to family and friends. A HECM for purchase allows them to buy what they need without worrying about a large mortgage payment, the FHA spokesperson says.

This type of loan may cost more upfront. One downside to this plan is that it requires a greater down payment than a normal mortgage. That's because you pay the difference between the loan amount and the cost of the home. The amount you're loaned will be based on your age, the price of the house, and the interest rate on the loan.

Typically, you'll end up paying around 50% of the house price. Many people use the profits from selling their old home to fund the large down payment.

You'll need counseling to figure out your options. Ready to get the ball rolling? The first step is to meet with a HECM counselor.

"Information is critical," says the FHA spokesperson. "Prospective HECM borrowers are required to receive HECM counseling. It is important to use this opportunity to run the numbers, learn about alternatives to the HECM, and see if a HECM is the right option."

You can find a counselor by calling 800-569-4287 or searching online at *entp.hud.gov/idapp/html/hecm_agency_look.cfm*.

Live big — and save big — with a small home

Ready to downsize? How small do you want to go? If you're ready to try a pint-sized home, you'll find options galore. Whether it's on wheels or built on solid ground, you'll save serious cash compared to buying a standard-sized home.

Join the tiny house movement. Tiny house events and TV shows have been grabbing everyone's attention, but have you considered one for yourself? Here's what you need to know.

- Typical tiny homes are 100 to 400 square feet — about the size of your standard family room. They usually cost $10,000 to $60,000, but you could save thousands if you build it yourself. That's significantly less than a standard home, which is typically 2,600 square feet and sells in the low- to mid-$300,000s.

- Although many tiny homes feature lofts to maximize space, you can find plenty that stick to one floor. Instead, to save space, they'll often have a Murphy bed or fold-out couch. In some clever models the bed is stored in the ceiling and lowered at the press of a button.

- Your main concern may be where to place it. First, determine whether your tiny home is classified as a recreational vehicle (RV), with wheels, or an accessory dwelling unit (ADU), on a foundation. Then look closely at your state and local zoning laws. A few places to consider settling are on family land or in a tiny home community.

Modular homes are the next best thing. These homes seem space age-like as they're plunked down onto your lot in big boxes. Built in units offsite, modular homes are then brought to your land and connected. If you're interested in downsizing but not sold on going tiny, these prefab homes fit the bill.

- They can be built more quickly than site-built houses and are usually less expensive. A typical small, not tiny, modular house will cost $36,000 to $88,000 and measure about 900 to 1,100 square feet.

- Custom modular homes will be more expensive depending on how you upgrade. Be sure to check whether the unit price includes other costs like foundation-laying and installation.

- Be aware that it may be difficult to purchase a lot in certain areas because of zoning laws.

Make the whole country your home with an RV. Give up one view to have them all when your downsized home sports wheels.

Depending on whether you buy new or used, you'll typically spend $15,000 to mid-$100,000 for a recreational vehicle.

To save on the road, join a discount camping club like Passport America to get cheaper overnight rates at campgrounds across the country. Save even more by staying in one place longer. You'll reduce gas and utility costs.

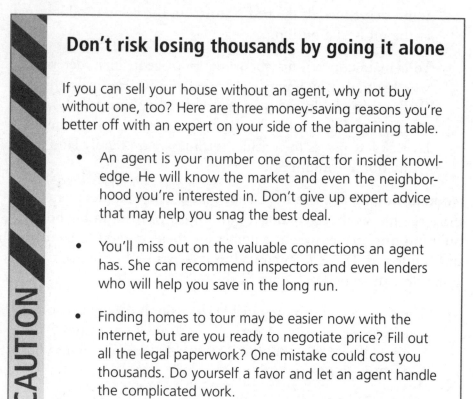

Don't risk losing thousands by going it alone

If you can sell your house without an agent, why not buy without one, too? Here are three money-saving reasons you're better off with an expert on your side of the bargaining table.

- An agent is your number one contact for insider knowledge. He will know the market and even the neighborhood you're interested in. Don't give up expert advice that may help you snag the best deal.

- You'll miss out on the valuable connections an agent has. She can recommend inspectors and even lenders who will help you save in the long run.

- Finding homes to tour may be easier now with the internet, but are you ready to negotiate price? Fill out all the legal paperwork? One mistake could cost you thousands. Do yourself a favor and let an agent handle the complicated work.

CAUTION

Get the best deal on the (auction) block

You've seen them in the newspaper and online — homes on the auction block for bargain-basement prices. In fact, according to the

National Association of Realtors (NAR), foreclosed properties can sell at 15 percent below market value. That's a savings of $30,000 on a $200,000 home. Try a few pointers to get in on these deals.

Pinpoint your search. Where do you want to buy? Type that city's name, along with terms like "foreclosures" or "REO properties" (real estate owned), into an online search engine such as *Google.com*. Websites like *homepath.com* and *realtytrac.com* are also great resources for finding foreclosed houses.

Base your offer on local comps. Sometimes the bank lists the price too high or too low. That's why you should research the selling prices of other homes in that area. You can always try to negotiate a better price. But remember, if you submit a low-ball offer, you could lose out to another buyer.

Get prepared ahead of time. Found your diamond in the rough? Then it's time to get prequalified for your loan. Bank-owned properties can sell very quickly, so it's best to be prepared. Be ready to show proof of how much you are eligible to borrow.

Head to the auction site. If the bank has been trying to sell the home without success, it may go up for auction. That means buyers like you could have a chance to bid on the property. Auctions can be held in person at the courthouse or county clerk's office, or online.

Watch out for the pitfalls. REO properties are generally sold as-is. Unless you're able to schedule an inspection (and you're not always allowed to do that) you may end up with more problems than you bargained for. All those thousands you thought you had saved could be swallowed up by renovations and improvements, in order to make your new money pit livable.

Do a title search. Don't skip this step. You need to know if there are any liens against the title or problems with the deed.

Don't be afraid to ask for help. No need to go it alone. Pay a qualified real estate agent to help you navigate the ins and outs of buying foreclosures.

How to bargain for the repairs you need

You've signed the contract, but negotiations aren't over yet. The home inspection revealed the house needs some repairs. Of course, you've already included the obvious defects in your purchase offer. So how do you handle the hidden flaws the inspector turned up?

- First of all, know which issues are worth negotiating. For instance, fixing outdated sewer pipes could be critical to your health and safety. Replacing old fixtures is not as important. Make sure your requests are reasonable.

- Don't show your cards to the seller. You may plan to renovate the kitchen, but if you mention that, you'll lose bargaining power. It's unlikely they'll agree to pay for scratched cabinets if they know you'll just replace them.

- Instead of having the owner do the work, ask for a cash-back credit to be paid at closing. That lets you customize the repairs and make sure everything is done to your standards.

Keys to a smart move for less

How to pick your dream retirement spot

If you're considering relocating during your retirement, you may feel overwhelmed by your options. Thousands of cities are open to you, so knowing where to start can save you a lot of trouble. Here are three things to focus on as you search.

Pinpoint the right location for you. Beach or mountain? That's the go-to, sometimes fanciful, question people ask about their dream home. But knowing where you feel comfortable is key to enjoying your retirement.

- Evaluate your lifestyle. Are you more suited for the city or countryside, all four seasons or full-time summer? A love for hiking may bring you to the mountains, but a passion for water sports could steer you toward the coast.

- Consider the community. Are you interested in a 55+ active adult community or would you prefer a mix of generations? College towns, for instance, are a great option if you're looking for a range of demographics. Plus you'll find a wide variety of activities, from concerts to low-cost classes.

Research the regions that spark interest. When you've found a few areas you might be interested in, it's time to do some sleuthing.

Trina Searcy, a broker associate, recommends researching thoroughly and consulting an expert in the area. "I would say take your time and do your due diligence," she says. "Do your homework. You've really got to think about where you want to be especially if you're going to buy because you might be stuck there for awhile." Here's what to look into.

- Find out how far you'd be from friends and family, and weigh the pros and cons.

- Look into the area's crime rate on sites like *city-data.com* and *www.crimereports.com*.

- Review entertainment and learning opportunities that can fill your time.

- Keep a sharp eye out for transportation options — buses and subways will make your life easier as will walking and biking.

Before moving, try a dry run of living there by renting a space or taking an extended vacation. Searcy says that can help you make sure you like the living situation before buying.

Pre-Move Must-Dos
Drop "moving stress" from your schedule when you use this checklist to organize your plans.

✔ Sort your possessions and sell what you don't want. Donate whatever is left.

✔ Measure the doorways, hallways, and staircases in your new home to make sure your furniture will fit through.

✔ Put special items like financial documents and medical records into a file. Keep the file with you instead of loading it on the truck.

✔ Make a plan for protecting fragile and expensive items like art and instruments.

✔ Take pictures of complicated electronic plug-ins so it's easy to set them up again.

✔ If you receive your Social Security as a mailed check, change your address ASAP.

Consider your budget. It's one of the most important parts of moving, but don't just look at house prices.

- Investigate the cost of living. Utility and grocery expenses are a good place to start.

- Look into tax rates. Texas, for example, doesn't have state income tax, but its high property tax would hurt your savings.

- Don't forget about mortgage rates. Lenders in some areas offer lower rates which will save thousands over the life of your loan.

Retire abroad and live better than ever

Don't let retirement confine you — redefine your life by moving abroad. You can often receive your Social Security benefits in foreign countries. Stretch this money at hot spots around the globe that beckon retirees with scenic views and low-cost living.

The Caribbean Sea calls. Pricey vacations to Caribbean islands like the Bahamas and U.S. Virgin Islands may discourage you from looking for your beachside paradise. But you can find a view with valuable savings in these areas.

- Roatán, an island in Honduras, is 30 miles offshore and has an international airport. Plus, English is widely spoken. A couple can buy a beachfront condo for under $200,000 or rent and live on $2,000 a month total.

- Isla Colón, an island in Panama, offers all sorts of water recreations to its expat community. Buying can be a little confusing though, so try renting first. You and your spouse will be able to live on a monthly $1,400 budget.

The Caribbean has the bonus of being relatively close to the U.S. And you'll find a welcoming balance of laid-back scenes and tourist hubbub.

A European room with a view. If you think retiring to Europe is out of your price range, check again. You'll pay a pretty penny to move into a metropolis like Paris, but small towns scattered throughout the continent have lower everyday prices.

- Spain promises sunshine and one of the lowest costs of living in Europe. Including rent, a monthly budget of around $2,000 is all a couple needs to live in Alicante. If you're keen on buying, an apartment there runs about $100,000.

- France is more than deliciously inexpensive wine and bread. Outside the city, you can find houses for sale for less than $100,000. If you want to test the waters before buying, renting may be less than $1,000 a month in Montpellier and around $565 in Sarlat-la-Canéda. Even in expensive Bordeaux, a couple can live on a total budget under $2,000.

The hardest part of retiring in Europe may be getting the right visa. Look into options for people who don't need employment, and consult with the appropriate embassy so you're prepared for the paperwork.

Around the world in a day to Southeast Asia. If you're feeling daring, you can keep your savings account strong by moving far into the Eastern Hemisphere.

- Vietnam's low-cost living can halve your expenses. Rent, food, and restaurants all have prices that are at least 50% lower than in the U.S. A couple in Vietnam only needs $800 to $1,200 per month when sticking to less expensive housing options like a fully furnished apartment for less than $400.

- Cambodia is one of the best places for retirees to get the most out of their money. In the capital of Phnom Penh, you may only spend $380 on rent and utilities.

The biggest potential drawback of this region may be distance from family and friends. Plus, in some areas you may encounter a significant language barrier.

Keep in mind you'll still have to file taxes if you move abroad, and working with a tax specialist could help.

For helpful details about a country you're interested in, check out *internationalliving.com*. Connect with other expats at *internations.org*.

Go green: Spend less on moving and save the Earth

You've spent hours of your precious moving time hunting down free, used cardboard boxes from restaurants and recycling centers. But with only a couple of dingy ones to show for it, you contemplate spending $180 on a set of new packing materials.

Dump that idea with those wasteful cardboard boxes and opt for reusable plastic ones that could help you save money — and the environment. Companies like BungoBox and Bin It make it easy. They drop off and pick up the rental boxes for free.

- Pricing will depend on how many boxes you need and how long you need them. Bin It says they're 25% cheaper than buying cardboard boxes. It will cost about $85 to rent 30 bins for two weeks. BungoBox says they're 50% cheaper.

- The boxes come with secure lids, so you'll save on tape, too.

- Unlike reused cardboard boxes, they're sanitized between uses.

- They're also sturdier, so fragile possessions won't get crushed.

Let specialists take the stress out of moving Mom and Dad

It's finally time to move Mom and Dad into an assisted living facility. They're going from 2,500 square feet to half that much — along with a lifetime of household stuff. Mom and Dad know it's time. So do the kids. But nobody knows what to do first. It's time to call in the senior move manager.

So what exactly do they do? To start with, they'll plow through the trash and treasures, helping you and your parents sort, organize, and pack up decades of family belongings. They'll go to your parents' new digs and set up their living space. Traveling with Mom or Dad can be part of the package, too. They'll even find a mover or real estate agent if that's what you need.

You're not alone in this. Over 50,000 families hired senior move managers last year. For keeping the family peace, and your peace of mind, it may be well worth the cost. Price points vary, depending on your family's needs. Most senior move managers charge by the hour, with rates ranging from $40 to $125 per hour.

Focus on Mom and Dad. These specialists can help families work together, and they make sure your parents' best interests are at the heart of all decisions. So how do you find one you can trust? Here are some questions to ask before you hire anyone.

- How long have you been providing senior move management services?

- Have you participated in any formal training programs? What kinds of training?

- Are you fully insured for liability and workers' compensation?

- How do you charge? Will you give me a schedule of your fees in writing?

- Will you provide a written contract?

- Can you provide references?

- Are you a member of the National Association of Senior Move Managers?

For more information about senior move managers, visit the national association's website at *nasmm.org*.

Home sweet home: Open the door to better insurance rates

Protect your biggest asset with the right homeowner's policy

You've just said goodbye to your last dinner guest, who proceeds to trip down your front steps as she leaves. Several hours later — after a trip to the emergency room, a diagnosis of a broken hip, and profuse apologies to your friend — you slump into your recliner with a sinking feeling of what's to come.

Are you covered for what just happened? Independent insurance agents Bill and Lee Knight say this scenario is a good example of why you need to set up your homeowner's insurance policy correctly. They have some advice for how to do that.

Find an agent that fits your needs. The Knights recommend independent insurance agents because of their access to choices in the insurance marketplace. "They can choose the market and fit the person to the coverage," says Lee.

Your independent agent knows which products are best for older adults. "Some of our carriers market directly to seniors," the Knights say. This means they are less likely to charge an "up rate" and probably have a premium designed with older adults' needs in mind.

Don't get caught with "canary" insurance. "Cheap, cheap, cheap" insurance is not always the best choice. "Price points are good, but it's not the most important thing, particularly when you get to be a senior," the Knights say.

If your premium's cost is your only consideration when deciding your policy, you risk being penalized for not properly insuring your property in the event of a total loss.

211

"We try to get people into the mindset that, hey, you have a nice home, let's insure it right the first time. It may not be the cheapest, but it will be done correctly because we want to protect you."

Pick the coverage that most fits your needs. Your choice of coverage level matters. Most carriers offer these options.

- Actual cash value. You'll get the amount you need to replace your home or property, minus a deduction for depreciation.

- Replacement value. You can rebuild your home with no depreciation penalty up to your policy limits. Ask for an inflation guard clause to offset increased building costs.

- Guaranteed replacement value. Your property is replaced regardless of depreciation up to 25% above the policy limit.

> If you are retiring to a new state, ask your current insurance agent to network for you and refer you to an agent in your new town. Or when searching for an agent, filter your search specifically to look for companies that say they specialize in serving ages 55 and up.

Lee cautions homeowners to take their coverage seriously. "Your insurance policies are very important. You might think it's just a numbers game, a policy that you don't want to pay. Until you have a claim situation come up. And then I've never heard anybody say, "Well, I paid too much for that." They say, "I am so grateful that I had this coverage."

3 tried-and-true ways to lower your homeowner's premium

Home insurance is not likely to top anyone's list of conversation starters. Unless you've figured out how to save over $2,000 on your premium — then you might be the talk of your next party. So get these pointers ready to share with your friends.

Choose policy limits wisely now to save later

It's painful to lose your home or personal property but worse to be reimbursed at a fraction of its value. "Your insurance agent tries to help you understand the value of your home," says Lee Knight, agent and co-owner of Knight Insurance Agency. "We try to look ahead. If a loss were to happen, what would be the best outcome?"

Preparing for the future means thinking about these details that affect your policy.

- Inflation. The cost of rebuilding depends on current materials prices.

- Depreciation. Property often drops in value from 20% in the first year to 60% in the 10th year.

- Additional living expenses. This feature pays the costs of temporarily relocating. Coverage varies but usually runs about 20% of your home insurance.

- Personal liability limits. These usually fall between $100,000 and $300,000. "You can extend this to $1 million for as little as $150 a year," according to Bill Knight.

- Possessions. Personal property coverage generally falls between 50% and 70% of your policy. Look at whether that's enough to cover your valuables.

Look into switching policies. If you live in Montgomery, Alabama, your premium could run as much as $3,538 with a $500 deductible. That's $294.83 a month for $300,000 property coverage and $100,000 liability — a basic policy.

If you compared this premium with six others in the Montgomery area, you would hardly believe the difference. The same coverage

213

from a different provider is as little as $1,314 a year. That's a savings of $2,224 right off the top. An independent agent could help you make those comparisons in your area if you need help.

Consider raising your deductible. Have you been claim-free for at least 10 years? Your insurer loves low-risk clients like you, especially if you have a low deductible and high premium. You keep giving them more of your hard-earned money, and they don't have to pay out anything in return.

If that's the case, it may be time to think about raising your deductible. In the Montgomery example, choosing a $2,500 deductible instead of $500 drops your annual premium another $100. The new monthly payment would be $101.16, a difference of $193.67 monthly and $2,324 annually from your original policy.

Of course, with a higher deductible, you would have to absorb up to $2,500 in repair costs if you experience a loss. That's a good reason to be sure you have enough savings in place in case you need to make a claim.

Ask what credit score the agent used to decide your rate. Many states allow insurance agencies to use a person's credit score to help figure out their premium. If the score they used to set up your policy was old or incorrect, then you are likely paying more than you should be. Ask them to recalculate it based on your current score.

Never underestimate the cost of calamities

In the spring of 2019, homeowners in many U.S. midwestern states were hit hard with catastrophic flooding. Many of these people did not ever expect to need flood insurance.

How about you? Have you heeded the warnings and made sure you're covered for calamities? You would never buy a shoe advertised as "one size fits all," so don't buy a standard policy assuming it will cover all your needs.

Along with floods and earthquakes, here are a few other hazards to be concerned about. Talk to your insurance agent about these possible gaps in your coverage.

Sewer and drain backup. Many city governments place responsibility for the sewer line on the homeowner beginning at the lateral, the pipeline from the street to the home. Standard policies limit coverage of water damage, and sewer backup typically is not included. You'll be on the hook for repair costs unless you specifically add it to your policy.

Mold. This fungus can invade your home through openings or come in on clothing and accessories. Your policy probably won't cover it if it's something you could have prevented. If it's caused by a "covered peril" like a burst pipe, you may be limited to a certain amount of reimbursement. You can add mold to your policy as an optional rider.

Sinkholes. You've heard the horror stories of cars and even houses being swallowed up by giant holes. These occur when ground water dissolves underground rock or erosion causes a collapse in the ground.

The U.S. Geological Survey provides information about sinkhole risks. Go to *usgs.gov*, and search on sinkholes to see if you're in an affected area. Then talk to your insurer about whether you can do an add-on to your policy or if you'll need separate sinkhole insurance.

Insurance terms that come with extra price tags

Insurers use specialized words to talk about your coverage — like surcharge, rider, endorsement, floater, and umbrella. These fancy words all carry additional fees, so look closely at them to make sure they meet your insurance needs.

CAUTION

Property taxes: How to save on the homefront

How to turn your taxes into treasure

Did you buy or sell your home this year? Have a lot of medical expenses? Chances are you'll be itemizing deductions on your tax return. Don't forget about your property taxes when you do.

Under the Tax Cuts and Jobs Act, from now until 2025, you can deduct property taxes and state and local income taxes up to the new limit of $10,000 if you are married and filing jointly or $5,000 if filing separately. Adding property taxes to your deductions is one more way to put money back in your pocket. Here are some things to keep in mind.

Make sure you count all eligible property. Think beyond your home when considering property. If you own cars, recreational vehicles, a vacation home, or land, you can include the property taxes paid on those in your income tax deduction. Just stay within the federal limit.

Take advantage of the timing. If you know you'll itemize on next year's taxes, you can pay your property taxes in advance to bump up your deduction. For example, say your semiannual tax bill is due next May. Pay it five months early — in December — and you can count it toward this year's deductions.

If your taxes are paid out of an escrow account, make sure the lender actually sends the money to the county before you claim the deduction. Don't assume the taxes are paid as soon as you send your check. As long as the taxes are paid within the tax year and reported on IRS Form 1098, you can deduct them.

Gather your receipts in advance. Keep a sharp eye on expenses related to all of your property. Be sure to store receipts for all of these items in a safe place for easy reference at tax time.

- car registration renewals
- taxes paid on a home you have bought or sold

Realize your rental's property tax potential. If you use a property exclusively for rental purposes, then you would report its expenses separately from your personal expenses by using IRS Form 1040 Schedule E, which means you can deduct your rental property's tax.

Abracadabra — make some of your property taxes disappear

Did you know you can eliminate some of your property taxes? It's true. Certain government programs help senior citizens face down this bill. Here's how to get in on the deal.

Work it off. Volunteer for tax credit? Sounds like a win-win. If your community participates in a Senior Property Tax Work-Off Program, you could perform chores for various nonprofit services or government offices in exchange for credit or compensation toward your next property tax bill.

Freeze it. Lock in the assessed value of your home, called a Property Tax Assessment Freeze, and your property taxes are calculated at a lower rate. A general Tax Freeze, based on income, will lock in the tax amount you owe so that it will not increase.

Defer it. Available in some states, a property tax deferral allows you to postpone your property tax bill until you sell your home. In most cases, the taxes are taken out of the proceeds.

Seniors: Get the tax breaks you deserve

Residents of Brookline, Massachusetts were thrilled to hear their property values had gone up 7.7%, since this almost immediately

217

translated into more equity in their homes. Unfortunately, it also meant their property taxes were going to increase — by a whopping 6.2%. But not to worry. The town made sure exemptions were available to help those most in need.

An exemption means you pay lower taxes on your property, usually by first reducing your property's value either a certain percentage or a dollar amount. After the exemption is applied, the remaining value of your home is then taxed.

But note, you won't automatically receive exemptions. You must apply and may have to show proof you:

- own the property.
- reside in the home.
- are of a certain age.
- meet the income requirements.

Because the number and type of property tax exemptions differ in each town and can change every year, your best plan of action is to ask your local tax assessor's office which exemptions could apply to you. These are some of the more common exemptions available around the country.

Property Tax Exemptions

Homestead — Must be primary residence

Senior Citizen — Eligible age range to apply is 61-65

Veteran — Honorably discharged armed forces personnel

Disabled Veteran — Usually 100% disability

Other Disability — Must qualify for Social Security disability

Widow — Applies if spouse had qualified for exemption

Floating Homestead — May have age/income limits

Unlock the value of rental properties

Boost your income with the perfect rental property

So you want to become a landlord. If you can handle the unusual work hours and spur-of-the-moment repairs, managing the property yourself is a good way to bring in extra income.

More than a third of U.S. households are renters, according to Harvard researchers. That's a lot of people needing somewhere to live. And every month they pay, on average, $1 per square foot of living space. Of course monthly rents depend on many factors, but if you'd like to get in on this cash cow, here are some things to keep in mind when looking for your regret-free rental property.

- Focus on appealing properties like single-family homes. These usually attract long-term renters.

- Search out homes close to where you live so you can get to the rental quickly and easily.

- Remember property taxes can vary within the same area — even the same neighborhood.

- The neighborhood you buy into also affects what kind of tenant you'll get. Factors to keep in mind are crime rate; school districts; amenities like public transport, entertainment, or shopping; and nearby job opportunities.

- Understand the rent you can charge will depend on average rents in the surrounding area, your location's popularity, and the number of nearby vacancies.

- Run the numbers before you buy. To make a profit each month, you'll need rent to exceed all your expenses, including a reserve fund for emergencies and to cover unexpected vacancies.

When you're set on a property, don't use your cash to buy it even if you can. Let your tenant's rent pay off the mortgage instead.

Look before you lease: How to choose a bankable tenant

You won't start making rental money until you've found tenants. And screening for good ones should be a careful task.

Focus on the financially fit. Get permission to run a credit check and make sure your potential tenant is able to pay your rent. Their credit report can provide information about payment history and bankruptcies. A few late payments aren't necessarily signs of a bad tenant, but a bankruptcy should be a red flag. A lot of current debt may prevent them from paying their rent on time, or at all.

> Your tenant cannot move in with more people than your established maximum. With some exceptions based on children's ages and room size, a max of two people per bedroom is reasonable. Have a conversation about this before things become final.

Double-check their employment information. You want to know they can continue paying rent. Verify they work where they claim, and if they told you a salary, ask their employer if it can be confirmed. Consider whether the tenant can afford rent and basic expenses with this salary.

It's OK to make it personal. You want to know your candidate's track record as a tenant, and the easiest way is to contact a previous landlord. Ask whether they had problems with your potential tenant or if their unit was damaged. If the tenant has eviction history, ask for details — you may want to reconsider.

Get your applicant's approval to run a background check. If any issues arise, consult the applicant first. Keep in mind the difference between an arrest, which does not mean they were guilty, and a conviction.

Stay on the right side of the law. Carefully follow the Fair Housing Act. It prohibits discrimination because of race, color, religion, sex, disability, familial status, or national origin.

Avoid bias by using the same application for each potential tenant and running the same checks on everyone.

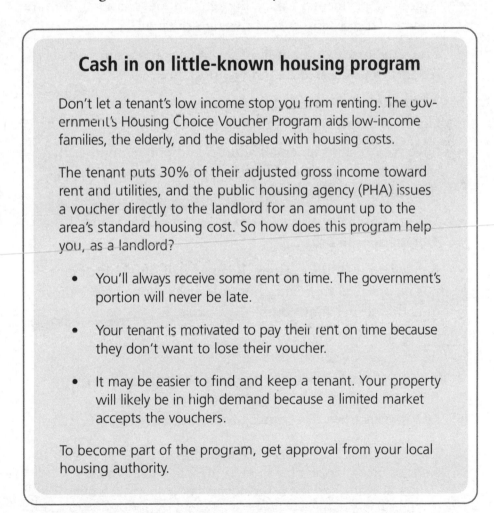

Cash in on little-known housing program

Don't let a tenant's low income stop you from renting. The government's Housing Choice Voucher Program aids low-income families, the elderly, and the disabled with housing costs.

The tenant puts 30% of their adjusted gross income toward rent and utilities, and the public housing agency (PHA) issues a voucher directly to the landlord for an amount up to the area's standard housing cost. So how does this program help you, as a landlord?

- You'll always receive some rent on time. The government's portion will never be late.

- Your tenant is motivated to pay their rent on time because they don't want to lose their voucher.

- It may be easier to find and keep a tenant. Your property will likely be in high demand because a limited market accepts the vouchers.

To become part of the program, get approval from your local housing authority.

Secrets to success as a long-distance landlord

It's challenging to manage a rental property when you live miles away. Here are some tips to make your life easier.

- Have a reliable team. Establish relationships with repair workers and cleaning crews in the area in case problems arise. Know your neighbors, too — they can be your eyes and ears when you're away.

- Automate payments. Collecting rent online is easier and more direct than receiving checks through the mail.

- Protect yourself with landlord insurance, and require your tenants to be covered by renters insurance.

- Make sure you're familiar with the property's local laws. Connect with a local attorney in case of concerns.

- Give your tenants an email address and phone number they can use to contact you. As with any long-distance relationship, communication is key.

- Visit the property at least once a year to see for yourself that everything is in order.

- Be vigilant with inspections. Regular walk-throughs might not be practical from afar, but at least have one before move in and one after move out.

Vacation rentals: A surprising source of revenue

Kelly rents out two lake houses to vacationers looking for relaxing getaways — one on Airbnb and one on Vrbo. These services connect homeowners hoping to lease out their space with customers looking for short-term rentals. Kelly's goal is to take advantage of the extra income her property can bring in. "I have had good experiences with both so far," she says.

Stretch your utility savings with smart home hacks

Bright ideas to power down
your electric bill 224

Put the freeze on high heating
and cooling costs 234

Plug the leaks in your water budget 242

Bright ideas to power down your electric bill

Effortlessly save over $400 with these easy changes

Ready to lower your electric bill by at least 30%? You'd be saving a lot. That's because Americans, on average, spend $1,340 a year to power their homes. Just follow these simple tips to find more than $400 in savings.

Don't get zapped by energy vampires. Most plugged-in appliances and electronics consume electricity around the clock — even when they're turned off. In fact, devices like computers, televisions, chargers, and printers account for roughly 20% of most electric bills.

A simple solution? Pull the plug. Or invest in a smart power strip, which cuts electricity to products when they slip into sleep mode. You'll be glad you did. All that wasted energy costs consumers, on average, $165 a year.

Go sleuthing through your bill. The first step to controlling costs? Understanding your bills. That's why it's important to review them each month. So take a pen and highlight any fees you don't understand or services you don't use.

Finding a single $5 error on your monthly electric bill would save you $60 over the course of a year. All it takes is one phone call to your utility's customer service department.

Smart lighting keeps your savings burning bright. Don't waste money keeping your house lit up like the top of the Chrysler building. Turning off lights in empty rooms, allowing the sun to brighten a space, and using task lighting — a desk or table lamp instead of ceiling lights, for example — could save you $30 a year.

Upgrade your tech. Ready to get a new computer? Opt for a laptop instead of a desktop. You'll save around $4 annually if you use the laptop two hours a day.

Hang this energy waste out to dry. Try air drying your freshly washed clothes. Do this four times a week and you'll have at least $65 extra each year.

Not ready to give up the convenience of your dryer? Toss a dry towel in with your wet clothes for 15 minutes. The reduced drying time will save you over $10 a year, assuming you run seven loads a week. And be sure to clean the lint from your dryer trap — the dryer's increased efficiency can put an extra $100 in your pocket annually.

Wring out savings from your washing machine. Around 85% of the energy used for washing clothes goes into heating the water. A simple way to save? Use cold water instead. You could hold on to as much as $63 each year with this easy switch.

And make sure you're washing full loads. You could save around $18 a year in energy costs by washing one less load a week.

Hot savings from your microwave. Use your microwave instead of your oven four times a week and add over $15 a year to your nest egg.

Take the load off your electricity bills

Electric companies want to save you money. It's true. Most have little-known programs that focus on saving power when demand is at its highest — stifling hot summer afternoons, say, when the widespread use of air conditioners causes energy consumption to skyrocket. And best of all, these utilities will pay you to help them.

Fortunately, it's easy to participate. Just ask your power company if it has a load-management program. You could see extra cash in your pocket if it does.

So how does the program work? A technician installs, free of charge, a signal receiver — often next to a home's outdoor air condenser — so that the utility can periodically turn off power to the air conditioner during times of peak energy use. The unit's fan, however, continues to circulate air inside the house.

And why would power companies want to control demand? It keeps them from having to buy power when it's in short supply — and more expensive. And it lets them hold off on building more generating facilities and transmission lines. That, in turn, helps prevent customer rate increases, they say.

Programs vary widely, so do your research before signing on. Sawnee EMC in Georgia, for example, offers a $36 credit, or $12 a month, to participants in its three-month summer program.

Otter Tail Power, which services communities in Minnesota and the Dakotas, provides a monthly credit of $8.25 for a similar program, while the city of Rocky Mount in North Carolina gives a $20 monthly credit.

Some utilities also offer load-management programs in the winter. For instance, you might get a credit on your bill if you allow the electric company to temporarily turn off your water heater during times of high energy demand.

Be a star saver with energy-efficient appliances

Quick. Do you know how many appliances you have plugged in right now? Did you count the washer and dryer? The refrigerator? Appliances like these use on average 13% of your home's total energy. (See graphic on next page.)

With Americans spending more than $170 million every year on residential electricity, it's important to get a handle on the energy hogs in your house. Do it successfully, and you'll put cash back in your pocket.

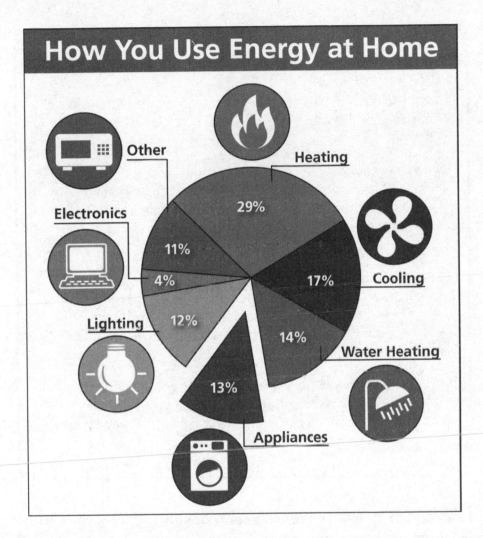

How You Use Energy at Home

Other

Heating

29%

Electronics

11%

Cooling

4%

17%

14%

Lighting

12%

Water Heating

13%

Appliances

A blue star is the key to saving energy. In 1992 the Environmental Protection Agency (EPA) introduced ENERGY STAR as a voluntary labeling program. It helps identify products that reduce energy use and greenhouse gas emissions. That makes them good for your wallet and the environment.

So how do you find ENERGY STAR appliances? Check out a list of certified products on their website at *energystar.gov/products*. You'll find everything from air purifiers to water heaters with details for specific brands and models. When you go shopping, look for the blue ENERGY STAR label.

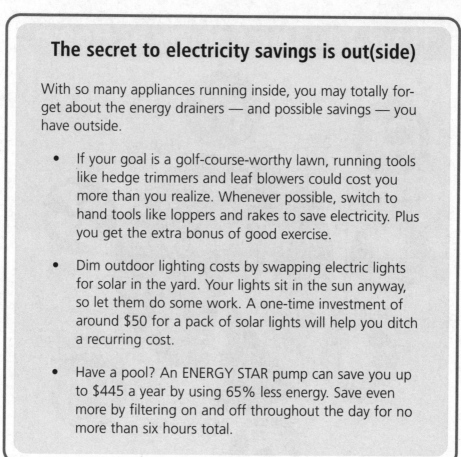

The secret to electricity savings is out(side)

With so many appliances running inside, you may totally forget about the energy drainers — and possible savings — you have outside.

- If your goal is a golf-course-worthy lawn, running tools like hedge trimmers and leaf blowers could cost you more than you realize. Whenever possible, switch to hand tools like loppers and rakes to save electricity. Plus you get the extra bonus of good exercise.

- Dim outdoor lighting costs by swapping electric lights for solar in the yard. Your lights sit in the sun anyway, so let them do some work. A one-time investment of around $50 for a pack of solar lights will help you ditch a recurring cost.

- Have a pool? An ENERGY STAR pump can save you up to $445 a year by using 65% less energy. Save even more by filtering on and off throughout the day for no more than six hours total.

Undecided? Consider the long-term benefits. Your savings with an energy-efficient appliance will depend on how much you use each appliance and the price per kilowatt-hour (kWh) of electricity. The average residential rate is just over 13 cents/kWh.

Since ENERGY STAR appliances are often more expensive, you have to consider your savings over the product's lifetime. Here are a few examples.

- Your clothes dryer is one of your biggest energy hogs. An ENERGY STAR dryer uses about 20% less energy than a standard model, putting $215 back in your pocket over its lifetime.

- Replacing an old refrigerator with an ENERGY STAR model could save you $300 or more over the next five years.

- Save around $380 over the lifetime of an efficient clothes washing machine. They use about 25% less energy than their standard counterparts.

- ENERGY STAR certified air purifiers are 40% more energy-efficient than standard models, saving you about 225 kWh per year or about $30 on your annual utility bill. That could add up to $235 over its lifetime.

Get more money back with rebates. All those potential savings aren't the only benefits. You can find rebates for energy-efficient appliances across the country. Check *energystar.gov/rebate-finder* and *dsireusa.org* to find a program near you.

Stop your fridge from being an energy hog

Your refrigerator uses more power than any other kitchen appliance. But you can keep it from eating up expensive electricity with these four tricks.

Clean your coils. No one wants to move a heavy refrigerator, but here's why you should do it at least once or twice a year. The condenser coils in back or underneath your fridge get covered with dust and cobwebs, making them less efficient at releasing heat. Your compressor then has to work harder and use more energy.

You'll extend the life of your refrigerator if you regularly clean those coils with a vacuum or coil-cleaning brush.

Keep seals airtight. Don't let your pricey cold air out. Make sure your door is sealing tightly with this test. Close the door over a piece of paper. Leave half sticking out of the door and try to pull it out. If you can do that easily, you may need to repair the latch or seal.

Maintain the correct temperature. Goldilocks will tell you that the temperature of your fridge needs to be just right. Make sure yours is in the range of 35 to 38 degrees Fahrenheit. You can check by putting an appliance thermometer in a glass of water and leaving it in the center of the fridge for 24 hours.

Cover any liquids and food. Your refrigerator has to work harder to keep uncovered contents cold, so make its job easier by closing or wrapping everything before storing it. You'll also avoid spreading odors or exposing the food to harmful bacteria.

5 bright ideas to save money and energy

You have lighting in every single room of your house. All those lights increase your energy usage and your electric bill. Take these simple steps and pocket hundreds — even thousands — of dollars.

Switch to LED lights. It's time to make the switch if you haven't already. LEDs may cost more up front, but some last over 20 years, saving you money in the long run. There's no need to toss out perfectly good incandescent bulbs, though. Just replace them with LEDs one at a time as they burn out.

Buy three-way lamps. Consider getting a three-way lamp the next time you need a new lamp. You'll save energy by using the lowest setting when you only need ambient light. Switch to a higher setting when you're reading or working on a project.

Use sensors. Motion detectors aren't just for your home's exterior anymore. Occupancy sensors can tell when a room is empty and automatically cut off the lights. So if you're one of those people who constantly forgets to turn off the lights, these handy switches will do it for you.

Get smart bulbs. Just when you think you've seen it all, General Electric comes out with "smart" LED light bulbs. You control the C-Life and C-Sleep bulbs with an app on your phone or tablet.

You can dim or brighten them with the tap of your finger, so long as Bluetooth is on and you're within 50 feet of the bulb. Learn more at *cbyge.com*.

Put up peel-n-stick. Why spend hundreds of dollars wiring new under-cabinet light fixtures? Cut peel-and-stick light strips to the length you need and plug them into any outlet. Then plug in a remote-control unit with a radio frequency, so you can turn them on and off. Colors range from warm light to super bright.

Solar power brings savings — and a sunny financial future

How would you like to have free electricity for 25 years or more? You can if you go solar. Investing in solar panels may seem daunting, but tax credit and rebate offers are available to offset your initial investment. And once you pay off your system, your electric costs will drop to practically nothing.

5 ways solar power will benefit you — and your pocketbook. If your current electric rates are high and your state has funding for solar panels, you could hit the savings jackpot. That's because your rates will drop the most with the least investment. Here are five reasons solar is a stellar deal.

- It will stabilize your electricity costs. That means you won't be disturbed by rising electricity prices — ideal if you're living on a fixed income.

- You can draw energy even when you're not generating any — like at night — because you're

> You can greatly cut down the expense of solar panels by leasing them. A third-party owner installs them, and you pay them a below-market rate to use the solar power. Since you don't own the panels, your savings won't be as high. But you'll still likely save 10% to 30% on your monthly electricity bill.

231

still connected to the electric grid. If you overproduce power, you'll get credit for that extra energy, which you can use later when you need it. If your system produces less electricity than you need, you'll pay your electric company to make up the difference. This back and forth between the grid and your system is called net metering.

• You can rely on your system for the long run. Buyers often pay off their purchase in seven to eight years. That means an electricity bill of little to nothing for the rest of its 25-years-plus life span.

• Repairs are rarely needed. Solar panel systems are durable and typically have very long warranties. Plus they don't usually need to be cleaned.

• You'll add value to your home. If you decide to move, the solar system may increase your house's resale price by 3% to 4%.

Get enlightened about all your options. To get started, see if your electric company offers solar audits. The Georgia cooperative Coweta-Fayette EMC offers guidance before interested members commit, so they can determine if solar power is a good fit for them.

Two important factors to think about are your home's efficiency and your roof's age, says Jimmy Adams, vice president of energy services at Coweta-Fayette EMC. "Not every home is meant for solar on their rooftop," he says.

If yours is not, consider another option — a community solar garden. With this program the panels are owned privately by a cooperative of individuals or a utility company. You can

If you're interested in a community solar garden, make sure you read the contract thoroughly, especially if you buy from a utility. You don't want any costly surprises. Look for details such as length of contract, minimum subscription size, transfer requirements and fees, scheduled rate increases, and early termination fees.

subscribe to a share of the power produced with the benefit of not having to install panels on your own roof. Check to see if one is available near you.

If you think solar power may be a good choice for you, do some research with EnergySage's Buyer's Guide at *energysage.com/solar-panels*. The website lets you compare panel prices and features and will connect you with a network of prescreened installers.

Save the Earth — and your wallet — with a little solar assistance

You've made your decision. You want to save money — and maybe even the planet — by using the sun's energy to power your home. Now how do you pay for it?

Look into local financing options. Some city or county governments offer PACE (property assessed clean energy) loans for home energy projects. If you qualify, you would repay the loan through assessments added to your property tax bill.

Take advantage of federal tax credits. The federal government offers the Investment Tax Credit (ITC) for private residences to help offset your expenses. But hurry — it's set to end by 2022. A 26% credit is available for construction started in 2020 and a 22% credit for 2021 projects.

Check for government rebates. State help is also available to solar shoppers. For instance, one program in Colorado offers up to $1,500 for systems with a 3 kW capacity or less. Go to *dsireusa.org* to find a program near you.

Put the freeze on high heating and cooling costs

The secret is out: A home energy audit can save you big

You turn the lights out when you leave a room, run the dishwasher only when it's full, and hang your clothes out to dry. So why are your utility bills so high? A home energy audit will give you the answer. It's an easy way to cut your electric bill and reduce energy waste.

Call in a professional — for free. A home energy assessment will tell you how much gas and electricity your house uses and identify any problem areas that, if corrected, will make your home more energy efficient.

Jimmy Adams, vice president of energy services for Coweta-Fayette EMC in central Georgia, says measuring a home's air leakage — the outside air that enters a home through cracks and gaps — is the most important part of an audit. "It's the air leakage of the home where a lot of energy wasting takes place," he says. "And those items are easily fixed at a low cost."

Adams says customers see immediate savings after updates and repairs. "I don't think it's out of the norm to feel good about a 20% reduction in their utility bills," he says.

These cheap and easy tricks can trim your high air conditioning and heating costs. In summer, generate a cool downward breeze by setting your ceiling fans to rotate counterclockwise. Opt for oven-free dishes or grill outside. In winter, shut the doors and vents of rooms not in use. Hang insulated curtains and sleep with flannel sheets.

That can really add up. While electricity rates vary widely, the average Californian pays about $2,000 a year for power. A few simple changes could mean annual savings of nearly $400.

Many utilities, like the Coweta-Fayette EMC, provide their customers with free audits. Other professionals charge between $200 and $600. Fortunately, low-income seniors may qualify for funding — including a free audit — to help weatherize their homes. For information, see *On a fixed income? 3 ways to lower your utility bills.*

This power play saves 10% on utilities

Saving money is right at your fingertips. According to experts at the U.S. Department of Energy, you can lower your heating and cooling bills by simply adjusting your thermostat.

In the winter, set your thermostat to 68 degrees while you're awake. Set it a little lower while you're asleep or away from home. In the summer, set the thermostat for 78 degrees when you're home, and set it a little warmer when you're out for the day.

Raise or lower your thermostat by 7 to 10 degrees for just eight hours a day, and you'll trim your bill by a cool 10%.

Do-it-yourself audit on your own time. Of course, you could always take matters into your own hands and perform a few simple tests to see how airtight your house is. Try these for starters.

- Grab a partner and a flashlight and look for leaks at night. Have one person stay inside and shine a light over potential leaky spots. The other should stand outside and look for rays of light passing through the siding.

- Try closing doors and windows on a dollar bill. If you can slide it through, you're losing heat.

- Having trouble finding leaks? Hold a piece of paper in an area in which you suspect a problem. The paper will move if air is coming in.

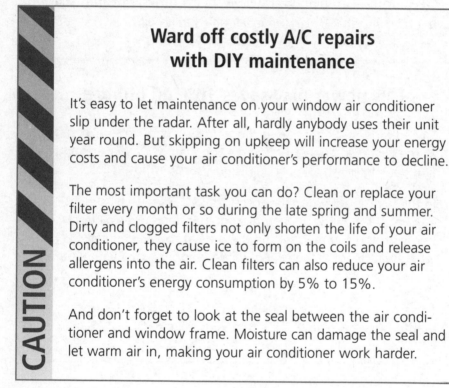

Ward off costly A/C repairs with DIY maintenance

It's easy to let maintenance on your window air conditioner slip under the radar. After all, hardly anybody uses their unit year round. But skipping on upkeep will increase your energy costs and cause your air conditioner's performance to decline.

The most important task you can do? Clean or replace your filter every month or so during the late spring and summer. Dirty and clogged filters not only shorten the life of your air conditioner, they cause ice to form on the coils and release allergens into the air. Clean filters can also reduce your air conditioner's energy consumption by 5% to 15%.

And don't forget to look at the seal between the air conditioner and window frame. Moisture can damage the seal and let warm air in, making your air conditioner work harder.

Top 2 places to save energy in your home

You may think of windows and attics as first lines of defense against heating and cooling loss. But if you don't watch out, they can kick your HVAC system into costly overdrive. These tips will help keep your utility bills within budget.

Put up hardworking window treatments. Experts say up to 30% of the energy used to heat and cool a home is lost through the windows. So improving their efficiency is one of the most cost-effective ways to prevent energy loss. How? Focus on your window coverings.

- On sunny winter days, open the blinds and drapes in the morning to let the sun heat your home. But close them at night to prevent warm air from escaping.

- During the summer, keep your curtains closed to prevent direct sunlight from heating rooms.

- Hang your drapes as close to your windows as possible to reduce heat gain and loss.

- Slat window blinds are useful in the summer for keeping out the sun and controlling glare and natural light.

- Insulated cellular shades — the kind made of pleated material that folds up like an accordion — also help manage the temperature and can reduce your energy bill by 15% to 20%.

In the market for energy-efficient windows? Look for the ENERGY STAR label. But don't stop there. A separate label from the National Fenestration Rating Council will provide you with performance ratings on the window's ability to light your home and prevent heat from entering and escaping a room.

Get on top of attic repairs. You might find the biggest energy leaks in your attic, so plan to conquer three areas.

- The chimney. Does your chimney or furnace flue run through your attic floor? Then the conditioned air in your home might be seeping in. Seal gaps at the entrance point with metal flashing and high-temperature caulk.

- The ducts. Some 20% to 30% of the air that moves through duct systems is lost. Seal any leaks and holes you find in the ductwork with mastic or foil tape. Use foam to cover open spaces where the duct enters the attic. Finally, wrap the ducts with a foil-faced insulation that has an R-6 or higher value. It will keep the air running through the ducts at the proper temperature.

- The insulation. Don't know if your attic needs more insulation? You'll need extra if you can easily see the floor joists. Use insulation that runs about 10 to 14 inches deep. Fiberglass rolls are the easiest to lay down if you're doing the job yourself.

Block out pricey heating and cooling costs with trees

Want an eco-friendly way to dramatically lower your heating and cooling bill? Look no further than your yard. Well-positioned trees can reduce your energy consumption for heating and cooling by up to 25%. Just three strategically placed trees could save an average household $100 to $250 in annual energy costs.

Trees provide your home with shade in the summer and wind protection in the winter. You can maximize these benefits with proper planning. Trees do their best work when they're to the west of a house. Following that, plant them to the east and north.

If possible, plant a tree where it can provide cover for a deck or grill. Shade can also increase the efficiency of your air conditioner's compressor by 10%. Just don't let low-hanging trees restrict airflow around the unit or let leaves fall into it.

On a fixed income? 3 ways to lower your utility bills

Don't let extreme temperatures rule your life — or wallet. If you need help paying for heating and cooling, see if you qualify for one of these assistance programs that give seniors relief from sky-high utility bills.

LIHEAP keeps your costs down. LIHEAP, the Low-Income Home Energy Assistance Program, is a federal project that helps low-income households with their energy bills. Depending on where you live, your local LIHEAP office may provide funds for heating and cooling, as well as emergency assistance in case of a utility shutoff. The program also pays for energy-related repairs and improvements — such as fixing a leaky window or installing insulation.

The maximum household income for eligibility is either 150% of the federal poverty level or 60% of your state's median income. For instance, the 2019 poverty line for a two-person household was $16,910. So, you would have qualified for assistance if your total combined income was $25,365 or less.

Of course, LIHEAP won't cover all of your energy costs. But the average household receives about $500 a year — enough to cover their electricity bill for nearly five months. In most cases, benefits are paid directly to utilities or fuel suppliers.

You must apply with your state's LIHEAP office each year to be considered for assistance. Find your local contact at *acf.hhs.gov/ocs/liheap-state-and-territory-contact-listing*.

Weatherization Assistance Program cuts consumption. Want to lower your energy use — and costs — but need help getting your furnace fixed or windows properly sealed? Enter the Weatherization Assistance Program, a federal program designed to help needy families reduce their heating bills.

You're automatically eligible for assistance if you receive Supplemental Security Income or Aid to Families with Dependent Children. The states, which are charged with distributing the funds, also give preference to individuals with a disability and seniors over age 60. Program participants save, on average, $283 a year after updates.

The first step in the process? An energy audit — a professional assessment of your home's energy use and a list of measures that will reduce consumption. For instance, one house may need a brand new water heater. Another might require several new windows and weather stripping on all the doors. On average, the program spends $6,500 per home on improvements.

To find your local weatherization agency, go to the website *nascsp.org/about/state-contacts*.

Discounts are just a call away. Help from Uncle Sam isn't the only way to lower your gas and electric expenses. Just ask your utility company if seniors get a discount.

For instance, Georgia Power Company offers customers $24 in monthly discounts and credits — nearly $290 a year — if they're age 65 or older and have household incomes less than or equal to 200% of the federal poverty guidelines. That amounts to $24,980 for a single senior, and $33,820 for a couple.

Surprising tricks to save on a new roof

Your home's roof is like a hat — it can help keep you cool in the summer and warm in the winter. But unlike a hat, you can't take it off whenever you want. So when it's time to commit to a new roof, consider money-saving products that will cut your energy bill or outlast regular shingles.

"Cool" roofs. Your roof gets sunbathed almost daily, and that heat can make its way into your home. Switch gears and get a roof made of highly reflective paint, tiles, shingles, or a sheet covering, and feel the difference. They're known as cool roofs because they reflect more sunlight and absorb less heat.

Standard roofs can hit 150 degrees in the summer sun. A cool roof can stay more than 50 degrees cooler under the same conditions. The cooler your roof, the cooler your home, and the less money you'll spend running the air conditioner. Plus, cool roofing materials cost about the same as a regular roof.

Architectural shingles. These high-end products may cost about 25% more than regular shingles, but they can last up to twice as long. That's because they're thicker, heavier, and feature more layers that protect against harsh weather. They can also boost your home's curb appeal when the time comes to sell.

The swamp solution: Save with this cooling trick

Calling your home a "swamp" may not seem like a compliment. But if you live in an area with lots of dry heat, a swamp cooler might be just what you need to lower utility costs.

Swamp coolers — a type of air conditioner often installed on the roof — use the powers of evaporation to lower air temperature. That's why they're also called evaporative coolers. They cost half as much to install compared with central air conditioners, and require one quarter of the energy. Small and portable options are also available.

But not everyone will benefit from a swamp cooler. That's because the cooler's effectiveness hinges on the high temperatures and low humidity levels typically found in southwestern states like Arizona, New Mexico, and Nevada. People living in humid areas like Florida and Louisiana or locales with relatively cool summers, like Maine and North Dakota, should consider an alternative.

Plug the leaks in your water budget

Going green: How to save water while caring for your lawn

Most people take water for granted. You just assume you can get a drink whenever you need one. You let the tap run while you brush your teeth. You throw a load of laundry in whenever you feel like it. And you may pride yourself on your green lawn and lush garden. If you've never traveled to another country, you may not truly appreciate just how lucky you are.

The fact is, the average family of four in the U.S. uses over 300 gallons of water a day. And nearly a third of it gets sprinkled, sprayed, and dripped onto grass, shrubs, flowers, and homegrown vegetables. That's probably more water than you use for showering and washing clothes combined.

To make matters worse, you could be losing 50% of the water you use outside to wind, runoff, and evaporation. These tips will decrease that waste and lower your water bill, too.

- Water your lawn twice a week, instead of daily. Place an open tuna can nearby, and give the grass a slow soaking. Turn off the water when half an inch has collected in the can. Water your lawn for the same length of time later that week — it only needs a total of 1 inch per week.

- Sweep your patio and driveway with a broom instead of hosing them down.

> Experts say a leaky faucet can waste more than 3,000 gallons of water in a year. Fix it and you could save $35 on your annual water bill.

- Water in the morning or evening and you'll lose less water to evaporation. Adding mulch around shrubs and plants also reduces water waste and inhibits weeds and erosion.

- Avoid overwatering with this simple test. Step on your grass, and if it springs back up, it has enough water.

- Channel rainwater from your downspout into a covered barrel and use it to water your flowers and shrubs.

- Don't waste shower water while waiting for it to warm up. Save it in a bucket and use it later to water your plants.

- Let your grass grow out. Adjust your mowing height to 2 inches and leave clippings on the grass instead of bagging them. Your grass will retain more moisture and get additional nutrients.

- Aerate clay soil at least once a year to help it retain moisture. Sandy soil can be aerated every two to three years.

- Cut down on fertilizer when possible. If your garden needs it, use slow-release fertilizer.

- Add native, drought-tolerant plants to your yard. Once established, they'll need less watering.

- Place plants with similar water requirements together. You can then tackle each group without worrying about watering too much or too little.

- Reduce your lawn size by replacing grass with substitutes like plants and mulch. Bluegrass turf, in particular, requires a lot of extra watering.

- Set up a drip irrigation system to water trees and shrubs. They're more efficient than sprinkler systems when it comes to delivering water to roots.

- Plant trees and shrubs in the spring or fall, when conditions are best for growth.

- Stop your hose from running continuously by attaching a pistol-style sprayer.

243

- Sandy soils dry out more quickly than clay soils. Clay soils need less frequent irrigation but longer soakings.

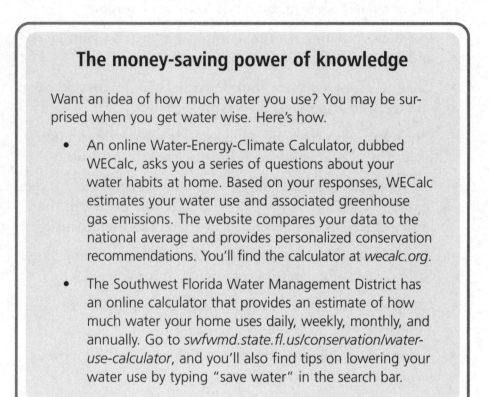

The money-saving power of knowledge

Want an idea of how much water you use? You may be surprised when you get water wise. Here's how.

- An online Water-Energy-Climate Calculator, dubbed WECalc, asks you a series of questions about your water habits at home. Based on your responses, WECalc estimates your water use and associated greenhouse gas emissions. The website compares your data to the national average and provides personalized conservation recommendations. You'll find the calculator at *wecalc.org*.

- The Southwest Florida Water Management District has an online calculator that provides an estimate of how much water your home uses daily, weekly, monthly, and annually. Go to *swfwmd.state.fl.us/conservation/water-use-calculator*, and you'll also find tips on lowering your water use by typing "save water" in the search bar.

4 shut-off valves that can save you serious cash

Can you put a price tag on water damage? Absolutely. It could take $500 to repair saturated drywall, $3,500 to refinish warped hardwood flooring, and more than $1,000 to replace waterlogged carpet. But preventing this costly disaster is free. All it takes is knowing how to shut off your water supply.

Terminate toilet troubles. If a backed-up toilet ever brings you dangerously close to a dreaded overflow, quick action on your part is the only way to prevent flooding. So take a peek behind the bowl and find the stop valve. Just twist the oval knob in a clockwise direction until the water shuts off. Newer valves may feature a lever that requires a 90-degree turn.

Avoid worrisome washing machine leaks. When setting out on a much-deserved vacation, locate and shut off your washer's water source — usually hot and cold knobs — on the wall near or behind the machine.

And make sure you're using those snazzy stainless steel connector hoses. They cost about $20, and you can install them yourself. Compared with rubber hoses, they're much less likely to burst or develop cracks and blisters.

Avert leaky dishwasher damage. Ever come home and find a pool of water collecting in front of the dishwasher? If so, a faulty door seal — also called a gasket — may be to blame. You can turn off the water supply by accessing the stop valve under the sink. It should be attached to a pipe or hose running through the cabinet into the dishwasher.

Monitor the main shut-off valve. A burst pipe can cause major structural damage to your home. That's why it's best to learn the location of your main shut-off valve early on.

It may be in your basement or garage along an exterior wall facing the street. It could also be found on the outside of your house. In some cases, the valve may be buried under an access panel near the street. Once you've found it, open and close the valve occasionally to make sure it functions properly.

Do less laundry, save more money

Quick quiz. Which of the following needs to be washed immediately after wearing — the suit you wore to church or the jeans you changed into afterward? The answer may surprise you. Unless either of them appears to be dirty, you can hang both up to wear again.

245

Most households do about 300 loads of laundry each year, but there's a simple way to cut back and save on water, energy, detergent, and your clothing's wear and tear. Just wash your clothes less often. Nobody's suggesting you walk around in dirty underwear, but you may be washing your clothing more often than necessary.

Wash after one wear. Of course, you should wash anything visibly stained, dirty, sweaty, or smelly. In addition, launder the following items each time you wear them.

- tank tops, T-shirts, undershirts, and shorts
- camisoles and underwear
- socks, tights, and leggings
- swimsuits
- whites and silks

Wash every few wears. Some items will break down faster if washed too frequently, like the elastic in bras. Experts suggest you wear bras a few times between washes, just like these other apparel pieces.

> Homeowners typically pay around $220 to fix a broken toilet. But you can bypass the labor costs and repair it yourself with the help of plumbers on *YouTube.com*. Open the YouTube website or app and search for "DIY plumbing toilet." Then click "filter" to select videos on the subject.

- pajamas
- dress shirts, if worn with undershirts
- skirts, jeans, khakis, and dress pants
- yoga pants
- fleece hoodies and sweatshirts

Wash one to three times a season. Winter outerwear can do with less washing. Check the tags for instructions on how to launder them properly.

- vests, coats, and jackets
- gloves, scarves, and hats

Handy hints to make your home last a lifetime

Clean sweep: How to make your
home sparkle for pennies 248

Around the house: Budget-friendly
guide to easy fix-its and fix-ups 255

Clean sweep: How to make your home sparkle for pennies

5 natural — and cheap — cleansers you can't live without

Forget buying high-cost, name-brand cleaning products. All you need are these five inexpensive household super-cleaners. They'll make your house sparkle from top to bottom for just pennies.

That's what Ruby discovered after deciding to make her own cleaning products. Tired of watching her money go down the drain, she collected recipes for common household items like dish soap, stain remover, and laundry detergent. With only a few basic ingredients, Ruby whipped up nine cleaners for $22 — over 50% less than the $46 she normally spent on store brands. Here are some of the low-budget items she used.

Baking soda. Use this mildly abrasive marvel, priced at a mere 20 cents an ounce, to scour your bathroom tub, shower, sink, and counter. And just like an open box of baking soda in the fridge absorbs foul odors, a small amount in a dish left in the open air works similar magic in your kitchen and bathroom.

> You can count on vinegar and rubbing alcohol for many household chores. But don't use them to clean all surfaces. Vinegar causes small cracks and indentations — called pitting — in marble, while rubbing alcohol destroys finishes like shellac, lacquer, and varnish that have been painted on your furniture.

Vinegar. Eliminate greasy spills and splatters in a New York minute with common white vinegar. And for just 3 cents an ounce, vinegar also adds sparkle to windows, mirrors, chrome faucets, and stainless steel sinks. But don't stop there. You can also use it to remove mildew, rust, and the mineral deposits commonly found on bathroom fixtures.

Liquid dish soap. Say goodbye to bathroom soap scum for only 5 cents an ounce. Simply sponge down your shower door with a mixture of dishwashing liquid and a little warm water. Or make a soft scrub by mixing baking soda with warm water and liquid dish soap. Rub it onto porcelain tile or an enamel table top for a gleam you can be proud of.

Rubbing alcohol. A natural disinfectant, rubbing alcohol — also called isopropyl alcohol — sells for around 7 cents an ounce. Use it to put a shine on stainless steel cooking utensils and shower tiles. This safe alternative to bleach also eliminates stains on furniture covered in microfiber fabric.

Borax. Also a natural cleaner priced at about 7 cents an ounce, powdered Borax isn't just a detergent booster. You can use it to clean surfaces, control odors, clear up carpet stains, and remove water spots. Borax also gets rid of mold and mildew.

Going green is getting easier — and cheaper

Ever felt hot and itchy after slipping on freshly washed clothes? If so, you might have suffered an allergic reaction to the chemicals in your laundry detergent and opted for a more natural alternative.

Unfortunately, not every cleaner with an "earth-friendly" label is 100% safe for you and the environment. While lots of companies make claims that their products are natural and eco-friendly, not all deliver on their promises.

So how can you spot the real McCoy? Read labels and look for words like "solvent free" and "no phosphates."

Spend the same greenbacks on green cleaners. Environmentally friendly and organic household cleaners now run in the same general price range — from about 7 to 19 cents an ounce — as competing products that contain chemicals and preservatives.

So with price no longer an issue, why else should you lean towards green?

- Health. Harsh chemicals can irritate the skin and trigger allergies and asthma. Cutting back on regular exposure lowers your chances of becoming ill.

- Home. Synthetic soap and detergents contain active agents — dubbed surfactants — that help lift off and wash away dirt. Modern surfactants are often petroleum-based or made with animal fat and contribute to the formation of soap film, or scum. Believe it or not, using too much detergent can cause gummy buildup, mold, or mildew in your appliances. That's why it's best to choose plant-based products whenever possible.

- Environment. The less toxic your waste water is, the more likely your local treatment center can properly clean it for reuse.

Do green products really clean as well? When one independent organization compared the cleaning power behind several all-purpose household sprays, both green and regular, their results were mixed. In some cases, green products held their own in basic cleaning tasks compared with more conventional cleaners.

But what if you're set on buying environmentally safe products? You can find the Environmental Protection Agency's Safer Choice product list at *epa.gov/saferchoice*. In addition, the Environmental Working Group provides a guide to healthy cleaning products at *ewg.org/guides/cleaners*. Both lists are updated regularly.

To make your consumer dollars count, read labels. Manufacturers are not required to list the chemicals in their cleaners, but they should tell you if their products are dangerous. Pay special attention to labels with product warnings and health hazards.

You want to use products that carry these kinds of labels:

- non-toxic
- bleach-free
- petroleum-free
- biodegradable
- dye-free
- chlorine-free

- made from renewable resources

- scented with natural plant derivatives or essential oils

If it's all a bit much to think about, consider making your own natural cleaning supplies. You'll find some great recipes in the graphic *How you can clean green* on page 253.

Make your housekeeping tools last longer

Are you cleaning with dirty tools? Then you're likely spreading germs and moving dirt from one place to another. It's time to give them a once-over. The cleaner they are, the more efficiently they work and the less often you have to replace them.

Mops. A clean mop won't spread dirty water all over your floors.

- Get a mop with a removable, washable head and toss it in the washer with bleach and hot water.

- Use a double-sided bucket or two separate buckets so you're not cleaning with dirty water.

- Make sure the mop head dries between uses, to prevent bacteria from breeding in it.

Dusters and dust mops. A dirty duster doesn't dust. (Try saying that 10 times fast!) Here's how to clean it.

- Vacuum it after each dusting, or place the head in a damp paper bag and shake it out.

- Hand wash it occasionally, or toss it in the washer if the head is made of removable fabric.

Brooms. Even your broom needs a good cleaning, so it works more effectively and lasts longer.

- Remove hair and lint with a wide-toothed comb.

- Store it with the bristles pointing upward.

- Soak straw brooms in warm salt water or a solution of warm water and gentle detergent. Allow to air dry completely, bristles up, before storing.

Sponges. They're probably the most unsanitary soldiers in your army of cleaning supplies. Sanitize them regularly and stop spreading bacteria all over the kitchen.

- Sanitize sponges by washing them in the dishwasher on a heated-dry cycle.

- Replace sponges once a month.

- Toss dishrags in the washer with bleach, and then in a dryer set on high heat.

Cleaning shouldn't make you sick

Remember those warnings about staying away from hand sanitizers with triclosan? Well, it turns out you don't want that chemical — or a few others — in your cleaning products either.

You may think you're being health-conscious by using disinfectants every time you clean. But those products are contributing to the growing global health problem of antibacterial drug resistance, making it more and more difficult for doctors to treat infections.

Antibacterial agents — including triclosan, triclocarbon, quats, and nanosilver — can be harmful to your health in other ways, too. They've been associated with asthma, allergies, and skin irritation. And they're harmful to the environment when poured down the drain.

Of course, disinfectants have their place. They're necessary to kill infectious organisms in public places like hospitals and schools. But in the home? Only if absolutely necessary. You're generally better off with regular soap and water to remove dirt, followed by a good rinsing.

CAUTION

How you can clean green

10 money-saving tips for making your own organic cleaners

sealed hardwood floors (not waxed)

1/2 cup vinegar + 1 gallon hot water + damp mop

toilet bowl

baking soda + 1 cup vinegar

sprinkle baking soda in bowl, pour in vinegar, let it sit a bit, scrub with brush, flush

stainless sink

olive oil + soft cloth

rub to get rid of annoying streaks

windows & mirrors

equal parts vinegar + water + spray bottle

tile

baking soda + damp sponge

grout

3 parts baking soda + 1 part water

make a paste and use to scrub grout

bathroom sink

lemon rinds + white vinegar

combine and let brew 4 weeks; strain; spray

shower door

dish detergent + warm water

use cloth to dissolve soap scum

mold & mildew

4 parts hydrogen peroxide + 1 part water

mix and apply directly on mold or mildew; sit for a bit, scrub

stains on laminate countertop

salt + 1/2 lemon

sprinkle salt on cut side of lemon and scour stain; rinse

253

Make these DIY laundry supplies for dirt cheap

With just a handful of ingredients and a few minutes of your time, you can make your own laundry supplies at a fraction of what it costs to buy them at the supermarket.

Powdered laundry detergent. Finely grate 2 cups of bar soap and mix thoroughly with 1 cup of washing soda and 1 cup of Borax. Use around 2 tablespoons per load.

Make a small amount first to see how it works in your water, in your machine, and on your clothes before investing in a big batch. Hard water may cause clothes to come out dingy looking. In that case, boost colors by adding 1/2 cup of baking soda to the wash cycle or vinegar in the rinse. Do not add vinegar to a load containing chlorine bleach.

Liquid laundry detergent. Powder may work better than liquid on heavily soiled clothing. Liquid detergent, on the other hand, may work better for cold-water washing and removing grease and oil.

Mix 3/4 cup of Borax with 3/4 cup of washing soda in a gallon jug. Add a few cups of hot water and shake or stir until dissolved. Pour 3/4 cup of blue Dawn Ultra dishwashing liquid into the container, and finish filling with hot water. Gently shake or stir again. Use about 1/4 cup per load.

Dryer sheets. You could start by cutting your store-bought dryer sheets in half. Or you can make your own by cutting rectangular strips from old T-shirts, washcloths, or flannel sheets. Add a few drops of essential oils and store them in a resealable plastic bag.

Stain remover. For a spot treatment comparable to Shout, combine 2/3 cup of Dawn dishwashing liquid, 2/3 cup of ammonia, 6 table-spoons of baking soda, and 2 cups of warm water. Pour into a spray bottle.

For homemade Oxyclean, try two parts water to one part hydrogen peroxide and one part washing soda. Use immediately, because it loses its stain-removing power quickly.

Around the house: Budget-friendly guide to easy fix-its and fix-ups

Aging in place: Home features you can update for $25 or less

You don't have to invest a fortune to make your home senior friendly. And it's never too early to start, says Steve Hoffacker, a certified aging-in-place specialist. "The idea is that everyone, and I do mean everyone, is aging in place their entire life," Hoffacker says. "It's wherever they are at the moment."

These five easy and inexpensive updates will make living at home easier during your golden years.

Widen your doorways. Think this is a major project? Think again. All you have to do is replace your existing door hinges with expandable offset hinges. They let your door swing out farther, which gives you more entry space and makes it easier for wheelchairs and walkers to pass through. Each hinge costs around $25.

Switch to lever door knobs. Round doorknobs can be difficult to turn, especially if you have arthritis or a poor grip. Hoffacker recommends switching them out for lever-style handles, which are easier to push down with your fingertips, hand, or elbow. You can find lever handles for around $15. Install them yourself or ask a friend to lend a helping hand.

Paint with contrasting colors. Painting your walls and baseboards in colors that contrast with your floors helps you distinguish between them more easily. You can also add a colored line to your steps to help with depth perception. A full-priced gallon of paint costs

255

around $20 and is enough to cover a small room. For more money-saving tips, see the box *6 crafty ways to save on paint*.

Not quite up to painting? Use non-slip tape as a border along the edges of your floors and stairs. You can also lower your risk of falling in the bathroom by using towels and bath mats that contrast with the color of your tub and tiles.

> Painting is a quick and easy way to enhance your quality of life. "If you throw a coat of paint on your living room wall, that's an improvement," says aging-in-place specialist Steve Hoffacker. "It's a modest one, it didn't cost you that much, but it makes you feel better. It enhances your attitude about your home and makes you more comfortable."

Change your address number sign. Swapping your address plaque for large numbers makes it easier for emergency vehicles to find your house. You can buy each number separately and pay about $20 total.

Glow up with LED lights. Now just might be the time to switch to LED lights. They don't get hot and aren't as harsh as traditional bulbs. Plus, they can last upward of 20 years. "It's the last time you ever have to worry about changing that light bulb," Hoffacker says. You can buy an 8-pack of bulbs for around $10, but expect to pay more for dimmable ones.

Skip the pro and save: 3 easy DIY fixes

Most homeowners would agree that major projects like roofing, plumbing, and electrical work are best left to professionals. But when it comes to easy repairs, a little elbow grease goes a long way. In fact, you can save hundreds of dollars by flying solo on these DIY projects.

Kick out crumbling caulk. Is the caulk around your tub cracked, discolored, or showing signs of mold and mildew? If so, it's time to reseal the grout lines between your tub and wall.

Just grab a utility knife and dig out the damaged caulk and any loose grout. Treat the mold — a mixture of bleach and water works well — and let dry. Then "mask the gap" by placing masking tape on either side of the groove you created. Apply the caulk — make sure it's labeled "for kitchen and bath use" — and smooth with a finger. Remove the tape while the caulk is wet.

Total cost for the project? Just $6 for caulk and $15 for a quality caulking gun. In comparison, a handyman would likely charge well over $100.

Solidify your shaky hand rail. The large newel post at the bottom of a staircase is often the cause of an unstable banister. If that's the case, you can stop the wobbling by drilling a hole into the post toward the stair frame beside it. Then insert a lag screw through the post hole and stair frame and tighten.

Plug the tip of the drill hole with the end of a dowel rod and then paint it to match the post. Repeat at the top of the staircase if needed. This DIY project will cost around $20, far less than the $300 to $900 a professional would charge to fix your stairs and rails.

Fill in driveway cracks. Driveway cracks lessen curb appeal and, if wide and deep enough, can cause you to trip and fall. Seniors with an asphalt driveway can patch cracks less than 1/2 inch deep with asphalt repairing tar. Just clean the area of weeds and debris, fill in the crack, and level it for a smooth transition.

Have a concrete driveway? Fill hairline cracks with concrete caulking and wider ones with concrete sealer. Press the mix firmly and allow the patch to dry and cure. You'll want to seal the driveway later.

A repairman might charge between $300 and several thousand dollars for this project, depending on the damage. You could easily save half of what he would charge by doing the work yourself. The cost of 10 pounds of repair mix? Less than $20.

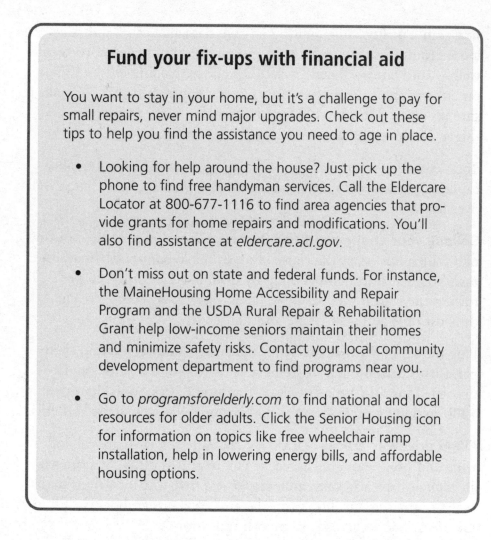

Fund your fix-ups with financial aid

You want to stay in your home, but it's a challenge to pay for small repairs, never mind major upgrades. Check out these tips to help you find the assistance you need to age in place.

- Looking for help around the house? Just pick up the phone to find free handyman services. Call the Eldercare Locator at 800-677-1116 to find area agencies that provide grants for home repairs and modifications. You'll also find assistance at *eldercare.acl.gov*.

- Don't miss out on state and federal funds. For instance, the MaineHousing Home Accessibility and Repair Program and the USDA Rural Repair & Rehabilitation Grant help low-income seniors maintain their homes and minimize safety risks. Contact your local community development department to find programs near you.

- Go to *programsforelderly.com* to find national and local resources for older adults. Click the Senior Housing icon for information on topics like free wheelchair ramp installation, help in lowering energy bills, and affordable housing options.

Savvy solutions to unsafe bathrooms

One in four Americans over age 65 falls each year. And for seniors with mobility issues, bathrooms are a prime — and particularly dangerous — location to take a spill. After all, they're tiny rooms full of sharp corners and unforgiving, slippery surfaces. But you can reduce the odds of a bathroom injury with these simple changes.

Grab onto help. Let's face it — sometimes seniors have a bit of trouble keeping their balance. So why not install grab bars in the shower and beside the toilet for a bit of extra stability? You'll want to look for bars that can support up to 250 pounds, and be sure to securely screw them into the wall studs.

Prices vary, but start at around $15 per bar. Professional installation of three bars will cost about $140.

Sit on a throne fit for royalty. Seniors with trouble sitting down and standing up can make their lives a whole lot easier by attaching a raised toilet seat onto their existing commode. Cost? Less than $50. You could also swap your standard toilet for a taller "chair height" version that costs between $150 and $300. Installation will run at least another $200.

Maximize tiny spaces. It can be tough to get around in the bathroom if you're in a wheelchair or use a walker. But you can make good use of all available space by rehanging your bathroom door so that it swings outward instead of into the room. This simple solution also helps with exiting and entering. You can hire someone to do the job for around $100.

Rinse off the right way. Trying to rinse off in the shower can be a nightmare if you're wobbly on your feet. A simple solution? The handheld shower head. It lets you direct the flow of water — even if you have limited mobility. Just make sure the hose is long enough to reach your feet when seated.

You'll find lots of models for under $50. Expect to pay at least $75 for installation.

Overhead heat lamps are the perfect solution to the chill seniors often feel when getting in and out of the bath. The lamps are especially useful for people who have to wait inside a walk-in tub while if fills and drains. Expect to spend between $50 and $150.

The best floors for seniors that won't break the bank

New flooring is a big investment, so you want to make sure you're getting the highest quality at the lowest price. Beware of stone and ceramic tiles — they're slippery when wet and provide no cushion from a fall.

And although hardwood floors are stunning, they're expensive to install and susceptible to water damage. But three options stand out for versatility and price.

Cork is easy to clean and naturally resistant to mold, mildew, and termites.

- Pro. It's good for accommodating wheelchairs yet offers cushioning underfoot.

- Con: It can be punctured and scraped by chair and furniture legs, along with certain types of heels.

- Cost: $2 to $6 per square foot. Installation runs $3 to $5 per square foot.

Linoleum is very durable and generally water and stain resistant.

- Pro. It's also good at accommodating wheelchairs. Pet hair and dust don't cling to it.

- Con: It offers little cushioning underfoot.

- Cost: $2 to $5 per square foot. Expect to pay between $7 and $12 per square foot for installation.

Carpeting is virtually silent to walk on.

- Pro. The cushiony surface gives some protection from fall-related injuries.

- Con: It's difficult to clean and hard to navigate in a wheelchair.

- Cost: $2 to $12 per square foot. Add 50 cents to $2 per square foot for padding and installation.

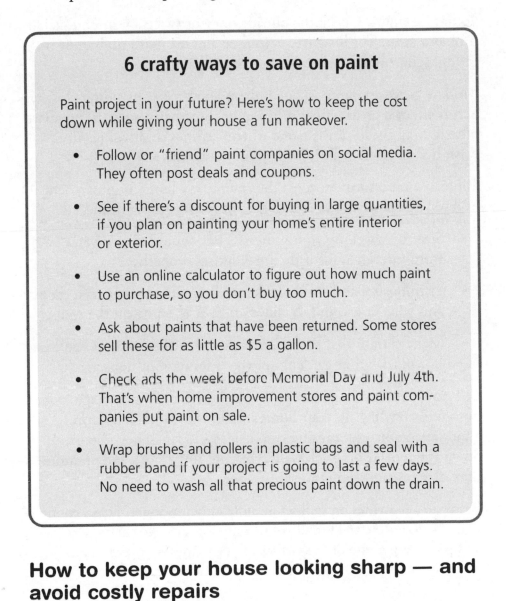

6 crafty ways to save on paint

Paint project in your future? Here's how to keep the cost down while giving your house a fun makeover.

- Follow or "friend" paint companies on social media. They often post deals and coupons.

- See if there's a discount for buying in large quantities, if you plan on painting your home's entire interior or exterior.

- Use an online calculator to figure out how much paint to purchase, so you don't buy too much.

- Ask about paints that have been returned. Some stores sell these for as little as $5 a gallon.

- Check ads the week before Memorial Day and July 4th. That's when home improvement stores and paint companies put paint on sale.

- Wrap brushes and rollers in plastic bags and seal with a rubber band if your project is going to last a few days. No need to wash all that precious paint down the drain.

How to keep your house looking sharp — and avoid costly repairs

Your home's exterior is just as important as its interior. And since an exterior paint job costs between $2,000 and $4,800 for a 2,000-square-foot home, it literally pays to take care of the outside now, before it needs a complete redo. Extend the life of your current exterior and boost your curb appeal to boot.

Touch up paint. Check the outside once or twice a year and tackle problem areas. For instance, if you see an area that's peeling or blistering, scrape it off, prime it, then apply paint.

Mildew grows in damp, shaded places so check your siding closely. Scrub affected areas with a solution of three parts water to one part bleach. Stay ahead of the game when it comes to dirt. Pressure wash before grime gets embedded in your walls.

Minimize moisture. Water is the enemy, say home improvement experts. So do what you can to keep it from coming inside.

- Start by checking your gutters. They should divert water away from exterior walls if they're working properly.

- Trim bushes and shrubs to keep air circulating between them and your house and to allow sunlight to shine on the walls.

- Make certain that sprinklers water what they're supposed to — your lawn or garden, not the sides of your house.

Cut down vines. They may give your house a rustic, cottage look, but vines crawling up your home's walls can do hidden harm. Vines trap moisture, causing wood siding to rot. They also break down the mortar on brick walls, creating tiny nooks and crannies that let moisture seep indoors.

Better to keep vines on trellises away from your house. Leave enough space between the trellis and your home for air to circulate. Do this, and you'll enjoy one of the virtues of your vines — they'll shade your house in summer and allow the sun to shine on it in winter.

Frugal food tips slash your grocery bill

Shopping secrets: How you can
outsmart the supermarket 264

Grow your own food for less 281

Kitchen hacks that save
you money 288

Dine out in style without breaking
the bank 298

Shopping secrets: How you can outsmart the supermarket

3 super-easy ways to cut your grocery bill in half

Bargain hunting at the supermarket is more exciting than ever. Store options, tech deals, and other incentives make the savings add up quickly. Here's how to trim 50% or more off your grocery bill — without cutting back on food.

Check out the competition and save 18%. At least 2 out of 3 Americans search for food deals in more than one store. Are you one of them? Shopping around gives you great savings options. Decide which of these features is most important to you to help pick the right place to shop.

- Cost. Discount grocers meet your low-price expectations for several reasons. They carry off-label brands and keep their overhead low. What they lack in perks they make up for in price. Consumer expert Clark Howard's comparison of Aldi's prices against Kroger and Walmart revealed a savings of at least 18%.

- Quality. When you've got a taste for fresh-off-the-farm or organic produce, detour to farmers markets and smaller stores like Sprouts and Whole Foods. You'll have fewer choices, but their carefully selected products are often offered at surprisingly competitive prices.

- Quantity. Warehouse clubs carry bigger sizes, which may not always be convenient. But picking up an occasional kitchen staple in bulk may be worth it. For example, *Consumer Reports* found organic coffee at Costco priced 19 cents per ounce cheaper than a conventional coffee brand.

Use your gadgets to gain up to 20% cash back. Do you find technology intimidating? Too bad because that means you're losing out on free money. Learn how to use it, and you'll stay on the cutting edge of new deals.

Cash-back apps like MobiSave, Ibotta, Checkout 51, and Ebates all give you rebates when you shop. After setting up your account, you scan your itemized receipt from any of the participating stores to receive money back. Some apps credit your Paypal account, while others send you a check.

Lenders want in on your food-purchasing action, too. Many promote deals on cash-back credit and debit cards. If you spend a lot on groceries, it might be worth getting a card with a high cash-back rate for supermarkets. Check out Lending Tree's comparison of cards and their incentives at *comparecards.com*.

Just be sure to look beyond the cash-back bonus for annual fees or interest rates. One card offers a whopping 6% back on supermarket purchases but carries a $95 annual fee.

Paying with coupons clips your costs an average of 20%. You can save even more if you use your coupons on sale items, combine store and manufacturers coupons, and shop on double-coupon days.

For example, if you have 50-cent coupons for 20 items and take advantage of double-coupon day, you'll save $20 right off the top of your grocery bill. Do that every week throughout the year and you'll put $1,040 back in your pocket.

Supermarket loyalty programs grant you an immediate discount off a product's regular price. One shopper saved $8.80 on her $127 bill without even trying — just by buying the store's promotional items. Check the bottom half of your receipt to find your exact savings each time you shop.

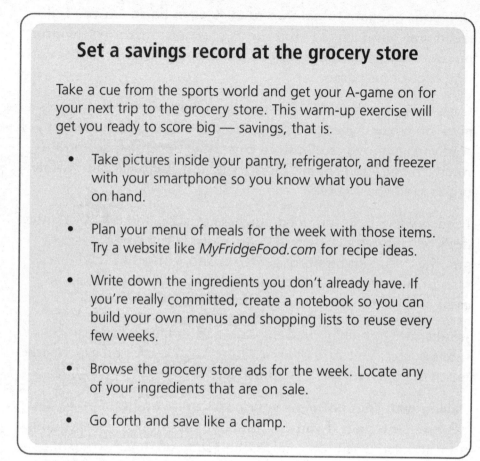

Set a savings record at the grocery store

Take a cue from the sports world and get your A-game on for your next trip to the grocery store. This warm-up exercise will get you ready to score big — savings, that is.

- Take pictures inside your pantry, refrigerator, and freezer with your smartphone so you know what you have on hand.

- Plan your menu of meals for the week with those items. Try a website like *MyFridgeFood.com* for recipe ideas.

- Write down the ingredients you don't already have. If you're really committed, create a notebook so you can build your own menus and shopping lists to reuse every few weeks.

- Browse the grocery store ads for the week. Locate any of your ingredients that are on sale.

- Go forth and save like a champ.

Use your calendar to save every time you shop

Product cycles at your supermarket stir up real discounts. Here's how to spot the best days to shop. You'll chuckle at the spendthrifts who shop on other days — they just paid a whole lot more.

The key to cheap groceries is knowing when to stock up. Learn the weekly or monthly sales cycles by doing this quick study.

1. Choose the top five products you buy all the time. Write them down.

2. Visit the website *Weeklyads2.com*.

3. Locate your neighborhood supermarket.

4. Select the ads for the past six weeks, and look for your products or similar ones.

5. Write down the sales you spot on your top five by week.

6. Look for the patterns.

Cycles will become more obvious if you track your item in table form. Here's an example of how to do it.

Cereal	Week 1	Week 2	Week 3	Week 4	Week 5	Week 6
Regular	$4.99	$4.99	$4.99	$4.99	$4.99	$4.99
Sale	2 for $6	2 for $4	35% off	$1.99/ea	35% off	2 for $5
Discount	$1.99	$2.99	$1.75	$3.00	$1.75	$2.49
Cost/box	$3	$2	$3.24	$1.99	$3.24	$2.50

Sales usually operate on six-to-eight-week cycles. Watch the trend on your products until you see the sale pattern repeat. Given the six weeks in the cereal sale example, you would want to stock up during the fourth week.

Take advantage of coupon cycles for bigger savings. Check out this coupon-user's secret that could save you hundreds. According to John Vernon, who buys groceries for a city mission, coupons also run in cycles. By being organized and learning your store's coupon policy, you could easily save 40% to 50%, he says. Here's what he recommends.

- Watch for a "stock-up" price on an item you usually buy so you can pick up a large supply. "By the time you run out of that item the sale is happening again," Vernon says. It's even better if you have a buy-one, get-one-free item and you can put both a manufacturer and store coupon with it. "Then you've got this perfect storm of savings," he says. "Sometimes you can get the item for pennies or even free."

- Be on the lookout for senior appreciation days where you might save an additional 5%.

What would his tips look like in practice? If you had a 50-cent coupon for your cereal, and you bought it at the store's lowest price of $1.99 on a double-coupon and senior-discount day, you'd get your cereal for 89 cents a box. At 82% off the regular price of $4.99, that is, as Vernon says, a perfect storm of savings.

Online shopping: Easy, quick, and cheap

Imagine a world where you recline in your lounge chair, snack in hand, and load up your grocery cart. You click submit and in about two hours, your groceries show up in your driveway. Curious to know more? Here's why you may want to give online shopping a try.

It's a piece of cake to find a place to shop. If you live near a city, many of your favorite stores already offer user-friendly shopping experiences. And to keep your business, they continue to work on newer, automated tools to help with other tasks as well, like meal planning and shopping preparation.

To find out if your favorite store is among them, check their website, or do a search for "online grocery shopping."

Convenient, quick ordering is at your fingertips. Gone are the days of juggling a paper list and a handful of coupons. Apps and websites can take care of all that for you. Here's how.

- Select coupons that are already linked to online products. If you shop through a delivery service like Instacart or Shipt, you may be able to use both the grocery store's coupons and the delivery service's promotional coupons at the same time. The first will be loaded on your store loyalty card, and the second will be advertised next to the products in your search.

- Apps like Favado, Shopular, Yroo, and BuyVia compare prices across stores with lightning speed. In under one minute, you can find the price of your favorite cereal at two competing grocers. This technology predicts your needs and tailors suggestions to help you save time.

- Choose home delivery. Almost anything on your grocery list can be delivered to your home within 48 hours. One-hour delivery options are fast becoming the norm. And it's a cost-saver, too.

> Finding good-quality products online is a snap. That's why you should never buy things like batteries, toilet paper, electrical cords, tools, and vitamins at the dollar store again. You'll find them for less online, plus you can read the product reviews to make sure you'll be happy with the quality.

Another benefit? You're more aware of what you spend so you're less likely to make impulsive purchases. The shopping cart total is always visible and instantly tallies your order. The cart summary is just a click away, so you can add, remove, or substitute items with one quick keystroke.

Leave more cash in your pocketbook. If you and your spouse are 51 to 70 years old, the U.S. Department of Agriculture estimates you spend between $110 and $137 a week on food. That amounts to $477 to $593 per month.

How does that compare to shopping online? If you buy the same 48 items at three major retailers, here's what you'll pay. Prices include the delivery fee for each service.

Store	Weekly cost	Monthly cost
Amazon Fresh	$165.85	$723.36
Instacart, Kroger	$154.49	$667.64
Walmart.com	$123.34	$493.36

In this shopping excursion, Walmart.com kept the cost in the range of what you'd normally spend. Surprised? With the added benefits of time saved and ease of shopping, getting your groceries online may be something to consider.

Don't forget the hidden costs of grocery shopping online

Like pizza delivery, having groceries brought to your door costs a little more. Here's how to decide if the fees are worth it.

Delivery charge. A standard fee applies to each order if the store does not require a membership. The fee averages $3 to $10 per order. Look for free trials or coupons to get delivery discounted. Promotional codes and manufacturer coupons also offset this cost and can be applied instantly while you shop.

Membership fee. A typical membership costs around $150 a year. When you divide that cost over 12 months and add up the membership perks, it looks more like a bargain, averaging around $3 a week. Most services offer free delivery with membership as long as you place a minimum order.

CAUTION

Bulk buying: Is it right for you?

Buying in bulk can save you anywhere from 20% to 83% a month on your grocery bill. The question is, do you have enough space to store all those extra boxes of crackers and cans of soup? If so, don't just tuck them away on a shelf and forget about them. That's a sure way to waste food — and money.

Here's how to make sure buying in bulk is a bargain, not a bust.

Freezing meals helps you use up more food. If you already crave your homemade spaghetti, why not make extra so you can freeze a few meals for later? This would be the perfect chance to buy in bulk, and even better if the ingredients are on sale.

- For example, you decide to make one spaghetti dinner to eat fresh and three to freeze. The ingredients cost you $20, which works out to $5 per meal. Experts say you'll cut between 25% and 50% off that per-meal cost by buying your ingredients in bulk and using them to prepare several meals.

- Once you get home with your ingredients, be sure to follow through and make enough for four meals. If you wait too long, your ingredients may end up expiring.

Take advantage of sales on staples for big savings. Look for honey, coffee, sugar, salt, corn starch, dry beans, white rice, maple syrup, pure vanilla extract, and white vinegar. These are examples of delicious foods that never go bad, so stock up when they are on sale and save.

Other good bulk buys include canned goods, meats, and frozen fruits and vegetables as long as you can eat them in a reasonable amount of time. Stay away from oils and nuts since these products are more likely to go rancid before you use the bulkier size.

> When you see a quantity or time limit on a sale, it's a dead giveaway that you're getting a good deal, so stock up on this truly unbeatable bargain. If you can add a coupon on top of that, you'll score a real home run.

Pick the store with the biggest discounts. Once you have a plan, compare the local sales. You can usually find bulk quantities in a lot of different locations. Consider these choices.

- Warehouse or wholesale clubs are the go-to places for larger packaging and quantities, although they charge membership fees. Compare the product price per unit to your local market.

- Supermarkets sometimes carry larger packaging, but if not, do not hesitate to buy extra regular-sized boxes if the price is right.

- Farmers markets are great places to look for flats or cartons of seasonal produce. Set aside time to preserve it when you get it home.

- Salvage stores generally carry large bins of items that are just slightly out of date, which means the prices have been slashed drastically.

- Online stores like Boxed.com and Amazon offer competitive prices, sell larger quantities, and will ship directly to you.

You don't need a telescope to spot these savings

Grocery bloggers track the rotation of product sales as faithfully as astronomers chart the earth's orbit around the sun. And like scientists, they discover patterns, which they are more than willing to share. Here's a summary of the cycles they find in common. Buy during the right month and you're sure to save.

Month	Products on sale
January	cereal, chips, crackers, diet products, dips, oats/oatmeal, soda
February	candy, oats/oatmeal, canned vegetables
March	corned beef, frozen food
April	candy, eggs, sugar, vegetables
May	BBQ sauce, beef, chips, hot dogs, ketchup, marshmallows, mayonnaise, mustard, salad dressing, tortillas, vegetables
June	BBQ sauce, beef, dairy products, hot dogs
July	breads, juice boxes, chips, hot dogs, ice cream, ketchup, mayonnaise, mustard, soda

Month	Products on sale
August	juice boxes, deli meat, lunchables, granola bars, snack packs
September	canned soups, canned vegetables
October	candy, seafood, canned vegetables
November	broth, butter, candy, juice boxes, chocolate chips, flour, gravy, nuts, canned soups, stuffing, sugar, condensed or evaporated milk, turkey, canned vegetables
December	baking powder, breads, butter, cake mixes, chocolate chips, whipped cream, crackers, deli meat, eggnog, flour, frozen pies, ham, marshmallows, soda, sugar, condensed or evaporated milk

Unit price — your secret to always getting the best buy

An advertiser's goal is to tug at your emotional connection to certain products. Show them you're not falling for it. Pull out your calculator if you're ready to get serious about saving money. You'll need to compare products and their prices.

Look for the bottom line. Literally. Always look for the unit price, because it's the best way to select the best buys at the grocery store. You'll find it tucked into the corner of the shelf tag. Online it will appear in small or lighter lettering near the price, usually inside parentheses.

Comparing unit prices can get complicated if the products have special ingredients. A detergent that is scented, has a softener, or contains a bleach will be priced to reflect these "value added" enhancements. If the unit price is higher, but those features are important to you, you'll have to decide if paying more is worth it.

The unit price could be the price per ounce, sheet, or load depending on whether you're buying canned corn, toilet paper, or detergent.

It will tell you if a sale really is a bargain or if the regular price for a store brand beats its national competitor.

Factor in sales and discounts when comparing prices. Products are often packaged in slightly different sizes and quantities. When nobody has done the math for you, divide the total cost by the number of items, ounces, loads, or other measure. For example:

- avocados are on sale at three for 88 cents. Divide 88 by three. Your unit cost is 29 cents per avocado.

- 64-ounce sodas are three for $5. Multiply three times 64 to get 192, the total number of ounces. Divide $5 by 192 to get a unit price of 26 cents per ounce.

Compare those prices to the regular costs or other sales to know if you're getting a good deal.

Shocking shopping secret you need to know. It may surprise you to learn generic products are not always cheaper, and larger sizes are not always the better deal.

In the laundry detergent example below, Detergent A is the store brand. It is sold in a larger package at a higher price than B, the

	Detergent A	Detergent B
Quantity	35 packs	50 oz bottle
# Loads	35	32
Price	$9.99	$9.49
Price/unit	29 cents/load	30 cents/load
Sale	None	$5.94
Coupon	None	$2
Total	$9.99	$3.94
Final unit price	29 cents/load	12 cents/load

national brand. Even though it's slightly more expensive, Detergent A usually is a better deal at 29 cents per load. But with the sale and coupon, the national brand B clearly comes out on top.

So don't automatically reach for the store brand or the largest package. Train yourself to look for the unit price on every item, and you'll come out ahead every time.

'Sense'able shopping: How to 'just say no' to impulse buys

Grocery stores are designed to take advantage of your urge to splurge. From signage to shelving, stores are set up to lure you in and entice you to buy. That's a sneaky secret grocers won't tell you.

Don't become one of those Americans who fritter away over $5,400 on impulse buys each year. By sidestepping the store's sensory overload, you'll spend less on groceries — without coupons — and maybe even cut your grocery bill in half.

Experts estimate that 50% to 67% of all grocery purchases are impulse buys. Here's how to put up some defenses and steer clear of the traps.

Shield your eyes. If the produce looks extra fresh, that's because the stores place it under special lights and mist it. Think of it as a glamour shot for your veggies. Only select the produce you need, and ignore the rest of the beautiful bounty.

Don't round the corner too quickly or you may bump into product displays and end caps — those featured products at the end of an aisle. They're conveniently placed to grab your attention, but they may not be the best bargains. Here's where it helps to track your favorite products so you know if that big display is the real deal.

Don't touch. Sometimes you need a friend to tell you to put that box of doughnuts back on the shelf. If you have a hard time resisting snack foods or other goodies, don't even pick them up. Researchers have found that handling a product makes you more likely to buy it.

Your best strategy is to take only the cash you need to cover what's on your shopping list. Then you won't be tempted to trade items you need for those that look more appealing.

Pinch your nose. Tantalizing aromas of freshly baked cookies float through the store, beckoning you. Some grocers diffuse inviting scents into the air to inspire customers' cravings. Whether natural or artificial, research suggests that pleasing scents can make you stay longer in a store, want to purchase products, and even pay more for them.

Your game plan? Get enough sleep so you can make good decisions when you shop. And make sure you take a list to help you focus on what you need.

> Are you an impulse shopper? Join the crowd. A Cornell University study found that impulse buying is common among Americans, especially when snack food and credit cards are in play. A Slickdeals.net survey confirmed this bad news when it found that 7 out of 10 respondents spend impulsively on eating.

Plug your ears. The music piping through the sound system may hardly be noticeable, but that's what works best for retailers. Studies have found that shoppers buy 38% more, and grocery stores can make an average of $4,000 more, when soothing background music plays.

Relaxing tunes slow your pulse and encourage you to linger in the store, which is how you spend more money. To fight the urge to hang around, set a timer. Get in and out of the market quickly to avoid browsing. Try to beat your own best shopping time.

Close your mouth. Why wouldn't you want to taste those yummy free samples? When you do, you are much more likely to take the product home. One study revealed shoppers tend to stick with that product for a solid year-and-a-half after sampling it.

Don't shop hungry, and you'll be more likely to resist. If necessary, munch on a snack while you browse the store.

Why you should always buy produce on Saturdays

Saturday mornings across America, truckloads of sumptuous fruits and vegetables — along with organic honey, fresh jams, and more — await you at local farmers markets.

And, surprise, their prices are often competitive with or better than the supermarket. Not to mention you get fresh, healthy, unprocessed food, especially during peak growing seasons. Why would you buy your produce on any other day?

For a chance at some real bargains, give these tips a try as you browse the aisles.

Befriend a farmer. Striking up a conversation with a local farmer is easier than you think. Sellers want regular customers. If they know you, they are more likely to negotiate when you ask for a discount or want to buy in bulk.

Test your bargaining power. Show them your sales flyer and see if they can compete with the grocery prices. If you plan to preserve what you buy, offer the farmer a deal on her flat of slightly bruised, vine-ripened tomatoes. You'll cut them up to store anyway, and you get the tastiest tomatoes at the lowest price.

Learn to barter. Why not trade a skill for a weekly supply of produce? If you can mend clothing or maintain a website, then your local farmer may be interested in making a trade. Once you've built the relationship, you'll know better what might best help that farmer and can make the right offer.

Take advantage of special programs. Low-income seniors at least 60 years old can save even more by enrolling in the Seniors Farmers Market Nutrition Program. You'll receive coupons for fruits, vegetables, honey, and fresh-cut herbs to use at participating farmers markets, roadside stands, and community service associations.

For more information, visit *Fns.usda.gov*, click on Programs, and choose Farmers Market Nutrition Program.

Organic produce — healthy eating or a waste of money?

Naturally, you care about your health. So how much do you know about your food? When it comes to organic produce, how much should you be willing to spend if it means you're getting better quality? Consider these points before you make up your mind.

Don't be fooled by "organic" labels. When you think of organic foods, you probably envision produce grown with little or no pesticides, herbicides, chemical fertilizers, antibiotics, hormones, additives, or preservatives. The only items that fit this definition are products labeled "100% organic."

Labels that simply read "organic" mean that 95% or more of the ingredients that went into the food are organic. On the other hand, if the label says "made with organic ingredients," only 70% must be organic. Sometimes the nonorganic ingredients are simply added vitamins or other nutrients. Other times, they're ingredients you'd rather avoid.

Stop playing guessing games. Just look for the USDA organic seal. It guarantees the produce was grown with at least 95% organic ingredients.

Some produce is already low-pesticide. An unpeeled banana may have pesticide residues, but when you throw out the peel, the suspicious chemicals go with it. Paying extra for an organic banana is basically a waste of money.

The moral of this story — spend your money on the top offenders. The "dirty dozen" are the fruits and veggies highest in pesticide residues. Conventionally grown apples, for example, tend to have more pesticides on them than mangos. To save money, buy the regular versions of low-pesticide produce, aka the "clean 15," and only splurge for the organic versions of the serious offenders.

> Grocery lists have never been easier to create. You don't even have to write them down anymore. Apps like GroceryIQ or Listonic let you speak yours into existence on your smartphone or computer. Set up your free account and create your first list before you head to the grocery store.

Beware of the dirty dozen. According to the nonprofit Environmental Working Group, people who eat the 12 most contaminated fruits and vegetables take in an average of 10 different pesticides a day. So buy the organic versions of these foods whenever possible.

- strawberries
- nectarines
- peaches
- tomatoes
- spinach
- apples
- cherries
- celery
- kale
- grapes
- pears
- potatoes

You're good to go with the clean 15. People who eat these 15 least-contaminated fruits and vegetables consume fewer than two pesticides per day. Go ahead and buy the nonorganic versions of these to enjoy healthy living at a reasonable price.

- avocados
- sweet peas, frozen
- sweet corn
- onions
- pineapple
- papayas

- eggplants
- cabbage
- broccoli

- asparagus
- cauliflower
- mushrooms

- kiwis
- cantaloupe
- honeydew melons

Clean up your diet on organic deals

All organic products — not just produce — must meet strict growing and processing standards set by the USDA. As a result, they bear the 100% organic seal. But do they always cost more? Not necessarily.

If you compare prices, you'll find that some organic products are the same or cheaper than their nonorganic cousins. Even if the organic product is slightly more expensive, it may be better for your health. Here are two things to consider when making your choice.

Store brands are a good option. A private label apple juice — 100% certified organic — sells for $3.49 compared to a name-brand organic apple juice priced at $3.89, a 40-cent savings.

Look at more than just cost. Juices labeled 100% natural or 100% juice are both priced at $3.29. Although cheaper than the organics, they're more likely to contain pesticide residue or heavy metals. In this case, the store-brand organic juice, at just 20 cents more, may be a better choice for your family.

Grow your own food for less

Create a gorgeous garden with a tiny space (and budget)

If you think you need huge tracts of land to grow your own food, think again. Carve out a small patch on your property to grow your favorite produce or herbs, and you'll taste the savings throughout the year.

Savory produce can grow in small spaces. Even if your available real estate is limited, you can grow enough food in containers to offset your grocery bill. Be sure your plant's container affords ample space and drainage for your growing plant.

Use your imagination and these tips to fashion homes for your plants at very little cost.

- Surf yard sales for containers. You don't have to settle for flower pots. Old colanders, broken pots or bowls, and even deep-set picture frames can be upcycled for pennies.

- Recycle old furniture as a planter. You'll add rustic appeal to your yard, too.

- Old ladders and shelving can help you maximize space by creating a tier of containers on the patio.

- Don't fall for overpriced planters. Beautiful, galvanized containers for under $10 will last for years.

- Fabric grow bags are portable and practical for under $2.

Simple and affordable raised beds give you room to grow. Your garden options don't have to involve back-breaking tilling of the earth.

Raised-bed gardens built on top of your existing surface are sizable enough to grow food for your family. Add the necessary garden soil and plant your crop.

Choose from two easy and affordable options to create your own bed.

- Build from scrap materials at home.

- Buy a kit. You can order one online for about $20, or bring one home from your local wholesale club for $40.

If dirt is not your thing, start a hydroponic garden. With a $75 investment, you can grow three plants at a time all year long using water and liquid nourishment, but no soil. These machines use seed pods and a grow light to yield a harvest in no time.

Grow plants from plants to save even more

Remember when you learned how to sprout potatoes as a kid? Well, you can still do it today — and with other vegetables as well. Discover how to regrow them and save money in the process. These veggie scraps make great starters.

Carrots. Snip the tip of a fresh carrot and drop it in water for a few days until it sprouts. Plant it and wait for it to flower. Once it goes to seed, harvest the seeds for planting next season.

Potatoes. Set aside potatoes to sprout. Once they do, plant them. Water them and keep them in a sunny spot. Expect about 7 pounds of potatoes if you plant them in a fabric grow bag.

Celery. Cut off the base of the celery stalk to place in a bowl of warm water. Leave it in direct sunlight, and watch for leaves to appear around the base. Once you see them, transplant the celery to the soil.

Ready to plant? How to cut your costs by 98%

A starter plant may not look that expensive at $4.98, but when you consider the same plant grown from seed costs only a dime, why would you want to pay an astonishing 50 times more? Start your garden with seeds instead of nursery plants and you'll cut your costs by 98%.

Find seeds for free. Communities across the country share their seeds with one another for free through seed libraries or exchanges. Find one near you by visiting *Seedlibraries.weebly.com* or *Seedsavers.org*.

Need to purchase seeds? Supplemental Nutrition Assistance Program — SNAP — benefits cover seeds. Any SNAP retailer, including farmers markets, can sell seeds and plants to participants. To see if you qualify for this program, use the prescreening tool available online at *Snap-step1.usda.gov/fns*.

Start your seeds with recyclables. Start seeds indoors or outdoors, depending on the time of year, according to the instructions on the packet. No packet? Visit *The Old Farmer's Almanac* online and look up your planting instructions. Seeds need the right combination of warmth, soil, and moisture to germinate.

- Recycled materials make perfect starter pods for your seeds. Empty used K-cups and fill the cups with potting mix. Plant about two seeds per cup.

- Mini cereal boxes also make great seedling cradles. Cut the tops off the boxes, fill with potting mix, and insert a couple of seeds per box.

- Try making seed tape, a similar planting hack, out of toilet paper. Roll it out, apply a flour-water paste in dabs every couple of inches, and secure seeds to the paste. Lay the tape in your garden row, and cover it when you're ready to germinate your seeds.

- For sowing directly in the ground, consider making seed paper. Search recipes online to see how to make it with recyclable paper, water, and seeds.

Remember that for every $1 you spend on seeds, you'll grow about $25 of produce. Now that's real seed money.

Dirt cheap home hacks to build the best soil

No fast food diets for your plants. They need to be fed with the right nutrients through their soil. The payoff? Lush, healthy plants that will provide you with enough produce to make your investment pay off.

Start with the right type of dirt. The blend of dirt you use is critical to your plants' survival. Pick one based on the type of garden space you have.

- When growing in containers, your plants need a special blend called potting mix or potting soil. It is sold in bags, usually measured in cubic feet or quarts, and costs an average of $5 for 8 quarts. Measure your containers before buying.

- When planting in the ground or a raised bed, use garden soil or topsoil. It typically costs more — about $8 for 1.5 cubic feet — but you'll get more soil for the price.

Give your plants their own blend of energy drink. Nitrogen, phosphorus, and potassium are nutrition boosters that help your plants grow stronger. Feed all your plants at the roots with this nutrient-packed smoothie once a month. Whip up a batch big enough by combining these common household staples in a 5-gallon bucket.

- 2.5 teaspoons ammonia
- 5 teaspoons baking soda
- 5 tablespoons Epsom salts
- 4.5 gallons water

Amend the soil with homemade compost. Another natural way to feed you plants is with compost. You can buy ready-made compost for about $4.97 per cubic foot. Or you can make your own compost at home for free out of yard debris and food scraps.

Creating a compost pile couldn't be easier. Convert an old trash can, or construct a small box for your pile in a corner of your yard. Toss in the right materials, water it occasionally, and aerate it. By the time your next garden needs to be prepared, you'll have excellent organic material to till into the soil.

Kitchen scraps, grass clippings and leaves, used coffee grounds, eggshells, fruit and vegetable plants at the end of the growing season — all these will help develop the rich, organic material your plants crave.

Prune your grocery bill with homegrown herbs

Have you seen the price of fresh herbs in the supermarket? Those clear, plastic containers lined up in the refrigerated produce aisle are oh-so tempting, with their feathery fronds and crisp leaves. But sticker shock could leave your bargain tomatoes longing for a side of pesto.

Why would you fork over a small fortune for packaged herbs when it's so easy and economical to grow fresh herbs at home? You don't even need much of a green thumb. The trick is to start small, choose herbs you really will use, and plan carefully so your garden doesn't cost more than you'd spend at the grocery store. After all, the goal is to not only enjoy fresh and flavorful seasonings, but save on groceries, too.

Here are a few popular perennial herbs you may want to try. Check out the price comparisons. By growing them yourself and enjoying a bountiful harvest for years to come, you'll save money in the long run.

Parsley. Easy to grow in any soil without much water, but does require sun. Re-seeds itself freely.

- Seed — $1.99 per pack

- Starter plant — $6.48

- Store bought — $3.64 per ounce

Thyme. Grows well in almost any condition, but prefers full sun.

- Seed — $1.59 per pack

- Starter plant — $4.98

- Store bought — $3.64 per ounce

Rosemary. Likes well-drained soil and sun. Pinch it back and it gets bushier as it grows.

- Seed — $1.59 per pack

- Starter plant — $5.47

- Store bought — $3.64 per ounce

Cheap — or free — ways to stop garden pests

Your garden is a regular vacation hotspot for pests like weeds, bugs, and diseases. When it comes to managing them, horticulture expert Brian Morris urges you to be proactive. "Prevention is always cheaper than treatment," he says.

Healthy plants naturally resist pests. Follow these tips to give your plants the best chance at success.

Plant low-growing flowers, herbs, or vegetables with taller ones. You'll suppress weeds with the ground cover, but you'll also allow air to circulate, which lowers their risk of disease.

Pests sleep in your soil. Rotate crops to prevent them from waking up and feasting on the plants they love. Just make sure the crops are from different families. "It doesn't help to rotate a tomato and a pepper because they are both in the nightshade group," Morris says.

Planting flowers like marigolds with your vegetables can push away bad bugs. Sunflowers, on the other hand, will pull in beneficial insects to eat the bad ones.

Water correctly for plant health. Do you usually take your hose and spray everything in your garden? Or set up a sprinkler to do it automatically? Those are both no-no's.

Insects and diseases thrive in hot, humid, and stagnant conditions. Watering plants in the morning at the soil level with a soaker hose lessens the chance disease can set up on the leaves. And your plants can make use of the water throughout the day.

Mulch to guard against weeds and backsplash. "Weeds compete for water and nutrients against your vegetables," says Morris. "They also serve as hosts for pests."

Organic mulch like straw, hay, leaves, or composted bark has several benefits, according to Morris. It maintains moisture, provides nutrients for the soil, reduces the threat of water-borne diseases splashing up onto the plants, and controls weeds.

Know your friend from your foe. "Not all bugs are bad," Morris says. You should be happy to see small wasps, ladybugs, mites, and praying mantises in your garden. They eat the insects you don't want around.

Another good way to get rid of unwanted bugs is to check the plants regularly. "If you spot a group of bad insects gathered on a leaf, pluck the leaf off and discard it. You've probably wiped out 99% of the population."

If that doesn't do the trick, try a homemade pest-repellant soap. Morris recommends a mixture of 3 cups of mild dishwashing liquid, a quart of water, and a tablespoon of cooking oil in a spray bottle. If it is 80 degrees or less outside, coat the leaves of your plants where you see an infestation of bad bugs. The soap suffocates the bugs and they drop off.

"It's a cheap and easy way to deal with a mild infestation of some insects," he says.

Kitchen hacks that save you money

Secret to whipping up delicious, low-cost meals in a jiffy

The sound of onions and garlic sizzling in their buttery pan beckons you into the kitchen. Inside, the scent of a delicious home-cooked meal-in-the-making has you hooked. The best part? Not only will it taste amazing, but it also costs next to nothing.

What's the secret? A pantry stocked with essentials that can be combined in dozens of new ways.

Stock your kitchen. Think of your pantry as a plate of healthy food. The U.S. Department of Agriculture (USDA) suggests you prepare your place setting with a balance of fruits, vegetables, grains, protein, and dairy. If you keep these kinds of foods on hand, you'll always have starters for your meals at home.

Unless you're in desperate need of that sauce pan to make dinner tonight, pass up the kitchenware at the grocery store. Why? Supermarket cookware comes with an average 30% markup. You're better off buying it from a big-box retailer or department store during a seasonal sale.

So how do you pick your go-to pantry staples? Choose foods you can use in many types of recipes. Here's an example of how you could stock your pantry with versatile foods in mind.

- Nonrefrigerated items — brown rice, whole-wheat noodles, canned tomatoes, pasta sauce, salsa, whole-wheat tortilla shells, canned black beans, onions

- Refrigerated and frozen items — butter, low-fat cheese, chicken, minced garlic, frozen broccoli and spinach

Put the essentials to work. Some instruments make beautiful music together no matter what song they play. Likewise, many pantry essentials work well together whether you combine them in soups, casseroles, or rice and pasta dishes. You can always personalize the recipes to suit your taste buds.

With your versatile pantry items on hand, you already have the basics for burritos, chicken stir-fry, broccoli casserole, salsa chicken over rice, lasagna, spaghetti, chicken noodle soup, and more.

Still stuck? Check off your pantry ingredients from the list at *myfridgefood.com* and click Find Recipes to discover tasty menus that let you skip a trip to the grocery store.

Select meals you love. When you crave something from your favorite restaurant, but the budget is tight, put your chef's hat on and turn your kitchen into your preferred eatery. Check out these websites for tasty copycat restaurant recipes.

- *sixsistersstuff.com/recipe/100-of-best-restaurant-copycat-recipes*

- *delish.com/cooking/recipe-ideas/g3219/copycat-recipes*

- *tasteofhome.com/collection/best-copycat-recipes*

Save space — and money — with these organization tricks

Have you ever pulled a jar of jelly out of the pantry, only to find others in a cupboard and the back of your fridge? Buying extras because you don't know what you have on hand can really spoil your budget. Here's how to organize your kitchen so you can streamline your shopping.

Develop a system that works for you. Food label makers are helpful but not required for a good system. Use a piece of tape and a marker to identify and date food when you take it out of its original package. Labels make it easier to rotate older items to the front so they won't spoil before you use them.

Repurpose items to free up space in your kitchen. These common household items can help you in your quest to get organized.

- You can use a magazine holder — cardboard, plastic, or metal — in every part of your kitchen to keep it tidy. An extra-wide magazine holder easily stores canned food in the pantry. Reusable water bottles and thermoses stack neatly in them as well. Position the long flat sides down in your freezer, and stack flat food packages in the makeshift "shelves." Or stand them upright under your sink to hold cleaning products.

- Valuable shelf real estate opens up when you install tension rods vertically between shelves to prop up baking sheets or cutting boards. Attach curtain rods to the insides of cabinet doors to hold pot lids in place. Or install them under sinks to dispense rolls of paper towels or trash bags.

Now you see it — make your kitchen stuff visible. Little spice bottles and condiments easily get lost and forgotten in the deep space of a pantry. Bring them back into the light by putting them on a multilevel shelf that's higher in the back so smaller items always stay in view.

Do bulky cereal boxes with one serving crumpled up in the bottom have you vexed? Try storing your cereals, grains, and pastas in clear canisters or glass jars. Label the containers and then you can see at a glance when you need to pick up more at the store.

Even favorite recipes get stuffed in nooks and crannies around your kitchen like last year's Easter eggs. Bring them all together in a joyous reunion by placing them inside sheet protectors in a binder.

Food you should never buy at the grocery store

Don't be tempted to throw your money away on convenience foods. Prepping your own snacks and sweets saves you from pricey pitfalls.

- Picking up snack packs at the grocery store will cost you as much as 50% more than buying the same munchies in bulk and portioning them yourself.

- Pre-cut fruit, vegetables, or meat could cost up to 370% more than the whole products.

- Buy special occasion cakes at warehouse clubs, which have more appetizing prices and deliver quality, decorated cakes or cookies. Better yet, bake your own delectable dessert — even from a box mix. Kick your cake up a notch by swapping water for milk, using butter instead of oil, or adding a few tablespoons of sour cream or mayonnaise to the batter.

Order up: Are meal kit subscriptions a good deal?

Dinnertime arrives with a smorgasbord of options. Do you go out? Grab take out? Order delivery? Cook for yourself? If you're tired of making decisions, maybe it's time to look into meal kits.

Five reasons you might want to subscribe to a meal kit service. You might be a bit hesitant to try out a meal in a box, but think of the time you'll save when you get to skip out on these tasks.

- Shopping. Refrigerated boxes arrive on your doorstep with everything you need.

- Chopping and measuring. Items are already sliced and diced in the right quantities for your meal.

- Fumbling around for recipes. The ingredients come with step-by-step instructions.

- Figuring out how to balance meals nutritionally. Chefs already figured that out for you.

- Fussing over dietary needs. Services allow you to select from gluten-free, vegan, vegetarian, and other dietary options.

The downside of delivery. When your box arrives, you still have to unpack and store the ingredients until it's time to cook. And you'll need anywhere from 20 to 45 minutes to prepare the meal. Although it probably won't cost as much as eating at a restaurant, you'll pay more than if you bought the groceries and prepared everything yourself.

How to get the most for your money. Ordering the meal kit subscription for a family of two generally costs more per serving than the subscription for four. So you'll get a better deal if you order the four-serving plan, prepare the extra meals, and put half of them away for later.

Your cost for 12 servings per week might be as low as $95.87. Or you could get 16 servings per week for $119.84. That's under $8 a serving for each meal delivered to your doorstep.

So if you want an inspired, restaurant-quality meal without the hassle — and you don't mind the price tag — a meal kit subscription might be for you.

Insider shortcuts to savings in the kitchen

You don't need expensive gadgets or elaborate setups to enjoy your cooking experience — just some basic tools and techniques, says culinary arts instructor Chef Carolyn Fludd. "It all boils down to having a good chef's knife and a paring knife."

After the basics are covered, consider inexpensive gadgets that make preparing a meal easier. Chef Fludd, for example, has a hard time living without her Benriner slicer, also called a Japanese mandolin. This tool helps with slicing and more challenging cuts, and it runs about $25 on Amazon.

Looking for other ways to cut costs in the kitchen? Follow this advice from Chef Fludd.

> Get creative with your plate and add appeal to your meal, says Chef Fludd. Eat lots of colors to get the vitamins and minerals you need. And make it fun. Swirl your spaghetti on your plate, for example, or lean those vegetables up against your meat.

Use restaurant secrets to save money and avoid waste at home. "Planning. We can't get away from it whether we have a restaurant or a family," says Chef Fludd. Luckily, you can plan well and save more by taking a hint from the pros.

"If you're making fried chicken one day and you don't eat it all, what a restaurant would do is take the skin off the chicken and have chicken salad the next day," she says.

In fact, restaurants plan ahead by creating cycle menus that repeat ingredients throughout the upcoming weeks so no food is wasted. Do the same, and build your shopping lists from your menu.

"When I do that, I eat out less because the food is already in the house and my husband and I already know what we're going to eat," says Chef Fludd. "It saves money that way."

For menu inspiration, check out Chef Fludd's go-to cooking sites — *smittenkitchen.com*, *cooksillustrated.com*, and *seriouseats.com*.

Quick hacks keep food from going bad. When your fruit is near its end, don't toss it. IQF it, says Chef Fludd. The individually quick-frozen (IQF) technique is an industry standard and is super easy. Place your washed and dried berries or sliced fruit flat on a baking sheet in a single row. Stash it in the freezer until solid, then store the frozen pieces of fruit in a freezer bag.

In addition, when your recipe only calls for a small portion of a canned good, freeze the remainder in single serving sizes. For example, portion out 1-tablespoon servings of remaining tomato paste in small freezer bags. This works for many canned goods.

You can also freeze fresh herbs in an ice cube tray with oil for easy, flavorful retrieval later.

Don't waste freezer space on these foods

You can freeze most foods, but don't try it with these. You won't be happy with the taste or texture when you thaw — and ultimately throw — them out.

- fried foods, except french fries and onion rings

- salad vegetables like cabbage, celery, cress, cucumbers, lettuce, parsley, and radishes

- baked or boiled potatoes

- desserts with meringue, cream, or custard fillings, or icing made with egg whites

- milk sauces for casseroles or gravy

- crumb or cheese toppings for casseroles

- sour cream

- gelatin

- fruit jelly, mayonnaise, or salad dressing

CAUTION

Cool down your spending by freezing food the right way

Do you buy in bulk to save money? It can be a smart move — unless you end up throwing away food because it goes bad before you can eat it. The solution to this predicament is right in your kitchen. All you have to do is learn how to freeze food properly. These steps help keep your freezer food safe.

Bypass food-freezing blunders. A bad experience with freezing and thawing food could mean you didn't do it right. Follow these simple rules the next time you want to save food for later.

- Banish freezer burn. Air can dry out the surface of food, causing gray ice crystals to form and your goodies to develop a bad taste. Squeeze out all the air from around the food when you seal it into bags.

- Keep it small. Divide food into small portions so it freezes more quickly. The faster food freezes, the fresher it will taste later. Also, you're more likely to find a use for small portions of frozen foods than for large ones.

- Bag it right. Freezer bags may cost more than other plastic bags or wrap, but they are worth it. Containers meant for the freezer are also durable enough to keep everything safe.

- Test for safety. Sniff or take a small taste of a frozen food before cooking. Make sure nothing is rancid or "off."

Three foods you didn't know you could freeze. Surprise! You can happily buy these foods in bulk, freeze them before they go bad, and enjoy later.

- Eggs. Break eggs into a bowl. Add either 1 tablespoon of sugar or 1/3 teaspoon of salt per cup of eggs, and stir until the yolks and whites are blended. Measure 3 tablespoons — the equivalent of one egg — into each cup of an ice cube tray.

This makes your frozen eggs a great size for baking. Let the mixture freeze solid, slip the egg ice cubes into a freezer bag, and keep in the freezer for up to six months. Thaw in the refrigerator before using.

- Cooked rice. This is a great idea for grains that take longer to cook, like brown rice. Make up a big pot when you have time. Let it cool thoroughly in the fridge, then divvy up into portions and store in quart- or gallon-size freezer bags or plastic containers. To use, thaw in the microwave or dump directly into a soup, stew, or stir-fry.

- Garlic. It's hard to go wrong here. You can freeze whole, unpeeled bulbs, individual cloves either peeled or unpeeled, or cloves that you've peeled and chopped. Best of all, no thawing is necessary. The only tricky part is keeping any garlicky odor from taking over your freezer. If this is a problem, try double or triple bagging your cloves.

Look for the Food and Drug Administration's handy refrigerator and freezer guide for more food items at *www.fda.gov/media/74435/download*.

Dodge storage slip-ups that spoil your savings (and your health)

Imagine you gather all the food in your kitchen into one big pile. Now divvy up one-fourth, cram it into trash bags, and throw it out. Just dump it straight into the garbage. This horrifying scenario is happening in most American households, according to the Natural Resources Defense Council (NRDC), an international nonprofit environmental organization.

You may not pile and sort, but you're probably tossing. The average family of four throws away an estimated $1,500 in food every year — mostly fresh fruits and vegetables, dairy products, meat, fish, and poultry. Why? Because it's spoiled or you think it might be.

Avoiding waste doesn't mean compromising food safety.
Foodborne illness, also known as food poisoning, will hit 1 in 6 people this year. The symptoms are devastating, often resulting in hospitalizations or even death. A variety of bacteria, viruses, and parasites cause most foodborne diseases.

Besides purchasing safe food and preparing it properly, you control your home's food safety in two ways.

- Know how long you should keep food. The USDA's Food Safety and Inspection Service suggests you follow sell-by and use-by dates at least on dairy and meat products.

- Learn how best to store food for best flavor and longest shelf life. Keep 'em covered. Store leftovers, meats, fish, and poultry in covered containers or sealed storage bags. Check daily for spoilage.

Whether it's a package of deli meat or a container of Friday night's chili, where, how, and for how long you keep food in your refrigerator could determine whether or not you get up close and personal with *Salmonella* or *E.coli*, two of the most common foodborne bacteria.

You may be surprised to learn that a food "gone bad" doesn't always sport furry growth, a funky odor, or even a nasty taste.

Three free smartphone apps — health and savings at your fingertips. Let these phone apps help you lower your risk of food poisoning, find out when it's time to toss that leftover, learn how to keep foods fresh, get tips on safe food handling and preparation, and reduce waste.

- USDA FoodKeeper (available for iOS and Android)

- Is My Food Safe? (available for iOS)

- Ask Karen from USDA (available for iOS and Android)

Dine out in style without breaking the bank

Wine and dine for pennies on the dollar

Five-star dining comes with a host of rules — wear nice attire, know where to place your napkin, don't use your fork like a scoop. Fortunately, a high price tag is not required. You can find gourmet food for a fraction of the cost if you know where to look.

Slice your bill by 82%. A three-course meal in an upscale restaurant could easily cost $100 or more per person, but you can get a taste of savory deals by visiting your nearest culinary institute.

Restaurants run by culinary schools are often open to the public with menus ranging from prix fixe (fixed price) and a la carte (priced separately) to buffets. The chefs are mostly students, which carves a big hunk out of your bill. The Oregon Culinary Institute, for example, offers a three-course meal at lunch for $9. You can also get a four-course dinner for $18 — about 82% less per person than at a fancy restaurant.

Get served specialties by a chef-in-training. The service is supposed to mimic that of high-end restaurants. "Our son has a culinary degree from the Art Institute, and we attended their restaurant one night," says Nancy Hills. "The students switch off cooking and serving so they get the 'front of the house' experience as well. It was fun."

Also, ask about their tipping policies. Not all school restaurants accept tips, and many of those that do put the tips toward their scholarship programs. You get a great deal on food and help someone's career — everybody wins.

7 savory tips help you eat out for less

Dining out can cost three to five times more than eating at home. But sometimes you crave a good meal you don't have to make yourself. If you're looking for ways to save when you eat out, try these seven strategies to score the biggest discount.

- Catch the early bird specials by eating during lunch hours, which are generally before 3 p.m.

- Split a meal with someone, or take half of yours home for later.

- Skip the overpriced drinks and order water.

- Join the restaurant's loyalty program for discounts and free offers.

- Instead of indulging in dessert at the restaurant, make your own. Or pick one up at the grocery store bakery on the way home.

- Look for coupons in mailers and newspapers, online, and on the backs of receipts.

- Support local fundraisers by buying discount cards or entertainment books, which often feature restaurant deals.

Food trucks: Discover a world of budget-friendly food on wheels

County fairs aren't the only places you'll stumble upon scrumptious meals on wheels. Today, you can find specialty food trucks downtown in most major cities with prices starting at $5 to $10 a meal.

Some towns even boast food truck parks that serve as destination points for both the curious and the hungry. Never thought mobile menus would be up your alley? You might be surprised by some of the benefits of sampling food truck fare.

- Depending on your town, you may find a huge variety of choices ranging from gluten-free fried oysters to authentic Persian chicken. And for dessert? Get a taste of delicious French crepes. Don't worry. Vendors also serve up classic foods like hamburgers, tacos, and freshly baked cookies.

- Want to know exactly what was in that special sauce? Vendors may not post their ingredients list, but you can usually get to know your "chef" and learn more about the food. That transforms your dining experience into an exciting social outing.

- Sometimes you find foods you can't get anywhere else. Exclusive dishes at a popular price? Yes, please.

- If you're out on a day trip to the city, you can't beat the convenience of dropping by a food truck rather than waiting in slow-moving lines at a sit-down restaurant.

- Dining at a food truck is a savory, urban experience. Owners tend to experiment with new dishes, which adds to the adventure. Top that off with the sights, smells, and sounds of the city, and your low-cost meal takes on even more value.

> Worried about the safety of food trucks? Some towns regulate them more strictly than others, but all trucks are required to be licensed and inspected by health officials as any restaurant would be. Ask to see their inspection documents if you're concerned.

To find a list of food trucks that serve your area, go online to websites like *yelp.com*, *thumbtack.com*, and *roaminghunger.com* and search with your ZIP code. You'll also find them at festivals and corporate events.

Not ready to drive downtown for the culinary experience? With more than 200 vendors registered in some major cities, you may find a food truck that will come to you and cater your next special event at $8 to $30 a guest.

Think twice before you buy that restaurant voucher

You can spend hours online sifting through deals for restaurants only to buy a voucher that could later be turned down. Consider this advice before spending your hard-earned money.

Don't trust every coupon. Watch for limitations. Location details, expirations, and other restrictions usually appear in the fine print.

Verify the vendor. Does the seller meet the standards set by the Better Business Bureau (BBB)? Some vendors like LivingSocial or Groupon are accredited by the BBB. Go online to *bbb.org* to read reviews as well as warnings about companies that have a lot of complaints.

Call the restaurant if you're in doubt. Frustrated customers often complain online when a voucher is rejected or the conditions change. It was too late for them to avoid the aggravation. But you can call ahead to see if the restaurant will honor your voucher.

CAUTION

Net more merriment for your money with dinner theater

Does this sound familiar? You need a fun evening out, but you can't decide where to go. And you're not ready to drop your life savings on a meal, either.

Here's the good news. You can splurge a little once in a while as part of your budgeting strategy. One of the most reasonable treats you can give yourself for the entertainment value is a trip to the local dinner theater.

Get lots of bang for your buck. Really. Sound effects, clever staging, engaging acting — you get it all in one place. You can find professional dinner theaters in most cities with costs ranging from about $12 to $75. The show often comes with a full three-course meal and a two- to three-hour live performance. And some shows are interactive.

Look for discounts when you purchase your tickets. Some theaters offer special pricing for seniors, military personnel, and children. You might also attend a show at an off-peak time when rates are lower.

The action comes to you at a dinner theater. Whether you're looking for a good mystery, a dramatic one-act monologue, or a full-blown thriller, there's a dinner theater production out there for you.

- Smaller theaters furnish more intimate experiences. You're generally near the stage and the action no matter what ticket you buy. These shows may be the most affordable, especially if you go to a weeknight preview. Some are as low as $12 for the show and $7 for food.

- Larger venues usually aim to dazzle. In some murder mysteries, for example, the staged crime unfolds in real time, and anyone can end up being part of the show. You might even win a prize if you can guess who the killer is.

- Some medieval-themed shows feature specially trained animals, spectacular lighting, and sophisticated props. You'll pay up to $75 for some of these more elaborate experiences. Other themed shows encourage you to wear costumes or accessories, get photographs made, and interact with the cast. The memories you make will last a lifetime.

Your road map to owning a car for less

Insurance essentials: Steer your
way to cheaper rates 304

'Auto'-matic savings: Put the brakes
on costly care and repair 310

Buy, sell, or lease: Rev up the savings
on your next car deal 317

Insurance essentials: Steer your way to cheaper rates

Don't overpay: Smart ways to get car insurance for less

Think it's impossible to slash your car insurance costs by as much as 50%? Think again. A little fancy footwork on your part can make a big difference in how much you pay.

For example, did you know that plugging in a monitoring device that allows your insurance company to track your driving habits could cut your premiums in half? The same goes for safe drivers who keep their mileage to a bare minimum.

> Belong to a credit union? If so, you might be able to lower your auto insurance premiums. Many credit unions partner with companies like TruStage and MetLife to offer reduced rates. It's still best, though, to compare quotes from several insurance companies before buying a policy — even if you qualify for the credit union discount.

Of course, insurers look at lots of factors before quoting you a price — your age, driving record, and your car's make and model, for starters. They even pore over your personal life, taking into account your marital status, credit history, and occupation. That's why it's always a good idea to shop around for new quotes whenever you have a major life change.

But you don't have to wait until then to lower your payments. Increasing your deductible from $200 to $500 could reduce your premiums by as much as 30%. Or you could hold off on buying a brand new vehicle — insurance rates are generally lower on older, smaller cars. You'll also pay less if you drop nonessential coverage and get by with fewer cars in the family.

So how else can you put a dent in your insurance rate? It's worth asking if any of the following discounts can be applied to your policy.

Up to 10%	Up to 15%	Up to 20%	Up to 25%
• defensive driving course • federal employee, active or retired • auto-payment plan • payment in full	• military — active, retired, National Guard, Reserves	• bundling with other insurance coverage	• coverage of multiple cars • affiliate group membership • emergency deployment • accident-free record

Carry the right coverage to keep your costs down

The days of hopping on your bicycle to deliver papers for extra cash may be gone, but nothing is stopping you from earning extra income by transporting people and packages in your car. That is, unless you don't have the proper auto insurance. Without it, you could find yourself facing a thick stack of bills after an accident.

So what kind of coverage will keep you on the right side of the law — whether you have a side job or not? It depends.

Personal policies typically aren't enough. It turns out commercial car insurance isn't just for businesses anymore. Independent contractors who use their own cars for on-demand delivery services are often required to get this coverage as well.

Some companies, however, provide "Hired and Non-owned" coverage that makes the delivery company liable for damages during work hours. Driving for a company like Uber or Lyft? You might consider purchasing Rideshare coverage for when you're "on the job" but don't have passengers with you.

At least carry the minimum. Every driver — working or not — needs their state's minimum, mandated coverage. For many, this includes liability, underinsured, and uninsured motorist coverage. But it's generally a bad idea to purchase just minimum protection. While insurance can be pricey, falling short can mean insufficient coverage after a major accident.

Live in California, Hawaii, or New Jersey? You're lucky. They're the only states that provide insurance for low-income residents. If you think you might be eligible, ask your state insurance commission about program requirements.

Extra, extra — think about more coverage. The most common types of supplemental auto insurance provide for damages to your car, medical payments for injuries, roadside assistance, and reimbursement if your vehicle is totaled. If you financed a new car, your lender may require you to carry one or all of these extras. Some states require additional coverage, too.

Is optional coverage worth it? Sometimes. If you have a new or expensive vehicle, you'd probably want to spring for guaranteed auto protection to recover the cash value of your car in case of a total loss. On the other hand, you might be better off saving your money for a new car if your vehicle is old or in need of lots of expensive repairs.

Insurance scams are no accident — stay alert to protect your wallet

Auto insurance companies lose billions of dollars annually to crooks filing false claims. But they're not the only victims. Those same scams can cost law-abiding drivers hundreds of dollars extra in premiums each year. Even worse, they put the lives of innocent motorists at risk. But you can sidestep the following shameful swindles if you know what to look for.

Avoid policies that look too good to be true. They're called ghost brokers — con artists who pose as insurance agents and sell fake policies to unsuspecting drivers. You may not even know you've been a victim until you file a claim and learn that you're liable for damages.

The double-dealing has gotten so bad that the Arkansas Insurance Department is warning consumers about con artists peddling fake policies at dealerships. How do the crooks do it? They lure prospective car buyers by offering to help them purchase inexpensive coverage online.

Consider taking these steps before purchasing a policy.

- Contact your state insurance commission to find out if the business is legitimate.

- Compare quotes and be wary of someone offering premiums at a large discount. Don't allow yourself to be pressured by an aggressive agent.

Another sign of fraud? You don't receive your insurance card or a copy of your policy in a timely manner.

Stay alert for the swoop and stop. It happened to Elizabeth Rogers just after she passed through an intersection. A driver whipped around her car from behind, pulled in front of her, and promptly came to a full stop. Rogers slammed on her brakes, but not in time to avoid rear-ending the offending driver.

Fortunately, something unusual happened next. Witnesses took photos of the scene, shared them with Rogers, and described what they saw to a police officer.

"These witness testimonies were crucial, because on the surface, the accident looked like my fault," Rogers says. "The officer was convinced by the testimonies

> No matter how small the accident, always gather information at the scene. You'll need photos of both vehicles and their passengers, the other driver's license number, and his contact information. Also file a police report. It will make your case a lot stronger if you decide to submit an insurance claim.

to check the video surveillance of the intersection, where he saw what really happened."

Under other circumstances, Rogers would have gotten a ticket, her insurance company would have picked up the tab for damages, and her premiums would have risen. Instead, both insurance companies came to a resolution.

Lesson learned? Document everything, Rogers says, including the names of witnesses and their contact information. Otherwise the fraudster might have gotten away with his crime — he had already pulled the scam several times before.

Pricey car tech won't lower premiums

Your granddaughter's new ride seems to have more bells and whistles than the International Space Station. So you might be surprised to learn that the car's cutting-edge safety features and anti-theft technology translate into little, if any, savings on her auto insurance. In fact, they could even drive her insurance premiums up. After all, automobiles featuring fancy computers and sensors are more expensive to repair.

While added features may keep you mobile and independent, be aware none of the following safety equipment yields insurance savings.

- parking assist
- heads-up display
- rearview camera
- night vision system
- lane departure warning
- blind spot monitor
- driver alertness monitor
- collision preparation system

Some anti-theft technology will lower your premiums — but not by much. Tracking and disabling devices and audible alarms could each save you $10 or less annually.

CAUTION

Crash course: Special claim may recoup lost value

You've been in a fender-bender with the Kia Sportage you just bought for $16,500. Although your mechanic fixed the damage perfectly, you learn your car is now worth $13,500 — nearly 20% less than what you paid.

What happened? It's called diminished value — the perceived difference between your car's value before and after an accident. And it makes no difference if your vehicle looks as good as new and runs better than ever. In the eyes of a potential buyer or dealership, an automobile's value drops significantly once it's been in a wreck.

Fortunately, a diminished value claim can close the gap between these two values with cold hard cash. Rules vary by state, so find out what your insurance company might offer if you were at fault. If a third party caused the mishap, you can file a claim with his insurer. And if the other driver doesn't have insurance? Check with your insurance company to see if it will cover the claim under your policy's uninsured motorist coverage.

Consider these points before proceeding.

- Diminished value claims for expensive or new vehicles are generally worth fighting over. But if your car has excessive mileage, minimal damage, or wasn't worth much before the accident, the decrease in value may be too small to file a claim.

- If you decide to continue, get your car's pre-accident value from *kbb.com* or *edmunds.com*. Then get the trade-in price, preferably from a dealer who can say the lower value is due to the accident.

Problems with processing your claim or receiving compensation? Ask your state insurance commission for help.

'Auto'-matic savings: Put the brakes on costly care and repair

11 mistakes that pump up your gas bill — and how to fix them

Want to squeeze every last mile out of that dollar you spent on gasoline? Cassi Williams, owner of Kelly's Automotive Repair, advises you to keep up with general maintenance. You can also head off these potential problems before you get to the pump.

Driving over 50 mph. You'll shell out about 19 cents more per gallon for every 5 mph over 50. Maintain the speed limit and save.

Starting and stopping suddenly. Going steady isn't just for relationships — smoother starts and stops can save you 83 cents to $1.11 per gallon.

Carrying 100 pounds more weight. You'll spend about 3 cents more per gallon, so leave the extra baggage at home if you don't need it.

Adding rooftop carriers. You can save up to 47 cents a gallon by taking the empty cargo unit off your roof when you get back from vacation.

Paying for premium gas. See if the owners manual tells you to use premium gas. If not, don't spend the extra $100 a year on it.

Blasting your air conditioner. If you have to use your AC, choose the economy or recirculation setting for less drag on your gas mileage.

Using "gas-saving" products. The Environmental Protection Agency found that over 100 of these commercially available products do not produce any savings — and can possibly hurt your engine. Skip the $9 additives to save on every tank of gas.

Driving deflated. Keep your tires properly inflated and hold on to the extra 8 cents a gallon that's been leaking out.

Idling too long. You're spending 3 cents a minute to keep that engine purring in the parking lot. Shut it off and roll down the windows if you need to sit a spell.

Keeping it in low gear. Shift your car into overdrive out on the highway to improve fuel economy.

Not controlling your cruising. Use your cruise control setting since it's designed to help you save on gas mileage.

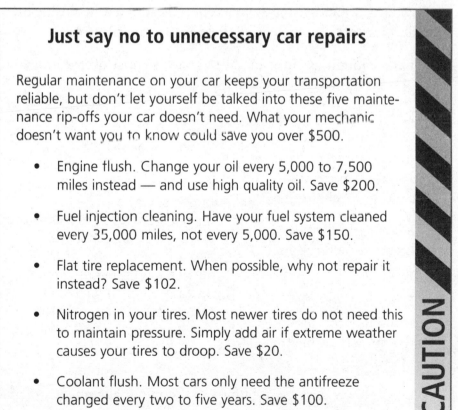

Just say no to unnecessary car repairs

Regular maintenance on your car keeps your transportation reliable, but don't let yourself be talked into these five maintenance rip-offs your car doesn't need. What your mechanic doesn't want you to know could save you over $500.

- Engine flush. Change your oil every 5,000 to 7,500 miles instead — and use high quality oil. Save $200.

- Fuel injection cleaning. Have your fuel system cleaned every 35,000 miles, not every 5,000. Save $150.

- Flat tire replacement. When possible, why not repair it instead? Save $102.

- Nitrogen in your tires. Most newer tires do not need this to maintain pressure. Simply add air if extreme weather causes your tires to droop. Save $20.

- Coolant flush. Most cars only need the antifreeze changed every two to five years. Save $100.

CAUTION

Secret to driving your car 200,000+ miles

Wouldn't it be grand to drive your car to a mechanical Fountain of Youth? Good news — you don't need to. The simple secret that will keep most cars on the road for 200,000 miles or more is to adopt good maintenance and driving habits.

Keep your car serviced regularly. When you follow the maintenance schedule in your owners manual, you'll find that fewer problems develop over time. Listen to your car. If you hear a suspicious knocking sound or see an unfamiliar light come on, get the problem checked out by a trusted mechanic.

Adopt good driving habits. You can help your car survive the long haul by making these simple changes.

- Maintain good visibility by keeping headlights, windshields, and mirrors clean. Replace them if they are broken.

- Keep enough gas in your car to guard against overheating and prevent damage to your fuel system.

- Rest your hand on the wheel, not the gear shift, to prevent wear and tear on the gear shifting mechanism.

- Leave extra cargo at home to preserve your suspension.

- Drive consistently without speeding up too quickly or braking too hard.

> Avoid potholes like the plague. These menaces cause $3 billion in damages every year. That breaks down to an average repair cost of $306 to fix things like steering, suspension, tires, and alignment. How do you know if a pothole has wrecked your ride? Watch for loss of control, pulling, or tire bulges, and get it checked out quickly.

- Drive slowly over speed bumps to keep your alignment straight.

Helping hands get you back on the road for less

Trying to stretch that paycheck to cover car repairs can sometimes be a challenge. But without transportation life becomes very difficult. Thankfully, organizations across the country offer a helping hand with car maintenance and repair to keep people moving.

Car repair ministries — real blessings for your wheels. Some church and nonprofit ministries offer routine help like oil changes, battery checks, tire rotation, or even diagnosis and repair for larger problems as part of their outreach to the community.

One Atlanta-area ministry provides such services. "We just ask them to bring the car

> Don't live near an organization offering maintenance assistance? You can apply for a grant to help with your repair costs at *ModestNeeds.org*. If approved, this nonprofit will raise funds through its community of donors. Or start your own fundraiser online for free with a GoFundMe page.

and let us evaluate it first and see what the car's needs are," says Ellen Mallorey, a volunteer in the ministry. "And then we do ask them, as they are able, to help us pay for parts. Sometimes they do and sometimes they don't, but we've never turned anybody away because they couldn't pay for their parts."

Some ministries — like St. Vincent de Paul and Catholic Charities — have locations nationally that may provide assistance with repairs and transportation. Other options will depend on your community, so ask around at local churches or your community action agency. You can also search online using the terms "car repair ministry near me" or "local nonprofit repair shops."

Let your car do some teaching. Public high schools and technical colleges that have automotive programs sometimes repair cars for the public for the cost of supplies. Call your local schools and ask if they have a "live work" program for car repair.

DIY auto repair. Maybe you're up for the challenge and satisfaction of fixing your own car? If you're ready to roll your sleeves up and get a little greasy, here are some places you can find help and tools.

- Repair shops like AutoZone, O'Reilly Auto Parts, and Advance Auto Parts have programs that allow you to put down a deposit on loaner tools, then bring them back for a full refund.

- *Cars.com* hosts a wide range of free DIY auto repair videos with step-by-step instructions that include illustrations.

- Rent a fully outfitted service bay by the hour at a DIY auto repair center, and work on the car yourself. In some cases, you can also get assistance with your repairs from a certified mechanic on site. Find a shop by searching "DIY auto repair shops" online.

Battery basics — rev up your savings under the hood

Renee left her new car in long-term parking for a week while she went off to enjoy a family cruise. Unfortunately the fun came to a quick end when she returned and found her car battery dead as a doornail.

"I couldn't believe it," she says. "The car was practically brand new."

"A vehicle that sits for long periods of time will have a higher failure rate due to the depletion of the battery," says Jeff Cox, president of the Automotive Maintenance and Repair Association. "This can also put extra strain on the vehicle's alternator which may cause it to fail prematurely."

Even a new battery can end up spent because the car's passive electronic systems — things like antitheft monitoring and GPS systems — drain it. That's why you may save your charge by disconnecting the negative battery terminal when you leave your car parked for an extended period. Here are some other smart moves to drive down battery costs.

Drop routines that kill your charge. "Batteries today are maintenance-free, so there is little we can do to extend the life of a battery," says Cox. "But to get the most out of a battery, it is important to start and drive the vehicle on a regular basis."

It's also a good idea to check your driving habits to make sure you aren't prematurely draining your battery. For example, don't leave your lights on when you get out of the car. You might also try to combine your short trips into a longer trip so your battery has a chance to fully charge.

Choose replacements wisely. "Battery life is determined by many different factors including temperature, number of drive cycles, and type of battery," says Cox.

If you buy the correct type of battery for the weather in your region, you should expect to get at least three to six years out of it. Price and brand don't necessarily equal the best quality. You can find good batteries priced from $50 to $240.

"If a consumer plans to keep a vehicle for a longer period of time, I would suggest buying a five-year or seven-year warranty," Cox says. "I would also suggest they purchase the correct type of battery based on the climate they live in and the vehicle." Quality batteries often come with a free replacement warranty of at least three years.

When you buy a new battery, you may have to pay a "core charge," which is essentially a deposit fee ranging from $5 to $20.

> Control pesky car battery corrosion and extend your battery's life. If your battery has no cracks, disconnect the cables according to the instructions in the owners manual. Mix a tablespoon of baking soda with a cup of hot water. Dip a toothbrush in the mix and scrub the corrosion away.

But you'll get a refund down the road if you return the old battery with your receipt.

RV upkeep: Steer clear of costly repairs down the road

Recreational vehicles (RVs) save families as much as 64% on vacation travel costs, according to a recent study. No wonder the RV Industry Association anticipates that 79 million Americans age 55 to 74 will own one by 2025.

An initial investment in an RV may seem pricey. But if you are careful to do regular, preventive maintenance to keep it in tiptop shape, you'll see your cost savings add up with every new journey you take.

Here are some examples of how you can take good care of your RV to prevent big-ticket repairs over the long haul.

Prevention plan	Cost	Benefit	Major repair avoided
Wash and wax	$20	doing this every six months may prevent the need to repaint	$12,000 to $30,000 to repaint a 26-foot RV
Tire pressure monitor	$320	helps you keep tires properly inflated to improve gas mileage and prevent early wear	$214 per new tire
Power surge protector	$87	guards electronics from voltage changes that could permanently damage equipment	$600 to $3,500 just to fix the refrigerator
Waste water treatment	$9	regular treatment breaks down sludge and clogs	$400 to $3,400 to fix waste system
Slide-out topper	$345	protects slide-out rooms from weather damage	$500 to $1,700 to repair slide out

Buy, sell, or lease: Rev up the savings on your next car deal

Electric cars get your motor running for less

In the market for a new car? Don't count out electric and hybrid vehicles. You may think they're for the well-to-do crowd, but these alternative fuel rides may be good for your wallet.

After tax credits, many alternative fuel cars cost about $30,000, or the price of a typical sedan. And they are easy to charge overnight at home from a regular outlet. Plus some public places allow you to charge your vehicle for free. With the cost of a 100-mile charge around $3.90, you can save about 64% of the money you spend on gas by driving an electric car.

The table below is an example of Honda's recent new line of sedans. You can see a big difference in fuel costs for hybrid and electric cars compared to gas-powered cars. If fuel economy is important to you, these types of vehicles may be a cost-effective choice.

Type	Price	MPG (city/hwy) or equivalent	Annual fuel cost
Conventional gasoline-powered sedan	$24,300	28/38	$1,600
Hybrid, powered by gas and electricity	$25,320	48/48	$850
Plug-in hybrid, offers extended electric range capability	$33,400	44/40	$700
Electric, uses energy stored in rechargeable batteries	lease $199 month	126/103	$600

Each year, the Department of Energy releases an annual report on fuel economy for new cars in the U.S. market. This report can help you make a better decision about the best car for your budget. Check it out at *fueleconomy.gov*.

Surefire way to never buy a lemon again

Before you spend your money on a car, wouldn't you like to find out what other buyers thought about it? Between websites and social media, you have all the tools you need to get the best car for you and save money.

Start with free professional reviews to narrow your car choices. Edmunds, NADA Guides, and Kelley Blue Book are all trusted sources for straight talk on prices, safety features, and more.

When you're ready to look for the right dealer or seller, you'll find helpful feedback at *autotrader.com* and *dealerrater.com*.

Finally, check out the opinions of influencers on social media who share their experiences with the cars you're considering. Search for your car in videos and posts on Facebook, Twitter, Instagram, and YouTube.

Better negotiations — get your new ride on your terms

If you've always loved the thrill of haggling with a salesperson at the car dealership, you probably have negotiating down to a T. But if the thought of spending hours trapped in a car dealership fills you with dread, don't despair. You have other options.

Buy online to avoid haggling. Did you know you can buy a car out of a vending machine? At *carvana.com*, you can choose your next ride online by looking through pictures, reading the car's history report, and arranging for financing. Have it shipped to you — often for a fee — or pick it up yourself at the nearest car vending machine. Fast-talking salesmen not included.

Other sites are in on this action, too. *Vroom.com* and *nowcar.com* offer virtual car shopping and buying experiences. Or shop on *carmax.com* to get a vehicle delivered to your door for a test drive, and complete the sale in your driveway.

Let's make a deal — with help from the pros. Striking a deal is hard work, but for a fee, businesses like CarBargains call around and get competing quotes for you.

Or do the grunt work yourself before you get to the dealership. With resources like the "Accelerate my Deal" tool at *autotrader.com*, you can submit an offer, apply for financing, and schedule a test drive from your computer.

When you want someone else to get the job done for you, send in experts like Authority Auto, whose professionals close the deal for a percentage of the discount they negotiate.

Be prepared when you negotiate it yourself. Going it alone? Get your facts straight before you visit the dealership. Know the fair value of the car and any trade-in you have. Research dealer incentives and expect fees and taxes. Be ready to walk out at any moment if you're not satisfied.

Dealers have an internet department, so try negotiating with them before going to the dealership in person. Or skip the dealership entirely and negotiate with other car owners. You can find used cars for sale online at *ebay.com*, *craigslist.org*, and *facebook.com/ marketplace*.

> Buying a car online and having it shipped to your door may be really convenient. Most companies even offer a five- to seven-day return policy. But as you prepare for payment, don't forget to factor in extra fees and taxes for your state.

Prevent costly collisions with a safer car

Accidents are expensive. Reduce the chance of having one by driving a car that fits your needs. An added benefit? It will keep you in the driver's seat longer and help you maintain your independence.

Upgrade your current car affordably. Getting in and out of your ride and operating the car safely become more difficult as you age, but assistive technology can help.

- Bar handles that insert into the door frame run $12 to $45 and help you brace yourself while lifting up out of the car.

- For $10 to $30, you can get an adjustable strap handle that buckles around your window frame and gives you added support as you get out of your car.

- A swivel seat gives you broader range of motion to turn in your seat and comes with a price tag between $20 and $40.

Learn about other gadgets that will increase your visibility, mobility, or control in your car by attending a free CarFit program where trained technicians evaluate your needs. Visit *car-fit.org* and click "Find an Event" to locate a program near you. Or contact an occupational therapist who specializes in driving rehabilitation.

Buy a newer car for improved design and safety features. Today many newer cars sport standardized features like rearview cameras and lane assist monitoring to keep the car inside the lines. Plus you can upgrade to get features like touch ignition and automated parking to work you into those tight spaces at the mall. Other aids like driving hand controls and specialized gas pedals can be installed.

Car designers are also making adaptive technology a priority. Ford Motors engineers, for instance, use a special suit to simulate the physical condition of a 104-year-old person so they can improve the driving experience for seniors. The result? Better doors and handles, automatic braking technology, seat belts that are easier to use, and more.

Plan for the future with a modifiable ride. Want to prepare for the worst? Consider a vehicle you can convert to accommodate a wheelchair. The Honda Odyssey, Jeep Grand Cherokee, and Chevrolet Silverado are popular models. Expect the conversion itself to cost $10,000 to $30,000.

Look for programs to help with the cost. Ford, Volvo, Toyota, GM, Chrysler, and Hyundai have mobility programs that offer up to $1,000 reimbursement toward adaptive equipment in new vehicles.

Secret to getting the best possible deal on a car

"Do your homework, research prices, and read reviews so that you will be well informed when sitting across the desk from the salesperson," advises Greg Faison, sales manager of Toyota of Newnan. But that's not all you need to do to score a sweet deal. To get the best car for you at the best price, follow this advice.

Prearrange your payments. Walk in with a down payment and preapproved financing in hand, and you'll be in a negotiating position that's hard to beat. Dealerships often offer financing options with marked up interest rates to build in profit for themselves. But finance with a lender of your choice and you'll know exactly what interest rates and conditions are available.

A good rule of thumb when loan shopping is 20/4/10. Make at least a 20% down payment. Only finance for up to four years. Cap your total monthly

> A new vehicle can depreciate by $6,000 to $7,000 after the first year, and lose an additional $1,500 to $2,000 the second year. Buy a car that's at least two years old, say money experts, and let the first owner take the depreciation hit. You'll save thousands in the long run.

car expenses — including principal, interest, and insurance — at 10% of your gross income.

Drive home with no car payment. When you pay in cash, you are in the best position to get the price you want. And you won't be troubled by interest charges over the life of a loan. Calculate how much you can set aside monthly to save up for the car you want. Then plan ahead and put a date on the calendar to pay in full for your car.

Choosing a used car gets you to your goal faster. For example, the 2019 Toyota Prius hybrid retails for $25,012, costs about $900 a year in gas, and has a consumer review rating of 4.8 out of 5.

An older 2014 model sells for $11,250, costs about $1,050 a year in gas, and has the same rating. Buying the used sedan cuts the cost by $13,762, but not the reliability or performance of the car.

3 reasons seniors should consider leasing a car

How can you drive a new car without the high monthly costs that come with financing and buying a vehicle? Lease it.

This option comes with lots of benefits for seniors. Check them out and learn how leasing could plump up your piggy bank.

All the perks but none of the pain of ownership. "All leasces will get more bang for the buck," says Greg Faison, sales manager of Toyota of Newnan.

"In my experience, seniors and retirees see the added bonus of being able to afford a newer car, for a lower monthly payment, that has all of the newest safety features." Plus basic maintenance, like oil changes and tire rotation, is often complimentary.

No commitment — love it or let it go. If you decide you want to buy the car when the lease is up, you simply arrange your financing and pay the price written into your contract. This amount is called the residual value.

Maybe you didn't love the car. When the lease is up, make an appointment at the dealership for an inspection. You can trade the car in and enter a new lease.

Or pay the disposition fee, a flat rate that covers cleaning and minor repairs, and walk away. You may have to pay additional fees if the car shows excessive wear and tear or if it's over the contracted mileage.

Dodge the climbing costs of an aging car. "Most leases will be up by the time any major repairs will be needed," says Faison. This means you come out ahead by leasing another new vehicle and keeping your monthly expenses low. "A safe, reliable car with complimentary oil changes will cost the customer less in the long run," he says.

The bottom line? Before you make your decision, weigh the pros and cons. For example, leasing often comes with a lower monthly payment compared to a loan. But those payments will continue as long as you keep leasing — they won't go toward paying off the car.

Selling your car? Be smart — and safe — to get the best deal

You've done everything right getting your used car ready to sell. You pulled together the car's history and got a written statement from your mechanic that says it's been taken care of. You priced it fairly using the NADA retail value, and you advertised it widely. Now that the calls are coming in, you want to take steps to keep the business arrangement safe, fair, and legal for you and the buyer.

Think safety first. Screen callers and field questions on the phone before showing them the car. You might consider creating an email address specifically for selling your car. Don't meet up with suspicious people.

"Always use safe practices when meeting potential buyers. Meet in well lit, populated areas — even the parking lot of the local police station," advises Greg Faison, sales manager of Toyota of Newnan.

When you allow a test drive, always ride along. Take a friend, if possible. If the potential buyer wants to have the car inspected, ride with them or drive to the mechanic's shop and meet them there.

Close the deal. When the time comes to accept payment, arrange to meet the buyer at the bank, if possible, and bring the bill of sale and release of liability form. You can get the paperwork notarized right there, and the banker can also verify whether you are receiving a legitimate check or cash payment.

Be sure to transfer the title to the new owner by signing it over and documenting the odometer reading.

Wrap up loose ends. The release of liability form makes sure you're not held responsible for anything that happens to the vehicle after the sale. For added protection, some states also suggest you notify the tax assessor's office of the title transfer.

Don't forget to cancel your insurance policy on the car once you know it is no longer in your name. Save your records when the deal has concluded.

Money-saving tricks to master technology

Hang up on high cellphone bills . .326

Cutting-edge gadgets at rock-bottom prices 333

Hang up on high cellphone bills

4 ways to save big on your cellphone plan

You love your cellphone, but you don't love the monthly bill. You can find lots of ways to lower it if you know the tricks. In fact, you may even be able to cut it in half. Here are some ways to trim your total expenses.

Find a plan to match the services you use. Here's one simple solution your service provider won't suggest. Check your bill to see how many phone minutes, text messages, and megabytes of data you typically use. Compare this information against the plans your provider offers to see if a cheaper plan will work for you. You can also use this information to comparison shop for a cheaper plan from another provider.

> Cellphone providers often update their plans without letting current customers know a cheaper option is available. Check your provider's plan offerings regularly to see if a new option would save you money.

For example, if you send lots of text messages and use lots of data, look for an unlimited plan for seniors. You'll have no restrictions on calls, text messages, or data for a much lower cost than someone who's not on the senior plan. Expect to pay about $35 to $50 per line.

What if you don't use your cellphone much? Look for a prepaid option where you pay a small fee for limited services.

T-Mobile, for example, offers a pay-as-you-go plan that includes calls and text messages, and starts at only $3 per month. Android users can get unlimited calls and text messages from Republic

Wireless for $15 and pay an additional $5 per gigabyte for data. Just be careful about exceeding the limits of your plan because the charges can add up quickly.

Check for extra discounts. If you're a senior, veteran, or member of an organization like AARP or AAA, you may qualify for extra discounts. Be sure to check whether your provider offers these discounts, and ask about your eligibility.

Use a wireless network when it's available. When you use Wi-Fi, you don't dip into the allotted data from your data plan. This saves those bytes for the times you need them most, and will help you avoid extra charges for going over your limit. Look for the Wi-Fi icon in the status bar at the top of your phone to make sure you're connected to Wi-Fi.

Buy an older-model or refurbished phone. Service providers often promote new phones with high-end features that require expensive data plans. And if you finance it, that's an extra $20 or more on your monthly cellphone bill. But if you just need a phone for necessities — such as calling family — an older-model or refurbished phone may have all the features you need.

An older-model phone is simply one that's been discontinued because the manufacturer has released a newer model. A refurbished phone is a used phone that's been wiped of old data and serviced so all the features work. Purchasing an older-model or refurbished phone can save you hundreds of dollars.

Dial down the cost of unlimited data

How much data do you really need on your monthly cellular plan? To hear the big four wireless companies tell it, the answer is simple. Go unlimited. After all, you live in an age where you can stay glued to your smartphone screen nearly every minute for news, email, social media, video streaming, and all the other trappings of the modern digital world.

According to Pew Research, 73% of adults ages 50 to 64 now own a smartphone, and nearly 50% of those age 65 and older have adopted them as well. But many still prefer classic comforts like a good old-fashioned telephone call over texting or Facebook, or watching news and movies on a big-screen television rather than squinting at a smartphone display.

If you count yourself among these old-school, penny-wise baby boomers, you'll likely agree — spending $75 or more on an unlimited data plan every month just doesn't make good sense.

Avoid the limits of unlimited. Here's what the big four don't want you to know. In 2018, the average smartphone user consumed about 4.1 gigabytes (GB) of cellular data each month. That means many used far less.

In addition, some carriers promising "unlimited data" actually limit your high-speed data to just a couple of GB per month. Once you use up that allotment, you'll have unlimited access, but at much slower speeds. This makes it more difficult to load pages quickly or to stream video, even though you're paying a premium for unlimited access.

Factor in the rapidly growing availability of Wi-Fi, which lets you access a wireless internet connection without consuming any data from your cellular plan, and it becomes clear for many users, unlimited plans are far more enticing than they are practical.

Flexible plans keep up with your lifestyle. While wireless companies keep coming up with creative new ways to encourage you to go unlimited, you can find real deals that provide what you actually need.

For instance, take a look at Consumer Cellular. This 100% U.S.-based provider offers no-contract cellphone plans including data plans that range from 250 megabytes (MB) to 20GB of data per month. Best of all, since your data needs can fluctuate from one month to the next, Consumer Cellular lets you change your data plan anytime you need to without paying any additional fees.

Unlimited anything sounds nice, but in reality, no one wants to buy more of something than they'll ever use — or pay more than they should. But that's exactly what most people with unlimited cellular data plans are doing.

Cellular competition is fierce, so make sure you're getting what's best for the way you really use your data. Check your current bill to find out how much you're actually using, then shop around. One size never fits all, so with a bit of smart research, you'll find all the data you really need, and for less. (BPT)

Buy used for today's tech at yesterday's prices

New phones are expensive. The latest, greatest gadgets can cost well over $1,000 if you buy them new. But why spend all that money when you can get the same tech for a fraction of the price? Websites like *gazelle.com*, *ebay.com*, and *amazon.com* sell gently used phones for a big discount.

Before you buy, get the serial number from the seller. You need to check with your carrier to make sure the phone will work with your cell network. And they will confirm that the device hasn't been flagged as stolen or missing.

5 tricks help you dodge early termination fees

You found "the one," signed on the dotted line, and thus began a long-term commitment to your new cellphone. But then one day you realize you want out of your contract, and don't want to pay the hefty early termination fee (ETF). Luckily, there are some steps you can take.

Read the fine print. Stay up to date with changes made to your agreement. By law, if a carrier changes its terms, consumers must be notified and given 30 days to break their contract.

Plead your case. If you're moving out of the carrier's service area for a noteworthy reason — job transfer, retirement, death of a loved one — you may find a sympathetic ear.

Transfer your contract. Find someone you know — through friends or family — that's interested in taking over your plan. It's usually easy to do and free. Call your provider to find out the process. Some online companies will act as go-betweens if you need help transferring or selling your contract. Check out *trademycellular.com.*

Switch carriers. Certain companies will pay your ETF just to get your business. Offers may vary throughout the year, so call around and ask for current deals.

Tweet or post. Airing a grievance on social media is like running a commercial during the Super Bowl. It's fast, effective, and can reach thousands within seconds. No company wants to look like the bad guy in front of its customers. Use Twitter, Facebook, or any other social media outlet to broadcast your desire to bail, and see if you get a response. Just always be polite and professional.

Protect your phone without spending a bundle

The average price of a new cellphone is an eye-popping $846. Just think what you could do with that money. Make a mortgage payment. Buy groceries. Take a trip to the beach. But if you lose or damage your phone, you just have to shell out the cash to replace it. Don't you? Maybe not — if you have cellphone insurance.

But wait a minute. That's expensive, too. Insurance plans through your carrier could cost anywhere from $7 to $19 a month, with a deductible capping out at close to $300. And sometimes you don't even get a new phone as a replacement, but a refurbished one instead.

To add insult to injury, many plans limit the number of claims you can file in a year.

You do have choices, though, when it comes to safeguarding your precious phone — from the obvious to the unusual.

Invest in some basic protection. Today's phones are a complex wonder of glass and electronics. Given that they travel with you everywhere, odds are yours will one day smack into something and crack the screen.

But a sturdy case and a glass screen shield can insulate and protect all those fragile components. For peace of mind, you could spend anywhere from $8 to $80, depending on features. Money well spent.

Compare before you repair. The charge will depend, of course, on the damage — less than $100 to fix a button or up to $300 to replace a cracked screen. Compare prices locally as well as those from mail-away services. Ask about lowest price guarantees and warranties, then go to independent websites, like *yelp.com*, to read customer reviews.

Check for an extended warranty. Did you buy your phone straight out using a credit card? If so, you may have an automatic extended warranty through the card service.

Add a rider to your homeowners insurance. Contact your insurer about additional coverage for your phone. For example, USAA will protect new phones registered within one year of purchase, and promise a new device within 24 to 48 hours. All for $99.99 a year plus a $199 replacement fee.

Get replacement insurance through your credit card. Some cards offer cellphone replacement insurance if you use that credit card to pay your monthly cellphone bill. If you find a card that does, here are some questions to ask.

- Does the insurance cover missing phones or just those that are stolen or damaged?

- What proof must you provide to get payment on your claim?

- Do you have to pay a deductible?

- How much coverage does your card provide?

If the insurance offered by one of your credit cards sounds worthwhile, start using that card to pay your cellphone bill. If your phone is ever lost, stolen, or badly damaged, that one change could provide a big payoff when you need it most.

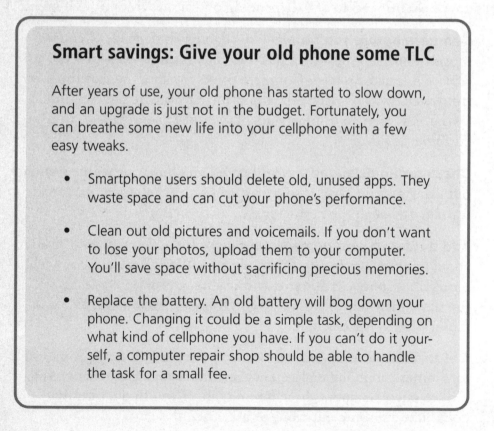

Smart savings: Give your old phone some TLC

After years of use, your old phone has started to slow down, and an upgrade is just not in the budget. Fortunately, you can breathe some new life into your cellphone with a few easy tweaks.

- Smartphone users should delete old, unused apps. They waste space and can cut your phone's performance.

- Clean out old pictures and voicemails. If you don't want to lose your photos, upload them to your computer. You'll save space without sacrificing precious memories.

- Replace the battery. An old battery will bog down your phone. Changing it could be a simple task, depending on what kind of cellphone you have. If you can't do it yourself, a computer repair shop should be able to handle the task for a small fee.

Cutting-edge gadgets at rock-bottom prices

How to pay rock-bottom prices on everything you buy

Never pay full price again. It's easier than you think with these websites and apps that find sale prices near your home for just about anything. You'll save more than you imagine.

Never miss a bargain again. The free Shopular app shows you the sale circulars, special deals, and coupons for any store you select. Add specific items to your Saved Deals list so you won't miss a bargain.

If you don't have time to study the sales circulars, go to Settings for deal alerts, and choose which offers come to you. Select bargains from nearby shopping centers, deals from only your favorite stores, or the hottest specials for the weekend.

Strike instant gold with discounts for your favorite stores. Use *RetailMeNot.com* or the free RetailMeNot app to get cash-back offers, coupons, and other bargains in-store and online.

- Search for promotional codes to get online shopping discounts. If you want a store's best cash-back offers and promotional codes to automatically appear while you shop online, download the Genie browser plug-in for Chrome and Firefox, and sign up for a free *RetailMeNot.com* membership.

- Find deals and thousands of coupons for restaurants and both online and local shops. This includes stores for clothing, electronics, home goods and furniture, office supplies, crafts, home improvement, sporting goods, and oodles more.

- Buy discounted gift cards for your favorite shop, then spend the card's full value. It's an extra discount on top of any sales or coupons you use.

Save as much as 80% no matter where you shop. Visit *Deal Hunting.com* to get great quality as well as low prices. Search for deals by store or by item, or search for discount promotional codes. *DealHunting.com* lists discounts and deals from many familiar retail names ranging from Ace Hardware to Zales. You can even find bargains on travel and eyeglasses.

See all your local sales in one place and rake in more coupons. Want to see the circulars for your favorite supermarkets and retail stores without slogging through the newspaper? Download the free Flipp app or visit *us.flipp.com*.

Tell the app your location and get all the local ads at your fingertips. Visit the app's Coupons tab to choose from dozens of digital coupons you can attach to your store loyalty card.

Find the biggest and best bargains every day. You can't hire hundreds of people to hunt down the best deals of the day, but you can download the free slickdeals app, or visit *slickdeals.net*. On this deal-sharing website, people post the best deals they find and vote on which deals are good enough to get top billing.

> Experts say to buy as much technology as you can afford. Put your money into the components that will give you the most bang for your buck. You can always upgrade and add on software later.

To view the best deals for you, create a free membership, and pick your favorite stores and product categories. Need a particular product? Create a deal alert to save both time and dollars.

Mine this rich source of money-savers. Visit *hip2save.com* or download the free Hip2Save app to catch the latest money-saving deals at your favorite stores, both in-store and online. It also lists restaurants plus entertainment discounts on movies, music, and more. Don't forget to check for freebies and printable coupons.

3 questions to ask before you buy that extended warranty

They put you on the spot every time — sales people and their extended-warranty offers. The what-if's are pretty scary, but do you really need the extra protection? Ask yourself these three questions before handing over more hard-earned cash.

Will it bankrupt you to replace it? If the item is worth less than a couple hundred dollars, a warranty is just not worth it. On the other hand, it might pay to purchase one for high-priced items, including high-end laptops and fancy smartphones, especially if the warranty covers everything from losing the gadget to dropping and breaking it.

Is the warranty from the manufacturer? Manufacturers tend to offer better coverage than retailers and other third parties. Plus, manufacturers have experts on hand who can troubleshoot issues with their own products.

Does your credit card already cover you? Before you swipe, find out what kind of coverage your credit card provides. Many credit card companies extend the manufacturer's warranty for an additional year. This extra coverage may ease your fears and keep you from throwing away cash on a warranty you'll never use.

Hidden gems: 2 little-known ways to save big on Amazon

Did you know Amazon has two essential websites every bargain hunter should be checking? See where Amazon hides jaw-dropping price reductions and huge discounts. You can shop for clearance items from home — no running around.

Prices plummet in Amazon's bargain basement. Discover the backdoor to the Amazon Warehouse where you can find like-new, returned, open-box, or used products discounted up to 70%.

If you shop on your laptop or home computer, find the Amazon Warehouse link hidden near the very bottom of Amazon's main page. On the Amazon app, search for "Amazon Warehouse" in the search box, and then tap the Amazon Warehouse link or ad.

Browsing the Amazon Warehouse is like shopping in a giant flea market or thrift mall. You can browse through items from up to 30 different departments including Arts, Crafts, and Sewing; Garden and Outdoor; Electronics; Clothing, Shoes, and Jewelry; and Home and Kitchen.

The products range from Like New to Acceptable condition, but you can return them under Amazon's usual 30-day return policy. Not every deal is worth having, but browse carefully, and you may find bargains to smile about for years to come.

What smart warehouse shoppers know. When you find a product you want, pay close attention to the item's condition. It is often listed above the "Add to cart" button. The less perfect the product is, the bigger your savings may be. Here is what each condition means.

- Used: Like New. The product is in good working order, but may have damaged packaging.

- Used: Very Good. The product may have small scratches or cosmetic blemishes, show slight signs of use, or have minor accessories missing.

- Used: Good. The product works well but shows some wear and signs of use. It may have minor cosmetic damage or missing instructions, parts, or accessories.

- Used: Acceptable. The product is worn, has signs of use, or may have scratches, dents, or other cosmetic damage. Manuals, parts, or accessories may be missing.

Amazon often gives specific descriptions of any shortfalls a product may have, but you sometimes have to click Details to see that information. Although the items do not come with a warranty,

Amazon claims to inspect and test each product before it goes on sale in the Amazon Warehouse.

Keep in mind that Amazon Warehouse items may not be available for long and their prices may fluctuate.

> Always ask about restocking fees on returns before purchasing — whether in a store or online.

Find the screaming discounts Amazon keeps under wraps. If you can't find the right deal at Amazon Warehouse, try the Amazon Outlet. You can save up to 50% on overstocked and marked-down products, and sometimes even up to 80%. Score bargains on all kinds of items including home goods, kitchen items, electronics, and much more.

Unfortunately, the outlet is even more hidden than the warehouse. You can't find this store on Amazon's main page. Instead, type "Amazon outlet" in the search box. When you find a great deal, keep an eye out for a timer or deadline because some deals may be limited-time offers.

6 things you must know about sales tax holidays

Sales tax on a $1,000 computer in New Mexico could range from around $50 to more than $90. But three days in August, you could pocket that tidy sum by shopping during a sales tax holiday.

These short events — usually lasting two to seven days — waive the sales tax on certain items. First introduced by Ohio and Michigan in 1980, they were meant to discourage shoppers from driving to nearby states in search of lower sales tax rates. The concept has had mixed success over the years, but as a purchaser, you need to make the system work for you.

- Only 16 states held a sales tax holiday last year, so don't assume it will happen where you live. The Federation of Tax Administrators (*taxadmin.org/sales-tax-holidays*) and the Sales Tax Institute (*salestaxinstitute.com/resources/sales-tax-holidays*) both publish lists online. Check one of them out every year.

- Each state has its own list of products you can buy tax-free. The sales that occur in late summer usually include back-to-school items, but at any time they may also allow appliances, bedding, and emergency supplies.

- Most states cap the tax-free perk at a certain dollar amount, say, $1,500 for computers. This varies by location.

- Sometimes, the price of each item is capped. For example, only clothing that costs less than $100 might be eligible for the exemption.

- Remember, you won't save money unless you purchase items you had planned to buy anyway, and if those items are on the tax-exempt list.

- Don't get blindsided by unexpected delivery charges or extra fees on exchanges, gift certificates, or layaways. Ask before you purchase.

Don't sabotage your next tech purchase

When you're in the market for a tablet, computer, laptop, or other electronic device, keep in mind these three shopping strategies that could derail a smart purchase.

- A yard or garage sale is probably the worst place to find current, functioning electronics.

- Don't shop while texting, making phone calls, or checking emails on your cellphone. A study published in the *Journal of the Academy of Marketing Science* found that those who did made more impulse buys and were more likely to forget to purchase planned items.

- Buying off-brand electronics online may save you some money upfront, but it's possible you'll be getting a poor quality product that won't last long and has no customer support.

CAUTION

First-class fun on an economy budget

Cable, satellite, and streaming: Ways
to watch that save you more 340

Cheap and easy entertainment
at your fingertips 350

Savvy travel: Great escapes at
the right price 356

Cable, satellite, and streaming: Ways to watch that save you more

Bright ideas to slash your cable bill

Cable costs keep going up — with no end in sight. Why? You can partly blame the networks. Every year they have to pay more for live events, like sports, and deal with increasingly large budgets for their shows. So they turn around and charge the cable companies more money to carry their channels. But if you're determined, you can cut your bill down to size. Here's how.

Compare and negotiate. Sometimes you're stuck with only one telecom provider in your area — but make sure. A website like *allconnect.com* searches within your ZIP code for all offers. With that information, you're in a position of power. Let your provider know you've found competing offers. Ask if they will price match. If not, be willing to cancel service.

Schedule a disconnect. You've found a better offer with another company and your provider won't budge. Go ahead and set up a date and time to disconnect your service — a week or two away. You may be surprised at the deals you'll be offered from your current provider as the disconnect date gets closer. At this point, it may be smarter and easier to take their deal and cancel your new service.

This tactic will be more successful if you are a long-term customer who pays on time.

Change your lineup. Really examine your viewing habits. Do you regularly watch all 300 channels in your package? If not, compare package lineups and switch to a cheaper one with fewer channels. Also be aware that companies change their packages frequently.

Decline free trials. These are tempting, but unless you are an excellent record-keeper, it's likely you'll forget to call and cancel this add-on when the free promotion expires.

Purchase your own modem. Renting one through your cable provider can add about $10 a month to your bill. Buy your own and you'll recoup your expenses within a year.

Inspect your bill. It may read like a foreign language, but the more you study the charges month to month, the more likely you are to catch an error or an added fee.

Of course, you should always start by calling your cable company and simply asking for a discount, promotion, or a lower rate. Be honest. Tell them your cable bill is too high and you'd like their help.

Bundling — the hidden cost of cable

The biggest mistake customers make when bundling cable, internet, and phone is not understanding that cable providers are not made equally. A company can have great phone service but terrible cable service. Or perhaps their internet speeds are lightning-fast, but their phone service is patchy.

By bundling, you're forced to take the good with the bad, instead of shopping around for the best providers. That can lead to additional money spent on service calls to fix issues.

Plus, once you're locked into a bundle, those cost savings that brought you there often disappear. Your bill climbs little by little each month, or you're subject to a large increase once a year. The money you saved by bundling is slowly chipped away. The bottom line — bundling may be costlier than you think.

CAUTION

Breaking up is hard to do — how to win when you cut the cord

So you're finally ready to call it quits with cable. Take just a moment and get all your ducks in a row to avoid unexpected charges.

First, know the terms of your agreement. Some cable contracts have early termination fees if you cancel before your contract is up. If your contract only has a few months left, consider waiting so you can avoid the fees.

Do your research. Before you call the cable company, know these three things — the terms of your contract, the cost of your new streaming options, and the fees you may have to pay to cancel cable. Have these items on hand when you call.

Take the plunge and call. Know that the cancellation department will try to offer you better deals to keep you as a customer. That's why the previous step is so important. Weigh the savings of other viewing options with the savings they're offering you to stay with cable. Make sure you're making the most cost-effective choice that still gives you everything you want.

Be prepared so you won't get scared. The cancellation department may also try to scare you with talk about extra fees and lost money. Knowing exactly what your contract states — and what it doesn't — can save you a lot of hassle.

Pay this once and watch TV forever

Forget monthly satellite or cable bills — you're ready to enjoy fee-free TV. But there's just one more thing. If your TV has a digital tuner, you need to buy an antenna to access the signal without cable. The good news is, digital antennas cost less than $100.

Get the same access for less money. All major networks broadcast over the air. So you get the same channels you would with cable.

How is that possible? Networks are paid by the advertisers who run the commercials in between shows. You, the viewer, don't pay for the broadcast at all. You pay for access to the broadcast. A digital antenna gives you that access for a lot less money.

No need to worry about finding channels. You'll find even more through a digital antenna, including shows you'd never otherwise see. Each channel now has "sub-channels." These sub-channels are often not offered in typical cable packages, or they are hidden in the higher channels you may not browse often.

Each sub-channel has additional programming beyond what you would find on the normal channel in a cable package. Some have regional content you might find interesting, such as local news. Other sub-channels have family friendly content or hobby shows, like cooking. Some even play reruns of popular shows. You'll discover a lot of great content with sub-channels.

Enjoy the best-ever picture and sound. Part of the reason the United States switched to digital was because of quality. Digital broadcasting gives you a sharper picture and better sound quality. But you'll often see an even clearer picture if you access over-the-air TV through a digital antenna.

That's because cable providers compress multiple high-definition signals into the same space one analog station used to occupy. Why? To save money, of course. But it ends up having a negative effect on quality. With a digital antenna, you don't have to worry about that compression, leaving you with a much clearer picture.

> You can choose between two types of digital antennas. Indoor antennas are small and work best within 30 miles of a broadcast tower. Outdoor antennas are larger and usually mount onto your roof. These give a much clearer signal and have a longer range.

Check your TV to watch for free

Was your television manufactured after 2007? Then you're eligible for free viewing. Say good-bye to your cable or satellite bill.

The Telecommunications Act of 1996 ushered in the age of digital broadcasting through "over-the-air" TV. Analog broadcasting was phased out, and networks had to begin transmitting digital signals. After March 2007, all televisions were required to have a digital tuner. This transition allowed for the better video and audio quality seen today.

So if you have a TV made after that time, you can access free TV over the air. Check the back of your television and look for the white sticker. Sometimes you'll find a manufacture date right there. If not, write down your serial number from the sticker and look it up online.

Or you can call your TV manufacturer's help line. The serial number will tell you exactly when your television was made. If yours passes the test, congratulations — you have the option to watch programs for free.

Save hundreds a year by streaming

Streaming is the use of technology to bring entertainment — movies, TV shows, music, and more — to any device that can connect to the internet. Once upon a time, you could only stream on computers. But now, with smartphones and internet-connected TVs, you can stream anywhere. All you need is an internet connection to get started. Get a load of these great benefits.

- You don't need to wait for a movie or song to download. You just click "play." The show is transmitted through your internet connection to your screen.

- The content is not "saved" on your device. This allows you to flip from show to show without worrying about running out of room.

- You can stream on any device connected to the internet — a phone, laptop, streaming box, or smart TV. You can also switch between devices without losing your place in your show.

With cable prices soaring 53% in the last 10 years, streaming has become a popular alternative. From Netflix and Hulu to Amazon Prime and Apple TV, you don't need a cable box anymore to watch your favorite network shows, blockbuster movies, or even sports. And often these streaming options are available for much less than your cable bill. Follow these three steps to get started.

Make sure you have a strong internet connection. You'll need a good one to get the most out of streaming. You don't need lightning-speed rates, but make sure you have a connection of at least 5Mbps. Many cable companies have websites for you to check your speed.

Find an internet-connected device. Of course, you need a device to stream to. Your phone and laptop are obvious choices, but you can also stream to a smart TV or a streaming box like Apple TV.

Make the call and adjust your plan. Many companies now offer internet-only or internet/phone plans for those who don't want cable. With a simple phone call to your cable or satellite provider, you'll shrink your bill tremendously.

Do the math and see for yourself. Even if you cut just $50 off your $150 per month bill, you'll save $600 in a year. And that's more money in your pocket.

Subscriptions are a budget-friendly hit

Streaming entertainment typically comes in two forms — free streaming, either using a digital antenna or accessing free services online, and paid subscriptions.

While subscription services do cost a monthly fee, you'll be paying a fraction of what you pay for cable. As a bonus, you also get to tailor your entertainment, only paying for the services you want to watch, not what the cable company has decided is most profitable.

Subscription services typically also have a broader range of shows and movies available, and include options like watching popular network shows right after they air.

Research the offerings. You'll find a lot of streaming subscriptions out there, and they all have different shows and movies available. These services make deals with the networks for the rights to certain shows and movies. So make sure the subscription you're signing up for has the shows you want to watch.

Calculate the costs. Next, figure out the fees. Most paid streaming services use a monthly payment plan, and many have levels within those plans. More expensive plans can include benefits like high-definition video, commercial-free viewing, and watching on multiple screens at once. Add up exactly how much each of these subscriptions will cost you per month, so you know what your new entertainment bill will be.

Create an account. Once you've decided on your services, it's time to create an account. Your streaming account will follow you across your devices, so you won't have to worry about separate ones for your TV, phone, and computer. Make sure to pick a secure password.

Pick your preferences. Many streaming services ask a few questions when you first get started to help make recommendations. What genres do you enjoy? What are your favorite shows? These preferences help customize what you see on your home page.

Build your watchlist. This has different names on different streaming services, but it is your best tool while streaming. Take the time when you first get set up to add favorite shows, movies you'd like to watch, and anything that catches your eye. Not only will it make them easy to find later, it also helps the streaming service provide better recommendations for you.

Stream entertainment for free

This secret could save you a lot of money. With streaming hardware — like a box, stick, gaming console, or computer — you'll find many apps that now provide content for free. How do they do it?

Advertisers pay for the cost. Much like the lower-cost subscription services, many free streaming services show commercials. Free services still have to pay for the rights to show their content. By showing ads, they pass that cost onto their advertisers instead of you. Ads are often shorter and less frequent than ads on cable.

Your favorite movie may not stick around. Another way these apps reduce costs is by rotating shows and movies on a regular basis. This means you trade off availability for new variety.

If you like discovering new shows and movies, free streaming services are a great choice. Look for those that show only "public domain" content, and you won't have to watch any ads. These videos are usually older films and shows that are past their copyright.

They give access to some content. A lot of news organizations and other entertainment apps offer smaller snippets of free content in addition to their paid content.

A "paywall" limits the content you watch to what's available for free, unless you decide to pay the subscription. So you can still watch sports highlights, news broadcasts, and selected shows for free without moving past the paywall.

Netflix steals the spotlight, but these free streaming services may give you everything you need. Which ones are right for you?

- Crackle — Watch shows like *Seinfeld* and *Married with Children* as well as popular movies and original content.

- Viki — Find older favorites like *The Lone Ranger* and *Ozzie and Harriet.*

- Rewinder — Enjoy classic movies and TV like Alfred Hitchcock's *The Man Who Knew Too Much* and *The Lucy Show.*

- Pluto TV — Watch live TV without the cable bill, with access to hundreds of channels like BBC America and Bloomberg. It even has a guide for easy browsing.

- Tubi TV — Access over 7,000 movies and TV shows, without the Netflix subscription cost.

Save money with a digital library

Don't you just love sharing favorite movies with your family? A digital library makes this so easy to do, since many providers offer family accounts, where multiple users can share access.

Your billing information stays separate, but the digital content you purchase can be accessed by anyone in the household. That means books, movies, TV shows, music, and more can be enjoyed by everyone, without having to pay for them multiple times.

When you set up a household, make sure you have a device that can access that store. For instance, if your family all has Apple TVs and iPhones, you may want to consider creating an Apple family plan. But if you have a mix of Android or Amazon devices, you may want to set up a Google or Amazon family plan instead.

There are usually limits to how many family members you can add. Accounts for kids don't have purchase rights so you don't have to worry about spending sprees. And you can set parental controls on what they can watch.

Sharing your digital library is a great way for your family to save money.

Deal or no deal?
When streaming is worth the fee

You may be asking, "Why would I pay a subscription fee when I can stream shows for free?" Here are some reasons a paid subscription may be right for you.

You watch a lot of network shows. Many networks, both broadcast and cable, only sell the rights to their shows to subscription services. Remember, they still have to make money, even if you're not paying for cable anymore.

You love premium content. Premium cable channels like HBO, Starz, and SHOWTIME also don't want to lose money by offering their shows for free. While you can watch without a cable package, you still need to pay for a subscription to their service.

You hate commercials. Most free streaming sites have commercials to make money, instead of charging a subscription fee. When you pay for a streaming subscription, you're often paying for the right to watch your shows commercial-free. Although some paid subscriptions also require commercials, you usually only have to sit through one or two per show.

Cheap and easy entertainment at your fingertips

Seniors can have fun on a shoestring budget

Do you feel bad whenever you hand over a coupon? Of course not. Well, why would you hesitate to ask for a senior discount? Hundreds of places offer them and many kick in as early as age 50.

So no, it may not feel glamorous, but if you embrace your "senior-ness," you are going to save some money. Just relax and enjoy the cha-ching of coins dropping back into your pocket.

Don't be shy about asking. The first rule of acceptance? Start asking for your discount. It's not always advertised, and many places won't give you the discount unless you specifically inquire.

Rule no. 2 — ask everywhere. Senior discounts aren't just available at the usual places anymore. You may find them at pharmacies, department stores, eyeglass stores, toy stores, banks, insurers, and supermarkets.

> Want freebies and coupons for just about everything? Surf to *heyitsfree.net, freesamples.org, freecycle.org,* or *freestufftimes.com* and find all kinds of free stuff.

Ask for one from your cellphone service provider. Ask at greeting card stores, major and minor league baseball stadiums, outlet malls, fitness centers, amusement parks, zoos, beauty salons, museums, and rental car services. Ask at craft fairs and even the Goodwill store. Ask your plumber, roofer, and accountant.

The bottom line — you'll find opportunities for savings wherever you spend money. In tough economic times, even businesses that don't usually offer senior discounts may try this method to get you in the door. The chance to take a big bite out of your cost is worth the effort.

Chow down on significant savings. Government statistics suggest people over age 55 spend between $2,000 and $3,000 on food away from home every year. So even if your senior discount only saves a meager 10% at each meal, that may put $200 to $300 extra in your wallet.

Chain restaurants or stores, however, may not offer a senior discount at every location. Your best bet is to call ahead and ask before you visit. If they say no, see if they have any other senior benefits, such as a reduced-price senior menu, freebies, a designated night for senior deals, or early-bird discounts. Don't forget to find out the age requirement.

4 great money-savers you may not know about

Become a savvy senior by tapping into discounts whenever and wherever you have fun.

Federal recreation sites. Enjoy a lifetime pass to natural beauty, unique attractions, and fun for only $80. Most people pay $35 a car to enter Grand Canyon National Park, but you will pay nothing if you have an America the Beautiful Senior Pass.

For a one-time fee of $80, you get a lifelong benefit that lets you enter more than 2,000 recreation sites, like national parks and national wildlife refuges. Each pass also covers standard amenity fees and day use fees for a driver and three other adults in your car.

To get the America the Beautiful Senior Pass, you must be at least 62 years old and a United States citizen or permanent resident. Request it in person at a federal recreation site, or apply by mail and pay an additional $10 processing fee.

Check out all the details online by visiting *nps.gov* and searching for "senior pass."

Movie theaters. A night at the movies is no longer a cheap date. But throw in a senior discount, and you can afford to upsize to a popcorn built for two. Check your local theater to verify it participates in these programs, and take a valid photo ID with you to the ticket counter.

351

- Cinemark — save by going on their special Seniors Day.

- Regal Entertainment Group — receive up to 30% off the regular adult ticket price if you are over age 60.

- AMC Theaters — customers who are 60 or older get a discount.

- Marcus Theaters — every Friday anyone over age 60 receives special admission prices. And ask about their Young at Heart special.

- Showcase Cinemas — senior Wednesdays mean discounted admission, popcorn, and soda.

- Landmark Theaters — nearly all locations offer discount pricing for seniors.

Even if you don't see a senior discount advertised at your local movie theater, ask for one anyway.

Golf courses. Always ask about senior discounts when you golf. You may pay less for an annual card at a public course, receive a deep discount on a certain weekday when most other golfers are working, or get a great deal when you show your AARP membership card.

Museums. Are you on a continual quest for knowledge? Are you fascinated by the stars, ancient civilizations, and great works of art? Then visiting a planetarium, museum, art gallery, or hall of fame may be your idea of fun.

Of course, some don't charge admission at all, like many military museums, and the galleries, zoos, and museums affiliated with the Smithsonian in the Washington, D.C. area.

But otherwise, with a little planning, you can take advantage of free museum days, deals, discounts, and money-saving museum cards.

The internet gives you plenty of opportunities to save on tickets. If you enjoy live theater, check out *theatermania.com* or *cheaptickets.com/events* for big discounts in your area. Or buy and sell tickets to concerts, plays, or sporting events at *stubhub.com*.

- On the first full weekend of each month, Bank of America's Museums on Us program allows one free general admission with a Bank of America, Merrill Lynch, or U.S. Trust credit or debit card plus a photo ID. Over 200 museums participate, but you'll want to check out details concerning times and exhibits. Go to *bankofamerica.com*, click on About us, and navigate to What guides us. Look for the Arts and Culture heading at the bottom of the drop-down menu.

- Veterans may be eligible for free or reduced admission either on Veterans Day or all year long.

- If you have a disability, you, and possibly your traveling companion, may qualify for free entrance.

- Are you a local? Ask if that means you receive discounted admission. Make sure you can show proof of residency.

- And of course, always ask about senior discounts. Go online to *50plusworld.com* and click on the heading for Discounts, then choose Entertainment Discounts. Scroll down and choose Seniors USA Museum Discounts. Here you'll find a partial list of venues offering senior discounts organized by state.

Check it out: Borrow fun freebies from your Library of Things

Your public library just might be one of the most underused resources in your community. That's because it is more than just a repository for books.

Libraries in cities both large and small are filled with treasures just waiting to be collected or lent out. Called a "Library of Things," this section of a regular library contains fun, unique objects. Here are examples of some of the unusual items you might find.

- Bakeware. There's no need to invest in fancy-shaped cake pans that you'll use once. If you need to bake a Power Ranger cake or one in the shape of Cinderella's princess carriage, chances are they might be on a shelf in a storage closet of your library, along with other kitchenware.

- Sports equipment. Depending on the geography in your area, you might find anything from fishing poles to hiking gear to snowshoes, sleds, tennis rackets, and other sports apparatus.

- Humans. Having a "living library" has been gaining in popularity since the idea was introduced in Denmark in 2000. Nurses, social workers, and knowledgeable people from various fields offer their time and expertise to educate patrons during operating hours in the library.

- Museum passes. Public libraries in Chicago let patrons check out passes that allow free entry to various museums throughout the city.

- Musical instruments. If your library has a well-stocked music and arts department, you might be able to borrow a banjo, bongos, dulcimer, kalmia, or mandolin. Local residents can check out all these instruments and others at Forbes Library in Massachusetts.

- Tools. Libraries in Oakland, California lend out drills, tape measures, saws, and many other items for quick projects. They also take donations of unwanted tools that are in good shape.

- Toys. Board games, building blocks, and even dolls are waiting to be borrowed and shared.

This weekend, make a trip to your local library and discover what useful items are available for you to use.

Local entertainment provides more bang for your buck

Big towns and big venues mean big prices. Why not search out entertainment that's a little closer to home? Admission to an event that's in your community could be hundreds of dollars cheaper than attending a bash in the city. In some cases it could even be free.

Watch the amateurs play. Pick a sport — football, baseball, basketball, volleyball, soccer, or hockey. Pick a level — farm teams, minor leagues, or even high school. Sporting events like these can be more exciting than professional games and cost far less. You'll find the food and the seats are cheaper, the venues smaller and more personal, and even the commute and parking a breeze.

Focus on art that's close at hand. Your parks and recreation department is a treasure trove of free and inexpensive happenings — everything from local art exhibits to community plays and concerts. Check your neighborhood paper or go on your city's website for a list of great low-cost or free entertainment.

---

9 ways to get cheap tickets

Check out these tried-and-true strategies for low-cost entertainment.

- Volunteer to usher at a local theater or concert venue.
- Take in a matinee, or wait for your movie to come to a dollar theater.
- Be quick and call when your radio station offers ticket giveaways.
- Write to the Guest Relations departments of television networks to get free tickets to live tapings of TV shows.
- Buy coupon books with entertainment vouchers.
- Sign up on mailing lists of art organizations to find out about last-minute discounts.
- Check your membership benefits through AAA or any other clubs you might belong to.
- Subscribe early to the theater or symphony for deep discounts.
- Keep your eye open for free public events or festivals.

Savvy travel: Great escapes at the right price

Score unbeatable travel deals with insider secrets

They looked at over 2 billion flights and studied more than 50 billion online airfare searches. Now the Airlines Reporting Corporation (ARC) and the Expedia Group, two intelligence and technology leaders in the travel industry, are sharing their findings — all so you can save some serious money. Take a look at the five important takeaways from their latest Travel Pricing Outlook report.

Secure flights at least three weeks ahead of travel. Industry experts call this the "sweet spot" for fare savings.

Book your flight on a weekend. Average ticket prices for economy and premium cabins tend to be lower when booked on a weekend, usually on a Sunday. You could save up to 20%, even as much as 36%, by booking then. The most expensive days to book? Thursdays and Fridays.

> Curious what others think about various airlines, hotels, and internet travel services? Register for free and download a copy of the American Customer Satisfaction Index (ACSI) Travel Report at *theacsi.org/news-and-resources*.

Start your journey on a Thursday or Friday. You could save around 10% on airfares simply by choosing flights that take off on these days. Flying on a Sunday will put the biggest pinch in your wallet.

Make your hotel reservation on a Friday. Regardless of when you travel, you're likely to find the lowest average daily rate on Fridays.

But stay away from Sundays — they are generally the most expensive day to book a hotel.

Stay through Saturday night. Extend your weekday travel to include a Saturday night and you could save around 25% on airfare. This was true for three out of four trips the experts analyzed.

For some popular corporate travel destinations, return airfare was cut almost in half when a Saturday night stay was added to the itinerary.

Suite dreams: How to cut pricey hotel bills down to size

Don't let a tight budget keep you from enjoying your next vacation. Affordable hotel rooms are actually pretty easy to find. So easy, you'd be crazy to ever pay full price. Heed these eight super smart tips and you'll have money left over for that souvenir T-shirt.

- Off-season, off-peak, shoulder. Whatever you call it, call it cheap. Traveling during "unpopular" times can mean huge savings on lodging. Imagine New England in the spring — no leaf-peepers. Ski slopes in the summer — a mecca for hikers. The southeast in the fall — great festivals. Yellowstone in the winter — stunning scenery.

- Bundle your hotel with your flight or car rental for a stellar package deal.

- You'll never get it if you don't ask, so ask — about discounts for seniors, veterans, groups, associations, employees, memberships, and anything else you can think of.

- Time your booking just right. For best rates, pull the trigger on a hotel for your summer vacation within a month of your trip, says TripAdvisor, the travel planning and booking website. You may snag a great price further out, and that's OK, as long as you can cancel the reservation for a full refund and no penalty if a better deal comes along.

357

- Join a hotel's loyalty or rewards program, as long as it's free. You could receive discounted rates, points for each stay, and money-saving perks. Look for programs with plenty of locations to choose from and rewards that don't expire.

- The art of haggling is alive and well, and is a skill you need to develop if you want to save some serious travel money. The simplest method? Call the hotel directly, talk to the manager, and ask for a better price, a price match, or an upgrade. Know what competitors are charging and, for best results, try to be flexible on your dates or amenities.

- Scrutinize the fine print before you book and challenge any sneaky fees. You may have to call the hotel for clarification or to opt out of certain services.

- And, of course, you have to comparison shop online or with apps like Hotels.com, Priceline, HotelTonight, Booking.com, Hotwire, trivago, and yapta. Roomer, at *roomertravel.com,* is a site that lets you purchase hotel rooms from other people who bought nonrefundable rooms. It's a win-win.

Watch state taxes to save on gas

How much you spend on your next road trip will depend on where you fill your tank. While the federal tax rate of 18.4 cents per gallon won't vary, state taxes range from 14 to 58 additional cents for every gallon.

For instance, avoid hitting the pump in Indiana, where the state tax is 42.9 cents a gallon, and fill up in nearby Kentucky, which has a gas tax of only 26 cents.

You can find current tax rates online through the Institute on Taxation and Economic Policy at *itep.org/state-and-local-tax-rates-on-gasoline.*

CAUTION

Smart traveler tips for a happy — and affordable — homestay

Imagine a vacation where you can hang your clothes up in real closets, your family can share evenings in a cozy living room, and then you all wake up to Uncle Joe's famous buttermilk pancakes. No, you're not still at home. You're somewhere fabulous, but with all the comforts of a house. Welcome to the vacation home rental experience.

Whether you're looking for a single bedroom in a shared home or an entire house; whether your wish list includes a treehouse in Oregon, a houseboat off the Florida coast, or a yurt in the mountains, there's a vacation rental to satisfy every whim.

Is it a good match for you? Airbnb, one of the leading online companies arranging homestays, says the over 60 crowd is its fastest-growing demographic. So why might you find this idea appealing?

- You'd like to spend some time testing out a potential retirement location.

- You crave more privacy than you get in a regular hotel.

- One of your goals is to meet and interact with friendly locals in a new area.

- You travel with pets.

- You travel internationally and want to immerse yourself in another culture.

- You want a place for friends and relatives to come together easily — a reunion or wedding, perhaps. Multi-generational family travel, where seniors vacation with children, is an exploding trend, with a 75% increase in these kinds of bookings in the last year.

On the other hand, some normal hotel amenities you may give up with a homestay include 24-hour security, front desk services, and daily housekeeping.

359

Don't let a rental bust your budget. Does this sound like an experience only for the rich and famous? The average nightly rental rate in the U.S. is $217, according to BuildUp Bookings, a digital marketing team that specializes in the travel, accommodations, and real estate industries. But they say popular vacation destinations can range from $186 to $978 per night.

When crunching the numbers, don't forget to factor in all the fees. These can include a booking fee, cleaning fee, security deposit, pet fees, taxes, and cancellation fees.

So it's true homestays won't always be a bargain or cheaper than hotels. In fact, if you're a budget traveler, a typical hotel delivers lower rates and may be more cost-effective for short visits. But there are plenty of ways a vacation rental can save you money.

- When traveling with a group, you can split the cost.

- Kitchens allow you to do your own cooking and nix the pricey restaurants.

- You won't have parking fees.

Explore the possibilities. First off, you'll have to go online to search and book. You can't just call a main switchboard and secure a room. But the process is pretty easy on a computer or tablet. Here are a few places to start looking for a cut-rate, first-class vacation, that won't involve paying a travel agent.

- Airbnb *(airbnb.com)*

- AllTheRooms *(alltherooms.com)*

- TripAdvisor Vacation Rentals *(tripadvisor.com)*

- Booking.com *(booking.com)* offers alternative accommodations like apartments, cabins, cottages, villas, and more.

- HomeAway *(homeaway.com)* and VRBO *(vrbo.com)* are owned by the same company and share the same inventory.

- Tripping.com *(tripping.com)* lets you compare properties from the top vacation rental sites.

Start by plugging in anything from a specific ZIP code to a city. Then filter by your criteria — price, number of bedrooms and bathrooms, and even whether you want a fireplace or swimming pool.

Just understand the difference between how many people a rental can sleep and how many beds or bedrooms the unit has. Some properties offer extra sleeping accommodations in the form of sleeper sofas or futons.

Tip the odds in your favor. Minimize surprises by reading reviews and considering properties with a special upgraded designation such as Plus, Premier, or Premium. This usually means the home, owner, or property manager meets extra requirements, like more stringent or frequent inspections, lower cancellation rates, or higher review scores.

Looking for travel that's a little unusual? *Roadscholar.org* is the world's largest creator of learning opportunities in 150 countries and all 50 states. *Eldertreks.com* specializes in small group exotic adventures for travelers over 50. *Adventurewomen.com* offers unique adventure travel tours designed especially for women, by women. *Globalvolunteers.org* organizes international community-based service projects.

And finally, never book offline directly with the owner. Use the website's secure payment system to keep your private information safe.

Armchair travel is a free way to see the world

Imagine strolling around the grounds of Buckingham Palace, checking out the monuments and parks of London, and even walking right by No. 10 Downing St., home of the British prime minister — all without spending a dime or leaving your living room.

Google Maps *(google.com/maps)*. It's great for general exploring but also for travel. Visit landmarks, natural wonders, museums, and businesses. No baggage fees required.

With Google Maps open in a browser on your computer or your phone, search for a location, then click or tap the pin on your destination. The information panel will show you photos, sometimes including 360-degree images inside museums and other landmarks.

- Go for a bird's eye view by clicking on Satellite, often a small square in the lower left corner of the map.

- Get a closer look with Street View, which uses 360-degree images. Get this view by clicking on a labeled photo in the panel or zooming in on your destination. Many places will let you go back in time using Street View, at least 10 years or so. Click the clock icon, if it's available, in the upper left-hand corner and choose your time.

Google Earth (*google.com/earth*). This software lets you quickly fly from location to location, soaring into the atmosphere and landing easily on each place you want to see.

Launch it in a browser or download Google Earth Pro onto your computer. The opening is impressive, an interactive image of the planet rotating slowly in space. Zoom out to see Earth from a distance and zoom in to explore.

You'll be able to visit the same places you can on Google Maps but with 3-D imagery that lets you view everything from the Eiffel Tower to your local supermarket from different angles. Then take tours of interesting places with Google Earth's Voyager feature.

Visit your phone or tablet's app store to get the Google Earth app. It's a small screen for a big planet, but is still a useful tool.

Expand your sights to the universe. If you're really looking for something that's out of this world, try Google Moon (*google.com/moon*). Take tours of the lunar landing sites, narrated by Apollo astronauts, and explore the moon firsthand. If that doesn't quench your urge for exotic travel, try Google Mars (*google.com/mars*).

Google Images — let pictures save your vacation

Have you ever searched online for a hotel or vacation rental and been impressed by pictures of huge rooms or an amazing swimming pool? Then you got there and discovered it wasn't nearly as beautiful as it looked? Next time, do a quick image search on Google, and you'll spare yourself the disappointment.

Since Google Images can come from YouTube, Facebook postings, review websites, and more, you're apt to see accurate portrayals of a place — from real people, not just advertisements.

And remember, maps are images too. If you're traveling to Boston on vacation, for instance, you may want a sightseeing map. Instead of searching scores of tourist websites to find a good one, do an image search. Keying in "Boston tourist sights" will give you mostly photos, but add the word "map" and you'll get hundreds of Boston maps.

Travel insurance: When to disaster-proof your vacation

"Travel isn't always pretty," said celebrity chef and television personality Anthony Bourdain. "It isn't always comfortable. Sometimes it hurts, it even breaks your heart." And yes, the best trips can do just that. It's OK, though, as long as they don't break your wallet as well, right? Many think that's why you need travel insurance.

Basically, this type of protection is one way you can recoup money lost when things go wrong while you are traveling — covering everything from mishaps to calamities. But is travel insurance really necessary and what should you pay for it?

Know when to say yes. Experts say travel insurance might be a good idea under the following circumstances.

- You have health issues that could flare up while you are far from medical care. Confirm any preexisting conditions will be covered.

- You have close relatives back home in poor health. You might have to return quickly to handle an emergency.

- Your trip costs several thousand dollars or you've paid a large, nonrefundable deposit.

- You are traveling to a potentially dangerous destination — think wildfires, hurricanes, political unrest — or engaging in risky activities. In certain cases you'll need specific riders to give you the coverage you need.

Check for existing coverage. Does the credit card you used to pay for the trip include travel insurance as a perk? Look into the details because coverage may be limited to certain travelers and very specific situations.

What about your homeowners, life, auto, or, of course, health insurance? Occasionally these policies will provide some coverage while you're on the road.

Practice savvy shopping strategies. You might pay 4% to 10% of your total trip cost for a comprehensive policy, say industry experts. So do the math to get an acceptable range before you start shopping. Of course you can purchase insurance from the airline, cruise line, or travel agency, but it's smart to get several quotes.

- Use online sites like *insuremytrip.com* or *squaremouth.com* to compare third-party policies.

- Buy only the level of coverage you need. Don't overinsure.

- Don't wait till the last minute to purchase insurance, especially if weather is a factor. Once a hurricane is on the radar, in most cases it will be too late to buy protection.

- There's no value in plunking down a lot of cash for a policy with too many exclusions. So read the fine print.

Index

401(k) plan
  catch-up contributions 29-30
  converting to IRA 51-52
  maximizing 48-49
  withdrawals 46-47

A

Accounts
  retirement. *See* 401(k) plan; IRA
    (Individual Retirement
    Account)
  social media 117, 128-129
Adult Protective Services 135
Advance directive 112
Advocate, patient 171
Aging in place
  considerations 185
  updates, cheap 255-261
Air travel 356-357
Airline rewards 91
Amazon
  Outlet 337
  Warehouse 11, 335-337

America the Beautiful Senior Pass
  351
Annuities 30, 44, 114, 149
Antenna, TV 342-343
Apps
  for food safety 297
  for grocery shopping 265,
    268-269, 279
  for managing money 82, 93, 97
  for retail shopping 333-334
  for shopping online 93
Area Agency on Aging 161
Auction, home buying 202-204
Automobile. *See* Car

B

Banking
  automatic drafts 82
  avoiding fees 94-100
  online 98-100
  passwords 117
  switching 99
  virtual credit cards 93

Bargains. *See* Discounts
Battery
  car 314-316
  cellphone 332
Beneficiaries
  estate planning and 108-109
  taxes and 109
Bonds, municipal 57
Budget
  apps 82, 93
  creating 78
  in retirement 26-29, 31
  prepaid debit card 89
Bulk buying 270-272
Bundling 341
Burial. *See* Funerals

C

Cable TV. *See also* TV
  cord cutting 342-349
  saving on 340-341
Capital gains 39, 67-68
Car
  accident, what to do 307
  battery, extending life 314-316
  buying 23-24, 318-319, 321-322
  diminished value 309
  electric 317-318
  fuel, saving on 310-311

increasing longevity 312
insurance 304-309
leasing 322-323
maintenance 312-314
repair rip-offs 311
safety features 320-321
selling 323-324
Career. *See* Jobs, in retirement
Caregivers
  life insurance benefit 107
  Medicaid and 148
  military veterans and 187-188
  resources for 184
  tax breaks for 7-8
CarFit program 320
Cellphones. *See also* Smartphones
  insurance 330-332
  saving on 326-327, 329
  wireless plans 327-330
Cemetery, green 120
Certificate of deposit (CD) 57-58
Charities
  for car repair 313
  for health care 158-159, 171, 181
  scams 140
  taxes 60
Check fraud 128
Claims
  car accident 309
  homeowners insurance 6

Cleaning, cheap 248-254

Clothing, maintenance 225, 245-246, 254

Color, and homes 9, 195

Composting 284-285

Computer
buying 338
scams 138, 301

Concierge, doctor 167

Cord cutting 342

Coupons
for drugs 155
for groceries 265, 267-268

Credit cards
cash-back incentives 265
debt 86-88
identity theft and 126
mail offers 90
rewards 90-92
skimmers 132
virtual 93
vs. debit cards 125

Credit report
effect of inquiries 79-80
errors 88-89
free 78-79
identity theft and 122

Credit score
ID theft and 122
improving 78-85, 88-89

Credit unions 98, 304

Curb appeal 10

D

Debit cards 89, 125

Debt
collectors 111
credit card 86-88
in retirement 28

Decluttering 194, 210

Deductions, medical expenses 59-60

Dental care 172-174

Dependent care credit 7-8

Depreciation 321

Dining out 298-302

Disability benefits, Social Security 40

Discounts
car insurance 305
dental care 173
for seniors 12, 111, 350-353
glasses 177
home insurance 5-6
life insurance 105
online codes 11
online shopping 335-337
prescription drugs 155, 156-157
wireless plans 326-327

Do Not Call Registry 141

Doctor
  choosing 167-168
  telehealth 169-170
Documents
  organization 45, 61-63
  shredding 126-127
Downsizing 200-202
Drugs
  foreign, purchasing 159-161
  free samples 3-4, 155
  generic 155-156
  grocery store chains and 154
  mail order 159
  Medicare coverage 3-4, 153
Durable power of attorney 112,
  186-187

E

Earnings record, for Social Security
  36
Eldercare Locator 135, 188
Emergency fund 87
Employment. *See* Jobs, in
  retirement
Energy audit, home 234-236
Energy bill, lowering 17-18,
  224-233, 234-241
ENERGY STAR 226-229, 237
Entertainment, cheap 301-302,
  354-355

Estate planning
  beneficiaries 108-109
  creditors 111
  legal advice, affordable 110-113
  taxes and 109
  trusts 114-117
  wills 110-113
Experian Boost 83-85
Extra Help program 153
Eyeglasses. *See* Glasses, bargain
Eyes. *See* Vision loss

F

Facebook 128
Farmers market
  nutrition program 278
  saving at 272, 277
Fees
  banking 94-100
  hospital 182
  investment 49
  legal 110-113
  restocking 337
  travel 360
FICO score. *See* Credit score
Financial advisor 33, 58
Food. *See also* Groceries
  bulk buying 270-272
  farmers market 277

freezing 16, 271, 293-296
growing 281-286
meal kit subscriptions 291-292
meal planning 293
organic 278-280
pantry staples 288-289
safety 297, 300
saving on 15-16
waste, avoiding 296-297
Food trucks 299-301
Fuel, saving on 310-311
Funerals 118-120
Furniture 1-2

G

Gardening, cheap 281-287
Gas, saving on 310-311, 358
Glasses, bargain 177
Golf, saving money on 352
Google, for travel 361-363
Grandparent scam 134
Green burial 120
Groceries. *See also* Food
  bulk buying 270-272
  convenience foods 291
  home delivery 269
  impulse buying 269, 275-277
  saving on 15-16
  shopping online for 269-270
  unit pricing 273-275

Grocery store
  loyalty programs 265
  sales cycles 266-267, 272-273
  shopping around 264

H

Health
  advance directive 112
  care proxy 112
  insurance. *See* Medicare
Health savings account (HSA)
  55-56, 162
Hearing loss 178-179
HECM (Home Equity Conversion
  Mortgage) 199-200
Herb gardening 285-286. *See also*
  Gardening, cheap
Highway scams 307-308
Home
  auction 202-204
  buying 199-204
  cleaning 248-254
  energy-efficient 17-18
  exterior 261-262
  increasing value 9-10, 194-195
  refinancing 190
  selling 9, 197-198
  smart 195
  staging 196-197
  technology 195

Homeowners insurance
    coverage 211-212, 214-215
    discounts on 5-6
    lowering premium 212-214
Hospital bill, lowering 180-182
Hotel deals 357-358

I

iBuying 197-198
Identity theft. *See also* Scams
    avoiding 125-132
    credit report and 78-79
    red flags 122-123
Income
    health savings account (HSA) as
        56
    pension 43-44
    retirement 30, 69-71
Index funds 58
Inflation, and investments 27-28
Instacart 268
Insurance
    car 304-309
    cellphone 330-332
    dental 173-174
    health. *See* Medicare
    homeowners 5-6, 211-215
    life 102-107
    long-term care 184-185
    travel 363-364

Interest
    credit card 87-88
    on checking accounts 98
    on savings accounts 98-100
Internet
    banking 82, 94-100
    bargain shopping 11
    car buying 319
    passwords 125-126
Investments
    diversifying 28, 54
    health savings account (HSA)
        55-56
    inflation and 27-28
    mistakes 53-55
    senior-friendly 57-58
IRA (Individual Retirement
    Account)
    catch-up contributions 29-30
    Roth vs. traditional 50-51
    withdrawals 46-47
Irrevocable trust 114-115
IRS (Internal Revenue Service)
    tax records 62-63

J

Jobs, in retirement 69-76, 305

K

Kitchen
  gadgets 292-293
  organization 289-290

L

Landlord 220-222
Laundry, cost savings 245-246
Leasing, car 322-323
LED lighting 230
Legal fees 110-113
Library
  freebies 353-354
  seed 283
Life insurance
  borrowing from 103-105
  cashing out 102-103
  lost policy, locating 105-106
  mistakes 106-107
Lighting
  smart 224-225, 230-231
  solar 228
LinkedIn 76
Lions Club 176, 178
Living trust, revocable 112,
  116-117
Load-management program
  225-226

Loans. *See also* Mortgage
  for solar power 233
  life insurance 103-105
  nonprime 191
Long-term care
  insurance for 184-185
  life insurance and 107
  planning for 185-187
  tax deductions and 59-60
Look-back period, Medicaid 114
Low-Income Home Energy
  Assistance Program (LIHEAP)
  239
Loyalty programs
  for groceries 265
  for hotels 358
  for prescription drugs 156-157
  for restaurants 299

M

Maintenance, car 311, 313-314
Marriage, and Social Security
  35-36
Meal kit subscriptions 291-292
Medicaid
  applying for 149-150
  caregivers and 148
  long-term care and 113-115, 148
  look-back period 114, 147-148
  trusts and 114, 149

Medical
  care, free 170-171, 181
  costs 55
  dependent tax deduction 7-8
  patient advocate 171
  tests, at home 169
  tourism 152-153
Medicare
  Advantage plan 19-20, 59,
    144-145
  doughnut hole 157
  enrollment 19-20, 145-147
  fraud, reporting 152
  free services 147
  hospital bill and 180-181
  prescription assistance 153
  scams 149, 152
  State Health Insurance Program
    (SHIP) 146
  tax deductions 59
Medigap 59, 145
Mortgage
  recasting 191-192
  refinancing 190, 193
  reverse 192, 199-200
Movie, discounts 351-352
Moving 39, 205-210
Mystery shopper 69

N

National Foundation for Credit
  Counseling (NFCC) 27
National parks 351
Negotiating bills 182, 340
Nursing home, paying for 113-115

O

Online. *See also* Internet
  Cyber Monday 21
  discount codes 11
  grocery shopping 268-270
  hearing assessments 178
  prescription drugs 156, 160
  retail shopping 335-337
  Social Security account 36
  streaming TV 346-349
  telemedicine 169-170
Organic produce 278-280
Outlet, Amazon 337

P

Passwords 125-126
Patient Access Network (PAN)
  Foundation 158
Patient advocate 171
Pensions 27, 43-45

Phishing 130-132

Phones. *See also* Cellphones

   hearing loss and 179

   scams 139-141

Physician. *See* Doctor

Portfolio, diversifying 28, 54

Power of attorney (POA) 112,

   115, 187

Premiums

   health savings account (HSA)

     55-56

   homeowners insurance 5-6

   life insurance 103-105

   long-term care insurance 59-60

   Medicare 19-20, 59

Prescription drugs. *See* Drugs

Privacy. *See* Security

Probate, avoiding 108-109

Produce

   organic 278-280

   saving on 15-16

   shopping for 277-278

Products, refurbished 21-22, 327

Property

   rental 219-222

   taxes 216-218

   unclaimed 76, 106

Proxy, health care 112

R

Real estate

   best time to sell 9

   curb appeal 10

   increasing home value 9-10

Rebates 155, 233, 265

Records. *See* Documents

Recreational vehicles (RVs)

   201-202, 316

Refinancing 190, 193

Refurbished products 21-22, 327

Relocating. *See* Moving

Rental property, owning 219-222

Required minimum distribution

   (RMD) 46-48, 60, 66

Restaurants, savings on 298-302

Resume tips 75-76. *See also* Jobs,

   in retirement

Retirement

   accounts. *See* 401(k) plan; IRA

     (Individual Retirement

     Account)

   budget 26-29

   debt 28

   mistakes 26-29

   moving 39, 205-208

   postponing 30

   working after 69-76

Reverse mortgage 192, 199-200

Revocable living trust 112, 116

Robocalls 141
Roth IRA 50-51

S

Safety. *See also* Security
  car selling and 323-324
  food 297, 300
Samples, drug 155
Savings account, for health 55-56
Scams. *See also* Identity theft
  car insurance 306-308
  door-to-door 141
  funeral 119
  investment 56
  Medicare 149, 152
  phishing 130-132
  power of attorney (POA) 115
  red flags 137
  seniors and 133-135
  Social Security 123, 140
  tax 65
  victim resources 123, 135
  work-from-home 71-73
Security. *See also* Safety; Scams
  card skimmers 132
  document shredding 126-127
  home 5
  ID theft prevention 125-126

Seed libraries 283
Seniors
  benefits check 161
  car leasing and 322-323
  discounts for 12, 240, 268,
    326-327, 350-353
  elder law attorney 116
  Eldercare Locator 188
  eye care assistance 176
  hearing aids for 179
  investment options 57
  job resources 73
  move manager 209-210
  nutrition program 278
  prescription assistance 153,
    158-159
  scams 133-136
  tax breaks for 59-60
  tax filing mistakes 66
  travel packages 361
Shipt 268
Shopping
  Christmas 21-22
  for cars 23-24
  impulse buying 269, 275-277
  online 11, 21, 93, 126, 333-337
  store discounts 12
Skimmers, card 132
Smartphones. *See also* Cellphones
  data plans 327-329

improving performance 332
insurance 330-332
Social media 117, 128-129
Social Security
  disability benefits 40
  marriage and 35-36
  online account 36
  spousal benefits 32-34, 36
  Supplemental Security Income
    (SSI) 35
  survivor benefits 34-35
  taxes 38-40, 60, 66
  when to claim 26, 37
  working and 36-37
Solar power 231-233
Staging, home 196-197
Standard deduction 66
State Health Insurance Assistance
  Program (SHIP) 146
Stock, selling 67-68
Store brands, price comparison
  274-275
Streaming TV 344-349
Supermarket. See Grocery store
Supplemental Nutrition Assistance
  Program (SNAP) 283
Supplemental Security Income
  (SSI) 35
Supplements, dietary
  safety 164-165
  saving on 162-164

T

Tax Counseling for the Elderly
  program 60
Taxes
  breaks for seniors 59-60,
    217-218
  capital gains 67-68
  caregivers and 7-8
  charitable donations 60
  deductions 59-60
  dependent care credit 7-8
  document management 61-63
  estate 109
  federal, credits 233
  filing mistakes 66
  free help for seniors 59
  fuel 358
  preparer, selecting 63-65
  property 216-218
  retirement accounts and 46-47
  sales holidays 337-338
  Social Security and 38-40
  wills and 109
Technology
  buying used 21-22
  in cars 308, 320-321
  shopping for 329, 338
  smart home 195
Telemedicine 169-170
Telephones. See Cellphones;
  Phones

Television. *See* Cable TV; TV

Tenant, choosing 220-221

Tests, at-home 169

Theater
    dinner 301-302
    movie, discounts 351-352

Travel
    alternatives 359-362
    insurance 363-364
    medical tourism 152-153
    rewards card 91
    saving on 356-361

Treasury inflation-protected securities (TIPS) 57

Trusts 113-117

TV. *See also* Cable TV
    antenna 342-343
    streaming 344-349

Two-factor authentication 126

U

UltraFICO score 83-85

Unclaimed property 76, 106

Upcycling 281, 290

V

Vacation. *See also* Travel
    home rentals 222, 359-361
    saving on 356-358

VantageScore 80

Veterans
    discounts 327, 353, 357
    hearing aids 178
    home care assistance 187-188

Virtual banking 98-100

Vision loss 176-177

Volunteer
    job seekers 71
    travel opportunities 361

Voucher, restaurant 301

W

Warehouse clubs
    bulk buying 271
    for special occasions 291
    prescription drugs and 156

Warehouse, Amazon 335-337

Warranties, extended 335

Water bill, lowering 13-14, 242-246

Weatherization Assistance Program 239-240

Will
    beneficiaries 108-109
    do-it-yourself 110
    legal fees 110-113
    tax burden 109

Windows, energy efficient 237

Wireless plans 326-329

Working, during retirement 69-71